# the mediterranean cookbook

# the mediterranean cookbook

**BETTY WASON**

HENRY REGNERY COMPANY • CHICAGO

*Library of Congress Cataloging in Publication Data*

Wason, Elizabeth, 1912–
    The Mediterranean cookbook.

    1. Cookery, Mediterranean. I. Title.
TX725.M35W37              641.5'9                    72-11200

# Contents

Archestratus, that writer so curious in all that relates to cookery, travelled through all lands and across all seas to learn for himself the best foods they produced . . . entering into kitchens where the delicacies of the table were prepared and conversing with all those who could advance the art he delighted in.

— Athenaeus, *The Deipnosophists*

For men travel over the whole earth in the service of the King of Persia, looking to find out what may be pleasant for him to drink; and ten thousand men are always contriving something nice for him to eat.

— Xenophon, *History of Persia*

# Notes on a Journey

The Mediterranean has long been my favorite part of the world, ever since the year I spent in Greece when something of the Greek spirit became part of my blood. When it was suggested I do a Mediterranean cookbook, this presented an immediate excuse to revisit those Mediterranean countries I already knew and loved and to explore others I had not yet seen. The very word "Mediterranean" was evocative of fond memories, of afternoons on Phaleron beach nibbling on pistachio nuts and sipping ouzo while gazing out over the bright blue "wine-streaked" Aegean; of watching, from the deck of a ferry plying its way from Alicante to Ibiza, the elephantlike mountains of the Spanish coast recede into mist; and of a pension at Juan-les-Pins on the French Riviera, set among blossoming orange trees, where every day I was awakened by the gentle lap of waves on the beach and where a sun-dappled expanse of water was the first thing I saw when I looked out the window.

For months I worked on an itinerary that would include as many stops as possible on a 'round-the-Mediterranean tour. At one time or another I had been to every country on the northern shores of the Mediterranean, but the only Middle Eastern country I had visited was Turkey, and I hadn't stepped on North African shores at all.

The first part of my trip was by sea—five leisurely sun-filled days from Lisbon to Piraeus, the port of Athens, on the Italian Line's *Cristoforo Colombo*, with stops at four ports along the way (Malaga, Naples, Palermo and Messina). After an all-too-brief stay in my beloved Athens, I went next to the island of Crete by overnight ferry, and then flew to Israel from Athens. At first I had naively hoped to travel down the Levantine coast by bus from Beirut to Haifa. The state of war in the Middle East made that impossible—the only route from Lebanon to Israel now is via Cyprus, since the borders between Israel and the neighboring states are closed. To have at least a stopover in Cyprus seemed an unexpected bonus; indeed, I found it to be a lovely island. But my stay was unexpectedly prolonged. The travel agent who had explained the necessity of going from Israel to Lebanon (or vice versa) by way of Cyprus had forgotten to mention that I should ask the Israeli passport control officers to put entry and departure stamps on a separate piece of paper. This, it seems, is almost standard procedure; "everyone" knows about it, and the Israelis don't mind doing it. But I didn't know, and only after I'd reached Cyprus was I warned hysterically that those unfortunate stamps in my passport almost certainly would bar my entry into all Arab countries. There seemed to be nothing to do but postpone my departure from Cyprus until I could get a brand new, clean American passport, which I did. But then I found that flights to Beirut were not only booked to capacity, but over-booked, for days ahead. At last a special plane was produced to take stranded tourists to Lebanon. As I nervously approached the passport control desk, I wondered what embarrassing questions might be asked about that suspiciously new passport. (So many people are forced to follow this procedure that the taking of passport pictures has become a thriving business in Nicosia, and surely, I thought, the Arab security officers were not unaware of this.) The guards scarcely glanced at the empty pages. The suspicion still lingers that the hysteria was simply part of a centuries-old fixation, born of almost incessant wars.

Meantime, my carefully timed schedule was thrown off balance and I decided to skip Egypt entirely, a decision I've since regretted. Instead, after four days in Lebanon, I flew from Beirut to Tunis, which entailed a six-hour stopover at the Rome airport, than which there can be no more dreary place on earth. Whoever thought jet travel was glamorous?

I'd chosen Tunis as my North African stop because it had been under French domination for so long; I assumed its cuisine must be superior. Besides, I'd had an unforgettably delicious Tunisian *cous-cous* in a restaurant in Switzerland a year before.

The first impressions of Tunis were enchanting. I stayed in a small hotel in the resort town of Sidi Bou Said on a hilltop over-looking Carthage Bay, and the first evening, seeing the lights of Tunis far below in the darkness and breathing in the scent of jasmine from the garden of what had been a sixteenth-century Hispano-Moorish palace, I felt indeed that I'd chosen a perfect spot.

The hotel's cous-cous was excellent, if not much like the one I'd had in Switzerland, and Tunis was fascinating in its contrast to Lebanon, another Arab country. But communications in Tunisia are difficult. The country's telephone system might be improved if they started supplementing it with carrier pigeons. Perhaps it was the fault of my awkward French, but the conflicting information I was given on departing flight schedules became more confusing each day. Finally, I went to the Tunis-Carthage airport for the second time, hoping to get correct information direct from the source. This time I was told that all outgoing flights were "complete" for days ahead. A young lady tried to soothe my apoplectic reaction by suggesting, "If you can return here in an hour, madame, we might be able to get you on tonight's flight to Marseilles." I did the impossible, leaving various articles of clothing behind in my rush, and found myself whisked, by the too-swift propulsion of jet engines, out of a country where time stands still.

The Mediterranean is not yet attuned to the jet age, and I have a feeling it never will be. Those old men idly fingering amber beads in the cafes of Piraeus and Beirut as they watch the few remaining ships steam in and out of their harbors are much closer to an understanding of what travel in the Mediterranean should be. Timelessness has always been one of the most attractive qualities of this ancient inland sea.

After Tunis, Marseilles seemed strikingly modern and its traffic a model of control. From Marseilles I traveled by train to Arles and then to Avignon to feast in restaurants that the *Guide Michelin* considered good enough to rate with stars. This was, after all, a cookbook that I was compiling, and so I hoped to sample some of those dishes for which the French are so justly famous. I did have one truly memorable meal, in Avignon, and just to look at the beautiful foods on display in French markets was a treat. But the jet age has not improved French service. In this land where gastronomy is like a religion, I was shocked, in a three-forks starred restaurant, when, after I showed the sommelier that my expensive wine was full of cork, he merely brought me a clean glass and left me to pour more wine myself from the same bottle. The entrée was excellent, but its sauce much too salty, and the ill-trained waitress displayed little of that finesse which in other days was part of the joy of dining.

On the other hand, many of the customers, in what was supposed to be an elegant restaurant, came to dinner in dress so informal as to be an insult to the establishment. One man was in tennis shoes and a red tieless shirt; a young woman was in plaid slacks and a pullover. The age of elegance is indeed dead, and remembering the way it used to be, I can only sigh nostalgically.

Was the journey, with all its headaches and disappointments, worthwhile? Yes, because it gave me a "feel" for the Mediterranean world I'd never had before. Traveling by jet was too fast and too tiring, yet the bird's eye view I had of countries so diverse in culture and technological progress enabled me to see how basically interrelated they all are. The same heritage lies everywhere just beneath the surface: Greek, Phoenician, Roman and Arab, with an intermingling of Celtic in all the European Mediterranean lands. The same waves of history, visible in both archaeological remains and in architecture, have molded them all. And while each country has its own food specialties, it is astonishing to observe the similarities in all their cuisines. All are fundamentally olive oil cuisines, all make imaginative use of the same vegetables and fruits—artichokes, eggplant, sweet and hot peppers, tomatoes, garlic, lemon and oranges—and in nearly all, lamb is the most often used meat.

One change that I noted deeply disturbed me: fish has become scarce everywhere, and it used to be that the fish dishes of the Mediterranean were the finest anywhere. On the island of Cyprus only one kind of fish was available—and not every day. The Aegean coast used to be full of little fishing boats; now there's scarcely a sail on the horizon. Even in the Italian ports where our passenger liner stopped, we saw little else but freighters. What shellfish is available is expensive beyond belief. Only in Barcelona was it different. In the wonderful San José market, just off the Ramblas, the same beautiful arrangement of gleaming-fresh fish, interspersed with crustaceans and molluscs of every kind, was for sale that I remembered from my last time there. Only Portugal has fish in abundance, but Portugal lies on the Atlantic, not the Mediterranean, and its seafood supply is also dwindling.

What has happened to all the fish? Pollution, of course. I wonder how long it will be before the Mediterranean will have no more fish at all?

It was also enlightening to note the differences in agricultural advancement in the various countries. The reason usually cited for the Phoenicians of antiquity having developed into a maritime nation was that they had so little productive land, because of the high mountains rising just off their narrow coastline. But in the food stalls of the souk in Beirut (the Beryte of ancient Phoenicia), I was impressed by the lusciousness and the enormous variety of the fruits and vegetables on display: enormous grapes, crisp red apples, melons piled in pyramids, tomatoes large, perfectly formed and flavorful to boot, and everything else comparably beautiful and mouth-watering in appearance. Next day, on the bus tour to Baalbek, the fabulous Roman ruins on a high plateau in the Lebanese mountains, we passed through fertile fields, which the guide explained were the experimental farms of the American University in Beirut. I'm sure these farms had much to do with the quality of produce in the markets.

In contrast to the Tunisia of antiquity in which the pasture and fields were noted for their fertility, the soil of Tunisia today is worn out, the countryside is drab, and the cattle in the fields are so gaunt that the hide hangs loose on their skeletal frames.

The agricultural strides that Israel has taken are a modern miracle. Traveling through the countryside, one can see giant sprinklers throwing fine sprays of water over truck gardens, fruit orchards and banana groves. Avocados are so plentiful that they are served in many imaginative ways. Those incredibly sweet and juicy Jaffa oranges so in demand in European markets have become Israel's second most important export. One of many places I longed to see in Israel, and didn't have time for on my jet stop, was that part of the Negev desert where archaeologists, exploring the remains of ancient terraced slopes built between the second century B.C. and the second century A.D., rediscovered one of the most effective methods of controlling and storing rainwater ever invented. Restoring this 2000-year-old irrigation system has meant the creation of new productive farms in what for centuries had been desert. Other irrigation is by a system of modern pipelines and canals that carry water from the Sea of Galilee to the Negev. Reforestation is also helping to prevent erosion and to preserve soil nutrients in what twenty years ago seemed hopeless wasteland. If the soil-conservation program practiced by the Israelis were copied in all the Mediterranean lands it would do much to turn unusable lands into gardens of earthly delights.

The number of recipes I could pick up on my whirlwind Mediterranean tour was limited by the number of meals my ever-expanding waistline could take, but I bought local cookbooks wherever I went, and these proved invaluable in compiling *The Mediterranean Cookbook*.

Whatever the excuse, the reason for traveling is the same as it always has been: to taste adventure and to break the dull pattern of a stay-at-home routine. And for those who cannot make such a voyage, dreaming of it, with the adventurous flavors of foods from faraway places helping to make illusion seem real, is the next best substitute.

# the mediterranean cookbook

Dear to us ever is the banquet and the harp and the dance,
And changes of raiment and the bath and love and sleep.
. . . The stormy season of winter, a soft couch after dinner
By the fire, honey-sweet wine in your glass
And nuts and beans at your elbow.

— Homer, *The Iliad*


The cook . . . began to be so much esteemed and valued that, all bedabbled with broth and bedaubed with soot, he was welcomed out of the kitchen into the schools, and that which before was accounted as vile slavery was honored as an art . . . whose care is to search out everywhere the provocatives of appetite; the peacock from Samos, the Phrygian turkey, cranes from Melos. . . .

— Livy, *Historiae*

# Mediterranean Heritage

It was more than eight thousand years ago when the first bold mariner left the coast of Asia Minor to sail out into the blue of the Mediterranean Sea. He wouldn't have gone far: his little boat was probably made of hides and shaped like a canoe. But before 6000 B.C. the first of the Mediterranean trade routes, between the island of Cyprus and the Lebanese coast, had been established.

Later, maritime trade expanded down the coast to Egypt, across the seas to Crete, through the scattered islands of the Aegean, over to the Greek mainland and north to the Bosphorus, the site of the first of the seven cities of Troy.

It's not known for certain who were the first men to sail as far west as the Atlantic, or when the first ships from the Aegean passed between the pillars of Hercules, but they probably belonged to that ancient Greek world that Homer immortalized. The word "Greek" is used loosely here; some of the traders came from Crete, others from Asia Minor (the Levantine coast), others from the Aegean islands. These mariners didn't even speak the language in which Homer wrote, yet it was their exploits that formed the basis of the myths and poetic legends that so captured the imagination of all the peoples in the Mediterranean region.

Hercules, or Heracles, or Melquart as the Phoenicians and Egyptians called him, was the legendary embodiment of the first

1

bold sailor. According to myth, he used his immense wine goblet as a boat and a cow hide for a sail, and with no more than this and dauntless courage he braved the seas, performing the twelve labors set for him by the King of Argos.

One of Hercules' twelve labors was to capture the cattle of Geryon. There was a real King Geryon of Tartessus, the earliest name for that part of Spain now called Andalusia, and he was in fact a cattle baron. Erythia, the island on which Geryon pastured his cattle, was the pre-Phoenician name of the island of Gades (Cadiz). Geryon's kingdom of Tartessus was the land called Tarashish in the Bible, a land rich in copper, tin, gold and silver. It's far more likely that the real Hercules sailed to Tartessus searching for gold rather than for cattle, for it was the demand for these precious metals more than anything else that spurred the earliest adventurers to brave unknown seas. It's been said that it was not really Helen's face, but mercantile interests, that launched a thousand ships.

Two thousand years ago there was already spirited discussion among savants as to how much of the Homeric tales were factual and how much were, as the Greek historian Strabo put it, "embroidered with poetic imagination." The cattle of Geryon were said to give milk so rich "it had no whey." It's hard to believe that Hercules drove the cattle all the way back to Greece from Spain as legend affirms, even taking a wrong turn en route, which carried him down to the toe of Italy before he discovered his mistake. Yet Hercules may well have brought back the "golden apples of the Hesperides," because the kings of antiquity were always demanding new and exotic foods to whet their appetites.

What were those "golden apples" that Hercules brought back from the Hesperides? Oranges? Quinces? Citrons? There's no written record of oranges in the Mediterranean before 1290 A.D., although in the third century A.D., Athenaeus, in his twelve-volume book, *The Deipnosophists*, a treasure trove of information for all those interested in gastronomy, quoted "Jobas, king of the Mauritanians" (present-day Morocco) as having asserted in his *History of Libya* that "the citron is called among the Libyans the Hesperian apple," that "they were citrons which Hercules carried into Greece . . . the name 'golden apples' [was given them] because of their color."

Hercules was also credited in legend with having planted the first olive tree in the West. The wild olive was indigenous to the Mediterranean area. But the wild olive bore little fruit, and it had to be pruned and cultivated for a more bountiful yield. An olive seedling requires ten years of growth before it begins to fruit. Nuts by their taste are oily; but olives are not even edible until processed in brine. In ancient times, as well as today, the rich oil of the olive was treasured above all others because it remained fresh in a hot climate far longer than other natural oils. Olive oil was universally used, not only in cooking, but as a lotion for anointing sun-dried skin and as fuel for lamps.

Olive oil was a major product of Crete when that island was under the rule of one of the most colorful and important kingdoms of the ancient world. The Minoan dynasty had its beginnings about 2600 B.C., and for a thousand years its ships ruled the Mediterranean.

There were three separate dynasties on Crete, at peace with one another—the three rulers may have been brothers or cousins. Each king or prince lived in a degree of splendor that is enviable even today. The greatest of the palaces was at Knossos, on the north shore. Here lived the most powerful of the kings, one who always bore the name Minos. But the palace at Phaestos, though smaller, with only 100 rooms in contrast to the 1400 rooms at Knossos, was in an even more beautiful location—on a hilltop overlooking the sea and facing Africa. The coast of Libya can be seen faintly in the distance, with snow-capped Mt. Ida rising in magnificence behind it.

To stand among the palace ruins at Phaestos was a thrilling experience for me. Olive groves stretch over the fertile valleys today as they did in ancient times, and the sky seems unbelievably blue above the crags of Mt. Ida. Our guide pointed to an ancient olive press in the palace kitchen and to the immense amphorae, higher than a man's head, that were used to store olive oil. But olive oil, which had been so valued by the Minoans, helped to speed the destruction of this superb palace. During the last of several earthquakes that shook the island, the amphorae cracked and the spilling oil caught fire, turning the magnificent palacial rooms into a holocaust.

Phaestos was the first port for ships coming from Egypt or Africa, and as I stood on the heights where the palace once stood, it was not hard to imagine ancient high-prowed vessels pushing through the rippling sea toward the white beach.

From Phaestos, merchants traveled overland to Knossos, where goods were appraised in a customs house. Portions of the palace at Knossos have been reconstructed so that visitors may see something of its former beauty—vivid wall frescoes, decorated columns and door lintels. The multi-leveled palace has immense kitchens and storerooms (the legendary labyrinth), and it is evident that its plumbing system was extraordinary. The palace had flush toilets, even for the slaves, and the queen had two bathrooms, one where she bathed in asses' milk to whiten her skin; the other where she bathed in a marble tub filled with hot or cold water. The cement-lined pipes of the plumbing system, installed 3700 years ago, still serve to carry off rainwater. The pipes were shaped to create pressure that would bring water uphill.

Still more impressive than the Minoans' engineering skill was their art, which was joyous and carefree in contrast to the solemn, stylized art of the Egyptians. No kitchen scenes are depicted in the Minoan frescoes, as they are in the Egyptian frescoes of the same period, but inventories listed on stone tablets mention figs, honey, coriander, sesame, fish and wine as being among the palace stores.

Any people who loved the joys of living as much as the Minoans also must have made an art of dining. The pieces that remain of their tableware are attractive enough to grace a modern table: some cups are shaped like coffee mugs, others like delicate teacups, and each bears a different, equally gay design. Plates, bowls and pitchers are all decorated. Rhytons, vessels from which liquids were poured, have ingenious shapes, some like the heads of bulls, animals that the Minoans held sacred. Minoan cookware included portable clay ovens; bronze cauldrons; grills and braziers, such as we still use for barbecuing; and shallow bronze ramekins in graduated sizes, with handles on either side. These ramekins are identical in shape to the French copper pans commonly used today.

Earthquakes devastated the island of Crete three times, and each time the palaces were rebuilt in greater luxury than before, although by the final period the artwork had become obviously more crude and primitive. Then the Minoan civilization came abruptly to an end when the island was invaded by the Mycenaeans, an army probably led by Homer's Theseus. The Mycenaeans of mainland Greece, the new Mediterranean power, became the heirs of the Minoan civilization, and their ships followed the trade routes already established by Minoan vessels.

The Mycenaeans, unlike the Minoans, were warlike and aggressive. While they adopted many aspects of Minoan civilization, their art was bolder, and less carefree. Their citadels were constructed primarily for defense and only secondarily for pleasure. The Mycenaeans kept alive the bull cult of the Minoans. "Bull leaping" was their favorite sport, one which they would introduce throughout the western Mediterranean area. Bull heads fashioned exactly like the rhytons found in Crete have been found in Mallorca and along the southern coast of Spain. The bullfights, which still draw thousands of spectators in France, Spain and Portugal, are a last vestige of this bull cult. In the Portuguese bullfight, the forcadores, who approach the bull on foot and grab him by the horns to leap on his back, are performing a feat strikingly similar to that of the bull leapers of Knossos.

The Mycenaeans left no written records to prove their colonization of the western Mediterranean area, but monuments believed to have been erected by them abound. There are "cyclopean walls," so named by later folk who believed that only giants could have handled such immense rock slabs, dolmens, cromlechs, toalas and other mysterious structures, which were all built of enormous boulders and are to be found in a trail from Malta, to the Balearic Islands, to Spain and Portugal, up the coast of Brittany, to England and as far north as Denmark.

The Mycenaeans were attracted to southern Spain because of the richness of its ores. They seem to have been on good terms with the ancient kings of Tartessus, who were apparently rich in ores, since they ate from golden bowls and drank from silver goblets. But during the Bronze Age, tin was in even greater demand than gold, because tin was needed to mix with copper in manufacturing bronze. Bronze was used to make swords, daggers and shields as well as for pots and braziers. The reason Mycenaeans sailed beyond the pillars of Hercules north to England was that the richest of all tin mines were in Cornwall. A Mycenaean dagger etched on one of the pillars of Stonehenge was probably the graffiti of a Greek merchant, who came to England in search of tin.

At least a hundred years before the start of the Trojan War, the tin route to England had been established. It seems likely, therefore, that Ulysses, a Mycenaean prince, would have heard reports about the rich lands to the west. Was it more than chance that led him to keep on sailing westward instead of returning home? Just how far he sailed is a matter of conjecture as it was even among the classical writers of the Roman period. Strabo in the first century A.D. asserted that it was "well known" that Ulysses had been in Iberia, and that his tales of what the country of Tartessus was like had furnished material for Homer's epic. Did the Trojan hero's ship find its way as far north as Olisipo, the city now called Lisbon? One legend says it did; most historians still are skeptical. However, Trojan swords have been dug up on the Atlantic coast and heavy gold bracelets similar in workmanship to those of Agamemnon's treasure have been found in widely scattered places in Spain and Portugal.

After the debacle of the Trojan War, the Mycenaean civilization fell before the onslaughts of another warlike and more barbaric tribe, the Dorians, who came down to Greece from the north. Many of the Mycenaeans fled to Asia Minor; others went to small Aegean islands. Greek influence seemed temporarily in abeyance during this period, but a few hundred years later it would flower again.

About 1400 B.C., approximately the same time as the Mycenaeans were busily collecting gold, silver and tin from the West, the Hebrews were in exodus from Egypt en route to the Promised Land. When the armies of Joshua conquered Canaan, they left one tribe of Canaanites alone, those along the coastal strip known even then as the Lebanon. The Hebrews called these people Sidonites, after Sidon, one of their cities; to the Greeks they were Phoenicians. And the next great wave of colonization in the western Mediterranean would be theirs.

Myth has it that it was a Phoenician princess who became the mother of the first King Minos of Crete. Her name was Europa, and when Zeus, looking down from on high, saw her on the Lebanese shores, he fell madly in love with her. He disguised himself as a white bull, captured her, and swam with her to Crete. Does the myth suggest that there was Phoenician blood in the Minoans? Or was the legend merely the poetic explanation of the Phoenician role in colonizing Europe?

The Phoenicians were the most skilled mariners of antiquity. Their ships, built of Lebanon cedar, were the swiftest and most seaworthy of all. Besides following the tin route to England to exchange olive oil for metals, they sailed down the coast of Africa as far as the land of pygmies to gather ivory and traveled east through the Red Sea to India and China to bring back such spices as cinnamon, frankincense and myrrh, as well as the all-important black pepper. Apparently they also brought back sugar cane, for in the book of Jeremiah in the Bible there is mention of "sweet cane from a far country." Sugar as we know it, however, would not come into general use even in the Near East until the ninth century A.D., and not in the lands above the Pyrenees in Europe until after the Crusades.

One of the first of the western Phoenician colonies was Gades, at the mouth of the Guadalquivir River in Spain. It was the kind of site the Phoenicians always chose, with a crescent-shaped harbor for the protection of their ships. Other colonies or trading posts were established in many places: on the Atlantic coast of Portugal (Peniche, the second largest Portuguese fishing port, is a contraction of the word *Phoenician*), all along the Mediterranean coast of Spain and on the islands of Ibiza, Sardinia, Corsica, Malta and Sicily.

In 814 B.C., another Phoenician princess—Dido, niece of the biblical Jezebel—fled from her homeland in fear of a vengeful brother-in-law. She stopped off briefly in Crete (as had Europa), and then went on with her handmaidens to North Africa, where legend says she founded the city of Carthage.

During this period, the Phoenicians made no attempt to enforce their rule on native peoples in the West. They were content to allow other eastern peoples to establish colonies, often adjoining their colonies on the same coasts. About 800 B.C. a new wave of Greeks, these from Asia Minor, probably descendants of Mycenaean refugees, began to settle in the West. Before another hundred years had passed there were as many Greek as Phoenician colonies, some located in North Africa, others in Sicily, Italy, Spain and France. The two most important colonies were Massilia (now Marseilles) in France and Syracuse in Sicily.

Another influx of colonizers from the east was led by the Etruscans, who settled in Italy and gave their name, Etruria, to the Tyrrhenian Sea. Herodotus said that the Etruscans came from Lydia, in Asia Minor, in what is now Turkey; indeed, their princes lived in a splendor like that of Assyrian lords. Jews, too, were migrating westward in this period, but as individuals or family groups. They did not establish separate colonies. Even Rome began its climb to power under the leadership of Aeneas, the hero of Troy, who settled in Italy after several years of wandering from one Mediterranean port to another.

Before 500 B.C., all the waves of explorers and colonizers in the Mediterranean had come from the east. This is why there is such a distinctively Levantine flavor throughout the Mediterranean, evident in physiognomy, manners, morals, the status of women, art, architecture and, not least, cookery.

Many of the things we think of today as Roman were really Etruscan. The Etruscans were a gay, sensual people who, according to Diodorus, "twice a day partook of elaborate repasts at tables decked with embroidered cloths and vessels of gold and silver." "Plump" or "obese" are words frequently used to describe the

Etruscans. They preferred feasting to fighting, and did everything by music: their warriors set out for battle to the accompaniment of flutes; hunters are said to have hypnotized their prey with music; boxers fought out their contests to the twanging of harps; and even bakers and cooks had music to regale them as they prepared food for their pleasure-loving masters. Is it surprising that the province of Tuscany would later become the "mother of French cooking"? Or that today Italians trill operatic arias as they work?

About 500 B.C. the Celts began to appear in the Mediterranean area from the north. In Iberia they settled down, intermarried and acquired the name Celtiberians. In France, they became known as Gauls. Like the Dorians in Greece, the Celts were a crude, barbaric people who only gradually acquired the refinements of the earlier oriental settlers.

But of all these early Mediterranean settlers, none would have such a profound and lasting influence as the Greeks. Before the Mediterranean became the Roman *mare nostrum* it was a Greek sea. And this is the more surprising because the Greek conquest was one of culture, not military supremacy. Greek artists were hired by kings, emperors and potentates. Most of what is called "Etruscan art" is really Greek. The Greeks developed their alphabet from the Phoenicians, as did many other peoples, but it was Greek literature, not Phoenician, that survived.

The Greeks were also the first Mediterranean people to elevate cookery to an art. Archestratus, a friend of Pericles, wrote many books on cookery, of which one called *Gastronomy* was frequently quoted by other classical writers. Even after the Roman domination, Greek cooks were in great demand, as are French chefs today, and the Greek way of cooking was everywhere most admired. It was the Greeks, too, who introduced viniculture throughout the rest of the Mediterranean. Greek wines were prized even after the Romans had learned from them enough about viniculture to produce Falernian, the most long-lived wine of antiquity.

The Greek colonies in the West became more luxury-loving than the cities of Greece proper. The inhabitants of Sybaris in Italy were so given to the pursuit of pleasure that invitations for banquets were issued a year in advance, and cooks, paid far better than any other artisans, were awarded prizes at public festivals. The word *sybarite* became a synonym for debauchery. Sybaris was destroyed when the horses of its cavalry, trained to dance to music, were led into a trap by the enemy, who used pied-piper techniques. Dionysius, the tyrant of Syracuse in Sicily, not only awarded purses of gold to the cooks who prepared especially delicious offerings, but tried his own hand in the kitchen and declaimed poetry in praise of gastronomy at his banquets. Dionysius died from overeating.

It's easy to understand how colonies so given to lavish living were easily conquered. First, there was the rising might and military expansion of Carthage. Then, those Greek cities that survived Carthaginian attack later succumbed to Roman conquest. Yet the ruins of Greek temples are still to be seen rising against the skies of Sicily, and the extravagance of Sicilian and Etruscan banquets were not only copied but were surpassed by the Romans in their turn.

Feasting lavishly has always been an accepted form of entertainment. Darius, king of the Medes and Persians, maintained a staff of gastronomic detectives whose sole function was to search for new and delectable foods to tempt the appetite of their ruler. Xerxes, Darius' son and successor, demanded such variety for his table that the countryside, wherever he traveled, was laid bare. "Wherever Xerxes took two meals, dining as well as supping," wrote Herodotus, "that city was utterly ruined." King Thys of Paphlagonia demanded a hundred dishes to be set before him at each meal, "starting with an ox." Even Solomon maintained 12,000 horsemen to search the countryside for viands for his table.

In Greece proper, during the Golden Age, such ostentatious feasting was condemned by philosophers and savants. Plato returned from Sicily disgusted with the way of life he had observed among the overseas Greeks. Epicurus, the philosopher from whose name we get the word *epicure*, although he praised as the finest things in life the pleasures of the table, urged and himself observed moderation in both food and drink.

Alas, such wisdom was all too easily ignored. The Romans rose to power because they were austere and well disciplined, and the might of the Roman Empire is still impressive nearly two thousand years after its fall: towering Roman columns, the ruins of mighty Roman aqueducts, baths, theaters and arenas are to be seen wherever one travels around the Mediterranean. It is not surprising to come upon these remains in Italy, Spain or France, yet it is astonishing to see the extensive ruins of Dougga, in the interior of Tunisia, once a Roman city of 45,000 with half a dozen temples, a theater seating 15,000, and the inevitable gymnasium and baths, to say nothing of an elaborate brothel. The awesome grandeur of the Roman temples at Baalbek, high on a mountainous plateau in

Lebanon, must be seen to be appreciated: broad flights of sweeping steps lead to the sanctuaries, whose columns reach eighty feet into the sky, topped by sculptured capitals and friezes so immense that one wonders how they can have remained in place all these centuries. Many a Roman bridge, such as the one spanning the frontier between Portugal and Spain at Elvas, is still in use after 2000 years. Roman roads are to be seen wandering into nowhere over mountainsides in the north of Portugal.

The Roman Empire became so powerful that the wonder is not that its fall was so precipitous, but that the empire endured as long as it did. Its frontiers were over-extended, from Persia in the east to Britain in the west, and its peoples were constantly in revolt. One of the proud tourist sites in Israel is the fortress at Massada, whose inhabitants committed mass suicide rather than become Roman prisoners. Nubia, in central Spain, suffered a similar end: mothers killed their children and husbands their wives and horses before they fell on their own swords. When the Romans entered the city, they found nothing but corpses. The Lusitanians in "Farther Spain" kept up their resistance for 200 years and their last great leader, Viriatus, aroused so many other Iberian tribes to revolt that the Romans seriously considered evacuating the area. The rebellion was crushed only when Viriatus was assassinated in his tent.

The extravagance of Roman aristocrats cannot have endeared them to their people. Rulers of overseas colonies lived in luxury as great as, if not surpassing, that of Rome itself. The mosaics of Roman villas are constantly being unearthed by farmers' plows in the most unlikely places—North African hills, Portuguese fields, Greek olive groves, Serbian pastures and Spanish seaside resorts. The most fabulous display of Roman mosaics to be seen anywhere in the world is that in the Bardo museum of Tunis.

While mosaics covered the floors of Roman homes, walls and ceilings were painted with landscapes or scenes from favorite legends. Before attending a banquet, which would have been a stag affair up until the time of the emperor Augustus, who decreed that wives or mistresses should also be invited, men went to the baths, had their hair trimmed by barbers, who also cleaned their teeth, and dressed in silks imported from Egypt.

The guests were served at table by an array of slaves, while a veritable army of cooks, roasters and saucemakers toiled in the kitchen. As the diners were led to their couches, a *praegustator* tasted everything to judge whether it was delicious enough to serve. A *nomenclatore* then called out the name of each dish before it was carried to the tables and, since all food was eaten with fingers, a *scissor* stood by to cut the meat into small pieces for each diner. Musicians provided background music; slaves with fans made of peacock feathers kept the flies away and cooled the air. Cushions stuffed with rose leaves were often provided for the elbows of the guests as they lay on their couches. Goblets were refilled with wine again and again and if, by the end of the banquet, some of the guests were unsteady on their feet, servants would be waiting to escort them home.

We know a great deal about what and how the Romans ate because gastronomy was such a popular subject with writers of the age, and actual recipes have come down to us through the cookbook of Apicius, a Roman gourmet. This bon vivant squandered so much money on the luxuries of the table, that he at last found himself impoverished, and when he saw that he could no longer afford to entertain in the style for which he was famous, he committed suicide. His book, however, became immortal; it was read through edition after edition, century after century, and it was admired by such famous people as Lister, the private physician of Queen Anne of England, and Carême, the greatest of all French chefs. Apicius' book is still used today as a reference guide.

Herbs and spices were used in profusion in Roman cookery; almost nothing was served plain. Garum, that strange and evil-sounding concoction made from the entrails of salt fish, was used as unerringly as soy sauce is used today by the Chinese. Garum must have been more palatable than it sounds, because the remains of innumerable garum factories have been discovered all along the northern shores of the Mediterranean and even on the Atlantic coast of Portugal. Apparently only a pinch needed to be used, usually blended with concentrated wine that was reduced by boiling, herbs and a bit of honey, mixed into a condiment called *liquamen*.

Besides an abundance of written testimony, a graphic picture of Roman life was preserved in the ruins of Pompeii, when that city was suddenly buried under the ashes of the erupting volcano of Vesuvius. Having a chance to visit Pompeii was one of the highlights of my round-the-Mediterranean trip. Pompeii was both a vacation resort for wealthy Romans and an important commercial port. Cicero had a house there, so did Pliny the Elder, who lost his life in the disaster because his curiosity was so great he returned to the scene even after a successful escape by boat. Falernian wine, the most famous wine of antiquity, came from the slopes of Vesuvius. Olive groves ringed the city, and the Campanian countryside produced the finest vegetables and fruits. Merchants came to Pompeii from all over the Mediterranean. Its population, largely Etruscan, also included many Greeks and Jews. Originally, Pompeii was a Greek settlement; its oldest building was a Greek temple, and there was also a temple to Isis, the Egyptian goddess.

On that horrifying August day in the year 79 A.D., lava particles and ash, swept without warning by strong winds from the erupting volcano twenty-five miles away, covered the city like a suffocating blanket. The skeletons of approximately 2000 persons, out of a population of 20,000, were found in the ruins when it was excavated 1800 years later. Many people had huddled against doors they could not open. The ruins of bakeries, wine shops—or, more properly, bars, since drinks were sold on the premises—and corner groceries line the city streets. Even the grocery lists of shoppers have been found. Besides the wine shops, there were quick lunch bars where hot stews or soups were sold from receptacles built into the counters. These lunch bars were for the most part located near Pompeii's two theaters and were for the benefit of late theatergoers. In one house a suckling pig had been left stewing in the pot; in another bread was baking in the oven. In the House of the Vettii, through which all tourists are shepherded, one can see exactly what the wealthier villas of Pompeii looked like. This house has been preserved exactly as it was on the day of the disaster. Its vividly colored frescoes make clear that the enjoyment of sensual pleasures was one of the primary interests of its rich owners.

Enough, perhaps too much, has already been written about Roman orgies in the dying days of the empire, and it's all too easy to blame the fall of Rome on debauchery. Even when the empire was at the peak of its power, in the year 68 A.D., the emperor Galba was said to have required as much for his breakfast "as would have enriched 100 families," and his successor, Vitellius, was once offered at a banquet 2000 separate dishes, 7000 birds, and every delicacy which the Mediterranean could provide. Included among these delicacies may have been dates from Phoenicia, peaches from Persia, raisins from Rhodes, the crabs of Alexandria and crayfish of Smyrna, strawberries from the slopes of Mt. Ida in Crete, and Tartesian mullets and chestnuts from Iberia, to quote from various writers of the time, who also mentioned "well-fed pigs from Sicily and fat sheep from Euboa" as prized banquet food. Fish from distant countries was brought preserved in jars of honey. From Libya came selphinium, a rare herb, and assafoetida, considered a powerful aphrodisiac. Truffles, both white and black, were imported from Greece and Gaul. There probably were also tongues of hummingbirds and brains of ostriches, the cost of which probably made more impression on the diners than their flavor.

The spice trade had assumed such importance that when Rome was under siege in the year 409, Alaric the Goth asked for a ransom of 3000 pounds of black pepper; reluctantly the Roman Senate agreed to hand over the treasure for their freedom.

Rome fell before the attacks of northern barbarians, as the Mycenaeans had fallen before the Dorian invasion, and once again a highly developed civilization went into decline in the West. The emperor Constantine, recognizing the weakened position of Rome, moved his capital to the ancient city of Byzantium on the banks of the Bosphorus, not far from ancient Troy. He changed the name of the city to Constantinople, and here another empire grew from the seeds of the old. While Western Europe fell into the obscurity of a dark age, the Byzantine Empire waxed powerful and acquired oriental splendor. Constantinople was a Greek, not a Roman, city. The rich aristocrats, who lived in its splendid palaces and dressed in silks and brocades, spoke Greek and dined on a Greek cuisine. But Constantinople also was an international city; in its bazaars Persians, Indians and Jews met and traded with Armenians, Egyptians and Venetians. They conversed in a babble of tongues as they bartered goods from the far ends of the earth.

By the sixth century, Constantinople was the most magnificent and most cosmopolitan city in the world. It had hundreds of churches, great libraries and a university open to both men and women. But even in the midst of its glory, Constantinople began to go soft with too much luxury.

A mere hundred years later, a new force began to emerge in the Mediterranean: Arabian armies under the banner of Islam began their conquest and moved with astonishing swiftness. The Moslems conquered most of Asia Minor and advanced nearly to the gates of Constantinople. They sped west over all of North Africa, crossed the Straits of Gibraltar into Spain and, advancing almost as fast as their nimble horses could carry them, penetrated northward into France where Charles Martel, grandfather of Charlemagne, finally stopped them. Crete and Sicily also were taken over by the Moslems, as were the Balearics and Malta. At its peak the Arab conquest extended over almost as much territory as had the Roman Empire, and the Arabs retained their power in parts of southern Spain for almost 700 years.

Again an oriental people had become masters of the Mediterranean. And while the Arabs were cruel and ruthless, they were more civilized than the equally ruthless Goths and Vandals who had usurped power from the Romans. In fact, the ease of Moslem conquest in Spain stemmed largely from hatred of the German conquerors on the part of the Iberian natives, many of whom had ancestors or relatives in the lands from which the Arabian soldiers came.

Into the alcazars and palaces that they built, the Arabs brought oriental luxuries—delicate silks and rich brocades, soft leathers tooled in gold, gleaming porcelains, glass and lusterware, rich carpets and silken pillows—which would alter forever after the Mediterranean way of living. The Arabs were skillful gardeners, and, like the Romans, they made their courtyards or patios—with reflecting pools and tinkling fountains, flowers in profusion and boxwood trimmed into fanciful shapes—the center of family life.

The Moslems also began the cultivation of foods that had hitherto been known, if at all, only as rare imports from the east. Rice, sugar cane, bitter oranges (planted so widely around Seville that they became known in England as Seville oranges) and lemon trees were all introduced by the Arabs. They introduced irrigation, using the "Archimedes screw," a horizontal water wheel that is still in use today, to bring up water from underground sources. They enriched worn-out soil with fertilizers and developed new fruit varieties by grafting. From the Phoenicians, who were now part of the Arab world, the Moslems had inherited the spice trade, and the use of cinnamon, nutmeg, mace, ginger and saffron in Spanish cuisine is largely due to Arab influence.

In the tenth century, Córdoba was "the jewel of the West." It was almost as elegant and cosmopolitan as Constantinople had been in the sixth century. When Constantinople fell under the oppression of a reactionary regime, free-thinking intellectuals fled to Córdoba for sanctuary. Scholars of all nationalities were welcomed to the city by the benevolent Caliph Abd-al-Rahman.

Was it the Arabs who taught the Spanish how to make the elaborate rice dishes of Persia? It's easy to come to this conclusion, since the Spanish paella closely resembles the Persian pilaf, and both Persia and Spain were at the time part of the Arabian Empire.

It was not until 1095 that the first of the purely western invasions of the Mediterranean took place. The First Crusade to the Holy Land was proclaimed by Pope Urban II at Clermont, France. Altogether, eight major Crusades were launched over a period of 200 years, but in between there were so many pilgrimages over land and by sea, that there was a continuous coming and going to Jerusalem. The city of Jerusalem never remained in the hands of the zealous pilgrims for very long, and the Holy Land was most of the time a battleground littered with corpses. But the Crusaders did build great castles on hilltops and next to the sea, and these still can be seen today in Greece, Cyprus, Crete, Lebanon, Turkey, Israel and Jordan.

The pilgrims returning home from the Crusades took back far more than they had brought. The wealth of the Orient had dazzled them. Geoffrey de Villhardouin, describing his impressions of Constantinople in 1203, wrote that those who were seeing the city for the first time "were not able to believe there could be so rich a town in the whole world, when they saw those high walls and mighty towers, those rich palaces and lofty churches. . . ."

The returning Crusaders introduced many hitherto unknown foods to western Europe. The first mention of oranges and lemons in France was by a Crusader who had enjoyed these fruits while in Palestine, though it must have been sugar- or honey-sweetened juices that he had tasted, because only the bitter orange was then known, and it would be another two hundred years before the first of the sweet oranges would be brought to Europe from the Far East by one of Vasco da Gama's Portuguese sailors.

Other foods introduced to the courts of Paris by Crusaders were the damson plum from Damascus, saffron and a small plant at first called *ascalon* (after a city of that name in Syria), later to be known as the shallot, an herb which French cooks today consider indispensable in the making of delicately flavored sauces.

The Great Age of Discovery in the West, which began at the end of the fifteenth century, was sparked by Arab domination of the eastern Mediterranean and Arab control of the spice trade—that is, of those spices that came from the mysterious lands of the Orient; cinnamon, cloves, nutmeg, ginger and pepper. Just as today the closing of the Suez Canal has bottled up the Mediterranean and blocked east-west trade, so the stubbornness of the Arabs in the Middle Ages forced Western entrepreneurs to find other routes to the East. It was Spanish and Portuguese explorers, sailing west trying to find a way to reach the East, who discovered the

New World. The strange foods that they brought back from these voyages affected the world's cuisine far more profoundly than did the spices of which they went in search.

Can we imagine Mediterranean cooking without the tomato, pimientos, paprika, cayenne or chili pepper? And how did the Spanish and Portuguese get along before they had the white potato? As late as the 1700s in France, physicians cautioned their patients against eating potatoes, which were "toxic and the cause of many maladies." Imagine a world innocent of "French fries"! Yet none of these foods were known in Europe before the fifteenth century, nor were sweet potatoes, pineapples, avocadoes or what still in Europe is called maize—what we call corn.

When the Atlantic routes were opened, the Mediterranean became a kind of backwater, although the great western powers established Mediterranean colonies: Spain controlled much of North Africa (Spanish paella and gazpacho are foods as popular in Tunisia and Algeria today as in Spain itself) and Portugal, for a time, had a foothold in North Africa. Later the French would take over the Spanish North African colonies and establish their hegemony in Lebanon, while the English would impose their rule on Cyprus, Malta, Gibraltar and Egypt. Yet when one visits these countries today it is surprising to observe how shallow the western influences are in comparison with the deeper and more profound Levantine heritage.

Of all the countries bordering the Mediterranean, France is least like the others. This struck me when I ended my tour with visits to Marseilles, Arles and Avignon. My purpose in arranging the tour in this manner was to find out just how the earlier cuisines of countries had been transformed by the French, knowing that as a matter of history, almost every dish and every sauce that we think of as French actually originated elsewhere.

The southernmost provinces of France, the only areas in France that can be called truly Mediterranean, also had their Greek, Roman, Visigothic and Arabic periods. While the north of France was still barbarian territory, there were rich and densely populated cities in the south: Narbonne was an important Roman port; Bézier, Nîmes and Toulouse had schools of rhetoric and poetry as early as the fifth century; and Arles, as the capital of a *provincia romana*, had a theater, public baths and an immense arena where bullfights are still staged today. When a council was held in Narbonne in 589, the population of the province was reported to include, beside Romans and Visigoths, Syrians, Greeks and a large colony of Jews. Long after the Saracens had been stopped at Poitiers, friendly communication was maintained with Moorish princes across the Pyrenees in Spain.

Visiting a museum in Arles, which was given over wholly to Provençal traditions, I was struck by the faces in dozens of eighteenth century family portraits that filled one gallery. Most were women's portraits, only a few were men, but men and women alike showed a sharpness of profile and a stubborn individuality of expression, and there were far more blondes than brunettes among them. Was this true of the Ligurians, the aborigines already in France when the first Greek settlers arrived? Or has it been a matter of evolution and centuries of intermarriage with invading tribes from the north?

And what made the French cuisine so superior to others? Examining individual recipes does not provide the answer. Many of the "typical" dishes of Provence or Languedoc have their counterpart in neighboring Catalán on the west or in northern Italy in the east: Soupe au Pistou is simply the Gallicized name of a Genovese dish; Ratatouille has its counterpart in every Mediterranean country; the garlic soup of Provence is identical to that of Spain, and so on and on.

The answer is possibly to be found in the stubbornness and discipline that I noted in the Arlesian family portraits, as well as in the attention to detail and willingness to take hours to prepare one sauce if the results prove worth the time and trouble. Attention to detail is an important precept for any cook who truly wishes to master the art of Mediterranean cooking, which has inspired poets, sensualists and bon vivants throughout the ages.

There is nothing which is a greater provocative of drinking than almonds when eaten between meals.

—Athenaeus, *The Deipnosophists*


I took the hot hearth-cakes, how could I help it?
And dipped them in a sauce, and then I ate them.

—Athenaeus, *The Deipnosophists*


In former times a dinner of importance always began with oysters and there was always a good number of guests who did not stop until they had swallowed a gross [12 dozen].

—Brillat-Savarin, *Physiology of Taste*

# Appetizers

The most Mediterranean of all things to do is to sit idly at a cafe table, in view of the sea if possible, and sip at an aperitif, nibbling at nuts, olives or other snacks while watching the world go by. The waiter won't bother you with the check; it may even be hard to get his attention if you want refills. Relax, relax, relax seems to be the message of the hot sunlight, the soft air and the rippling water of that blue, blue sea.

The kind of snacks you will nibble on will differ a little from country to country, but not as much as you might think. There is a bigger difference between those foods served at a cafe with aperitif drinks and those offered as part of a lunch or dinner. In Spain tapas are served only with drinks; the same is true of mezes in Greece and of kemia in North Africa. Yet in France hors d'oeuvres generally means foods served as a first course at midday luncheon, which is also the meaning of antipasto in Italy and acepipes in Portugal. On the other hand, order mezes in Cyprus or Lebanon, and as many as thirty little dishes—a meal in itself—may appear.

In most Mediterranean cafes, both snack foods and hors d'oeuvres are on display inside refrigerated cases or on countertops, and the pointing of a finger tells the waiter the one you want to try. Snack bars are not new: they were a fixture in Pompeii, and

19

long before that, the Greeks of antiquity exchanged recipes for their favorite "provocatives to drinking." In modern times, snack bars have spread like mushrooms everywhere, until it's now possible to eat three meals a day without ever sitting down—if you want to be that American. Nuts, olives, bite-sized seafood, cheese, meat, sandwiches in all shapes and sizes, hot or cold croquettes and meat-, cheese- or fish-filled pastries are among the temptations offered. In addition, there may be salads of many kinds and such curiosities (to us) as pickled octopus, sea urchins, thumbnail-sized clams and *percebes* (barnacles), which look like a monster's black claws.

If it's a cafe in Spain, the aperitif is dry sherry; in France, it's vermouth or one of several other herb-flavored aperitifs; in Italy, it's campari; it's ouzo in Greece, raki or arak in Turkey or Lebanon and beer anywhere. You can, of course, have whiskey, gin or vodka, but these are tourist drinks, and only the more sophisticated natives touch them. If you ask for a martini, expect to be served sweet vermouth; cocktails as we know them have never found acceptance in the Mediterranean countries.

The further east you travel, the more frequently dips are encountered. The name may be American, but smooth, saucelike mixtures into which bread or crackers may be dipped have been in use since long before America was discovered.

Oysters are available in season in most Mediterranean cities, but no longer are they consumed in such quantities as they were in antiquity, when the emperor Vitellius is said to have eaten a thousand a day and Seneca put away 200 before lunch— "then complained of indigestion." Oysters are nearly always served raw on the half shell, but mussels are invariably cooked. Clams of all shapes, sizes and varieties are offered, sometimes raw, sometimes cooked. A bit of lemon juice improves the taste of every kind of seafood, but especially the molluscs.

Need it be added that potato chips are now as universal as ice cubes? And the word chips (pronounced *cheeps*) is understood by everyone, everywhere. Yet I must say that quality is a factor of inestimable importance. How lovely it was to sit on the terrace of the elegant St. George Hotel in Beirut as sunset reddened the mountains rising above the city and touched with pink the waves of the harbor, to crunch potato chips so crisp they might have come from a kettle of boiling oil moments before, and to eat peanuts so fresh they still had the sweetness of the harvest in their "fatness." The best packaging system in the world cannot preserve that kind of flavor.

# NUTS

Almonds, walnuts, hazelnuts, peanuts and chestnuts are all in plentiful supply throughout the Mediterranean. Peanuts are not native to the Mediterranean. They originated in central Africa, but before they were introduced to Europe, they had been to America and back. Chestnuts appear only in the fall of the year. The fragrance of roasted chestnuts filling the air from thousands of peddler's braziers is irresistible, and in Europe, at least, chestnuts cost very little. Pistachio nuts used to be plentiful in Greece and I'd looked forward to gorging on them on my return, but I didn't see any. Perhaps they now are all going to America.

Most Americans buy their nuts in cans, already salted, but the following tips for treating fresh nuts may be of interest.

Shelled almonds are quickly blanched if cooked in boiling water for 2 minutes. Then turn the heat off. After the water has cooled, the almond skins will slip off easily. If the nuts are to be shredded, now is the time to do it, while they are warm and soft.

To toast blanched almonds, spread them over a pie pan and place in a preheated oven until all are deeply golden—turn with a fork once or twice for even toasting. Avoid both under- and over-browning. Add no more than a teaspoon of butter or oil, stir to coat all the nuts and then sprinkle with salt. Almonds must be thoroughly cold before they become crunchy.

Chestnuts are marvelous hot from the oven. Slit the shell of each chestnut before placing in a preheated hot (425° F.) oven. Roast 20 minutes, or until the slits have opened wide. Serve hot, for guests to shell themselves and spread with butter as they are eaten.

# OLIVES

It wouldn't be the Mediterranean without olives, but it's surprising how those of the various countries differ in flavor. This is due among other things to the varieties of the tree itself. There are more than 300 varieties of olives in cultivation. Another factor is the way the trees have been cultivated. In Spain the trees are heavily pruned; in Portugal and Crete very lightly pruned. The brine or other preservative used in the cure also affects the taste.

Only in Spain are stuffed green olives commonly served. Occasionally, one will come upon spiced or herbed olives. In the souk of Beirut, I noticed baskets of green (untreated) olives for sale and was told that people buy them to put up in brine in their homes. To hasten curing, the olives are bruised just a bit. In a nearby tub, I saw olives combined in a brine with little hot chili peppers and took a taste of one—and immediately regretted it. They were fiery hot!

Whether one's preference is for the sharply salted black olives of Italy, the softer ones of Greece, or the tiny bitter black olives of Portugal is a matter of taste. Of them all, none can compare in my estimation with the Greek kalamata olives, almond-shaped, preserved in a mixture of olive oil and red wine vinegar, more purple than black in color. These olives are available in jars in Greek-American groceries.

# SEAFOOD

Anchovies, according to Archestratus, require so little cooking that they should be put into a pan already hot and taken off the fire "as soon as they hiss." It must have been fresh anchovies of which he spoke. Most of us know the anchovy only as it comes from a tin, heavily salted. Little finger-length fish that have been floured and then fried until crisp are often served with drinks in Mediterranean cafes. The flesh of these fish is sweet but there's mighty little of it. Everything considered, salted tinned anchovies have their advantages. So do tinned sardines, especially those that have already been boned.

Much more interesting than sardines right from the can are those that have been marinated in an *escabeche* (pickling) sauce, especially if they are to be served with an assortment of hors d'oeuvres.

# Sardinas Escabeche

| | |
|---|---|
| 2 cans Portuguese boned sardines | 1 bay leaf |
| 1 large onion, thinly sliced | 4 - 5 peppercorns |
| ¼ cup salad oil | Salt to taste |
| ¼ cup vinegar | Dash of Tabasco sauce |
| 2 tablespoons minced parsley or fresh coriander | 3 lemon slices |
| | ¼ cup water |

Drain sardines and place in a clean bowl. Combine remaining ingredients. Bring to a boil. Pour through strainer over sardines and let stand several hours. Serve sprinkled with sieved egg yolks or pimiento strips for garnish. Makes about 8 servings.

# Anchovy Antipasto

This is easy, colorful and a delightful flavor combination. Arrange in the center of a platter or around a plate, fillets of anchovy interspersed with quarters of hard-cooked eggs. Sprinkle capers over the top. Encircle this with a mixture of fried green and red sweet peppers. To prepare the peppers, cut seeded peppers in strips; sauté in olive oil until tender; sprinkle with salt and cool before serving. Or, use only canned pimiento cut in strips, dressed with olive oil and vinegar and sprinkled with minced parsley. This makes an excellent first course hors d'oeuvre, or a buffet offering at a cocktail supper. Sardines, well drained, can be used instead of anchovies.

# Shrimp

Nine out of ten times, in every Mediterranean country, shrimp are served in the shell at cafes. Tearing off the shell is considered no hardship at all, especially if it's done at the aperitif hour while one sits lazily watching the paseo along the street or seawall. I discovered that when shrimp are fried in the shell, they have a much richer flavor. When the shell is removed, you also lose the excess fat used in the frying.

It's probably useless to suggest this to Americans, who almost always buy shrimp already shelled and deveined and frozen in plastic containers. For the American supermarket shopper, the following adaptations of Mediterranean recipes are suggested.

# Shrimp—Oil and Lemon Sauce

Drop shrimp into boiling salted water; turn down heat so water is no longer boiling; cook until just pink. Turn off heat; let shrimp stand in water until it cools; then drain. Marinate shrimp in a mixture of four parts olive oil to one part lemon juice, with salt and pepper to taste. Use the best quality olive oil. Salad oil may be used, but personally I find it too bland.

# Shrimp in Sherry Sauce

Cook the shrimp as you did the Shrimp—Oil and Lemon Sauce, but when drained, marinate in a mixture of very dry sherry and an equal quantity of fine olive or salad oil, plus a quantity of minced parsley. Add salt and pepper to taste. Serve with lemon wedges.

# Gambas Alioli

The shrimp will be more attractive in appearance if purchased in the shell, and if, when it is shelled, the tail is left on. But this method can also be used with preshelled shrimp. Sauté shrimp gently in olive oil along with several cloves of garlic until shrimp turn orange; when garlic is golden, mash it into the oil with tines of a fork to release juices. Remove garlic before serving; sprinkle shrimp with salt and lemon juice. Serve piping hot, preferably in small earthenware casseroles.

# Fried Scampi

The Portuguese claim to have taught the Japanese how to fry batter-dipped shrimp, the dish the rest of the world now knows as tempura. (The Japanese themselves give credit to the Portuguese.) Did the Portuguese learn it from the Italians, or vice versa? The following is the way it's done in Italy, whatever the order of invention. Scampi is simply the Italian name for a variety of prawn that may be cooked in various ways.

| | |
|---|---|
| 1 cup flour | 1 egg white, beaten |
| 3 tablespoons oil | 1 pound shrimp, shelled |
| ¾ cup water | Oil for deep frying |
| Pinch of salt | Lemon wedges |

These shrimp, too, will be more attractive if they are purchased in the shell and the tail is kept intact—but frozen, already shelled shrimp can also be used, if thoroughly defrosted and well drained before dipping in batter. Put flour in a bowl; make a well in the center; add oil; and blend oil with flour. Add water gradually, making a smooth batter; then add salt. Do this in advance—let batter stand at least an hour before using. Beat egg whites until fluffy and stir them into the batter just before the shrimp are to be dipped into it. Oil must be preheated to 375° F. (If you don't have a thermometer, test oil with a small cube of bread; the bread should be golden in 50 to 60 seconds. Remove bread before adding shrimp.) This batter makes a crisp, light coating for the shrimp. Serve while hot with lemon wedges.

# Pasteis de Bacalau
*(codfish croquettes)*

| | |
|---|---|
| 1 piece salt codfish, about 6 x 6 inches | 2 tablespoons minced parsley |
| 2 cups cooked mashed potatoes (about 4 potatoes) | 1 egg, beaten |
| 1-2 tablespoons minced or grated onion | Olive oil for frying |

Soak codfish in water overnight. Drain; add boiling water to cover; bring again to a boil; cook until fork-tender. Drain again. When fish is cool, tear into shreds, discarding skin and bones. Combine with potatoes, onion, parsley and egg. Beat mixture until light and fluffy. If the croquettes are to be served immediately, shape with 2 teaspoons into small balls; drop into hot oil (½ inch deep) in frying pan; cook until golden on all sides. If you wish to serve them later, chill mixture; shape into thick fingers; roll in fine crumbs before frying. Drain on absorbent paper. Good either hot or cold. Makes about 30 appetizer-sized croquettes.

## Tamarasalata
(*Greek caviar dip*)

| | |
|---|---|
| ¼ cup red caviar; or ½ cup tamara | 1 cup olive oil |
| 2 - 3 slices bread, crusts removed | 2 thick slices onion |
| | 2 tablespoons lemon juice, or to taste |
| 1 or 2 cloves garlic, crushed | 1 tablespoon minced parsley |

Tamara is the Greek name for the roe of red mullet, available in cans in many Greek-American groceries (check yellow pages under Gourmet Shops or Imports—Food Products). Tamara is more delicate in flavor than the red salmon caviar sold in supermarkets and is preferable, if it can be located.

First, place bread and crushed or minced garlic in bowl. Add olive oil; marinate overnight; then crush together into a paste. Place the caviar or tamara in blender; add onion; beat to purée; then add bread mixture, lemon juice and parsley. Beat until very light and fluffy. Salt is usually not necessary, but may be added to taste. Makes approximately ¾ cup.

## Pastel de Gambas
(*aspic shrimp salad*)

It could be sheer luck, but in the course of four visits to Barcelona, one of my favorite cities, in every restaurant I've tried, the food has been superb—and in several cases, I walked into a simple-looking place off the street without knowing a thing about it. I can't say I've always had such luck in France. What's more, there is an originality, a true creativity that distinguishes Catalán cookery. The following is a dish I enjoyed at a snack bar one evening after having attended a performance of Antonio Gades' ballet troupe dancing impassioned flamenco. I was still feeling elated with the exuberant mood of the dance. It was impossible to go quietly back to the hotel, but I intended only to have something light to eat. When I saw Pastel de Gambas on the menu, it interested me, because that afternoon, while wandering through the public market, the sight of gleaming, fresh shrimp and other shellfish had made me hungry for seafood. The serving brought to me was as beautiful in appearance as in flavor. It was a molded salad topped with shrimp, held in place with a ruby-red glaze. For garniture, it was surrounded by grated carrot slivers, marinated artichoke hearts, black olives and tiny radishes. It's ideal for a buffet hors d'oeuvre.

| | |
|---|---|
| 6 ounces small shrimp, already shelled | 2 pimientos, well drained |
| 4 or 5 medium potatoes, cooked | 1 or 2 garlic cloves |
| ½ teaspoon salt, or to taste | ½ cup mayonnaise |
| ⅓ cup olive oil | ½ cup tomato juice or *Clamato*—blended clam and tomato juice |
| 2 tablespoons vinegar | |
| 1 medium onion | ½ tablespoon unflavored gelatin |
| ¼ cup chopped green peppers | |

Cook shrimp by adding to boiling salted water; bring water back to the boil; then lower heat so that water simmers very gently. Turn off heat as soon as shrimp are bright pink. Reserve enough shrimp to garnish top of mold; mince the remainder.

Combine olive oil, vinegar and salt. Add to cooked potatoes while potatoes are warm. In blender, beat onion, green peppers, pimiento, garlic and shrimp until very finely minced; beat until almost a puree. Beat in mayonnaise, blending well. Press mixture into a loaf pan (9 x 5 x 2 inches) to mold; then turn out on a platter. Smooth edges with the blade of a knife. Arrange overlapping shrimp over the top of the loaf.

Heat the tomato or clam-tomato juice, *Clamato*; soften the unflavored gelatin with 2 tablespoons of cold water, then add the hot juice and stir until dissolved. Spoon half the glaze over the molded salad; chill until firm. Repeat with a second layer of the glaze. Keep refrigerated until ready to serve. To serve, cut in ¾-inch slices. For garniture, arrange artichoke hearts, carrots and black olives around the base. Makes 10 to 12 servings. (Even without the glaze, this makes a very attractive salad, especially if Vinaigrette-marinated avocado slices are placed around the base as garnish. Or the salad mixture may be piled on top of artichoke bottoms.)

# MEATS FOR MEZES

"You must learn what our mezes are like," I was told in Cyprus, and happily I agreed, expecting to have perhaps four or five appetizers with ouzo. I thought the waiter would never stop delivering the little dishes and the platters of foods, both hot and cold. "Appetizers" is hardly the word for them; we were still at the table long after midnight, and there was still food on some of the platters, barely touched. By this time, several bottles of wine had been emptied and the men were dancing to music from the juke box, their feet tapping out intricate steps, their fingers snapping in the air. Women are not kept off the dance floor in Cyprus, but dancing is primarily a male prerogative in both Cyprus and Crete. The men dance superbly, leaping, twirling, slapping knees. Then suddenly there was a crash. One of the women had hurled a saucer at the men's feet, and soon saucers were littering the floor from all sides, with the men nimbly stepping over and around them. It must be counted as part of the overhead on the part of taverna owners, because no one present seemed to think the custom strange.

Early in the evening, I had written out detailed descriptions of the dishes we were served, but in the hilarity of the saucer-breaking and the ever more exuberant dancing, I must have left the notes behind me, for I haven't been able to find them since. I have only memory to go on, memories of wonderful food, and wonderfully spontaneous people. What more can one ask of an evening?

Tahina and hummus were both on the table (recipes for these are given later in this section), as were two versions of liver (one broiled, the other cold in a sauce), little hot kebabs of lamb, tiny fried fish like the ones Archestratus was probably describing, feta cheese marinated in an oil-lemon sauce, little spicy meat balls, shrimp, *taramasalata*, fried sweet peppers, eggplant "caviar," various kinds of pickles, sausages and cold cuts. Fruit—large sweet grapes and luscious peaches—was brought in later on.

A few days later in Beirut, when I ordered *maza* at the seaside restaurant, Nasr, the assortment consisted of exactly the same foods, plus some delicious little meat pastries. Arak, which is almost the same as ouzo, was served with the maza. The setting was beautiful, the food was good—only the hilarious joy was missing. The interesting thing was to observe that though one restaurant was Greek and the other was Arab, their cuisine was almost identical.

# Mi'laaq Mashwi bi Toum
(*liver kebabs*)

Crush several garlic cloves. Work in a teaspoon of salt, a few leaves of dried mint and ¼ cup olive oil. Cut chicken livers in half, or use fresh tender steer liver cut in 1-inch pieces. Marinate the liver in the garlic mixture for 1 or 2 hours. Thread liver on skewers and broil until nicely browned on all sides. Serve hot with lemon wedges, sprinkling lemon over the liver at the table.

# Souvlakia Kephtaides
(*appetizer meatballs*)

In Greece, these meatballs are called Souvlakia Keftaides, but in Lebanon and Syria, where they are made with almost exactly the same ingredients, the name becomes Dawwd Basha.

| | | | |
|---|---|---|---|
| 1½ | pounds ground lamb or beef | 1½ | teaspoons salt |
| 1½ | tablespoons minced parsley | ½ | teaspoon pepper |
| | | ¼ | teaspoon cinnamon or nutmeg (optional) |
| 1 | teaspoon crushed dried mint or oregano | ¼ to ½ | cup pine nuts, coarsely chopped |
| ½ to ¾ | cup minced onion | 1 | egg, beaten |

The meat should be put through the grinder twice (ask the butcher to do this for you). Mash the ground meat in a mortar or bowl with a pestle until pastelike. Work in the rest of the ingredients, forming a compact mass—use your fingers to make it smooth. Form small balls; place on small skewers and grill over charcoal, or sauté in hot fat until browned on all sides. Serve hot. Makes about 40 tiny meatballs. (The meatballs may be sautéed beforehand and kept hot in red wine in a chafing dish to be speared with cocktail picks. As the wine simmers it thickens into a delicious sauce.)

# Rosto Madgouga Martadella
(*Arabian meatloaf*)

| | | |
|---|---|---|
| 2½ | pounds ground beef or lamb | 1 cup water |
| 2 | teaspoons salt | 2 tablespoons lemon juice |
| 1 | teaspoon black pepper | 2 tablespoons tomato paste |
| ½ | teaspoon cinnamon | |
| ½ | teaspoon nutmeg | **Basting sauce** |
| ½ | cup fine dry crumbs | 2 tablespoons tomato paste |
| 2 | egg whites, or 1 whole egg, beaten | ¼ cup vinegar |
| | | ¼ cup water |

Put meat through grinder twice; then work ground meat with fingers or mash with pestle to make a smooth paste. Blend with all of remaining ingredients, working with fingers until very, very smooth. Divide mixture in half and shape into two oblong rolls. Brush outside of each roll with olive oil; then roll in additional fine crumbs. Place in shallow roasting pan, in oven preheated to 350° F. As meat begins to brown, baste with sauce of tomato paste, vinegar and water. Cook 1 hour. Remove from oven; cool in pan. When completely cold, slice very thin to serve with mezes. This meat loaf is also very good hot, served as an entrée; make gravy with the pan drippings. Makes enough for 20 to 30 appetizer servings.

Other meats that may be adapted for mezes are given in the chapter on Meats: small lamb kebabs, almost any meatballs, spiced ham or other cold cuts may be included.

# VEGETABLES

Everywhere in the eastern Mediterranean, I noticed how many dishes listed in Lebanese or Syrian cookbooks have their counter-part in the Israeli cuisine. One can only conclude that geography determines food habits and food tastes quite as much as do cultural traditions. Jewish cooking, of course, is international, but native Israeli cooking closely resembles that of neighboring Arabian countries. When I asked once in Haifa, at a cafe, where I could find an especially good restaurant, the waiter asked, "European or oriental?" By oriental of course, he meant those restaurants whose foods are typical of the eastern Mediterranean.

# Tahina Sauce
(*sesame oil sauce*)

Tahina (also spelled *tahineh, taheeni,* or *tahini*) is the name by which sesame oil is known throughout the Near East. It is also the name of the sauce made with sesame oil, lemon juice and garlic. The oil can be purchased in cans from Greek-American or oriental groceries (check the yellow pages of your telephone directory under Gourmet Shops or Imports—Food Products).

|   |   |
|---|---|
| 1 cup sesame oil | 1 to 3 cloves garlic, crushed |
| 6 tablespoons lemon juice | ½ to 1 teaspoon salt (to taste) |
| ½ cup water | ½ cup parsley, coarsely chopped |

The easiest way to make the sauce is with a blender. Place the oil in the blender first; add, with blender in motion, water and lemon juice alternately until the mixture is the consistency of thick cream. Crush the garlic separately in a mortar or bowl and work in the salt. Add the garlic-salt mixture to the tahina. Do not overbeat. Serve in a shallow saucer or small bowl, with parsley sprinkled over the top. If a more tart flavor is preferred, add more lemon juice. Makes about 2 cups.

# Hummus
(*chick pea dip*)

| | |
|---|---|
| 1 large can chick peas | Garlic salt to taste |
| ½ cup Tahina Sauce | Chopped parsley for |
| Lemon juice | garnish |

Thoroughly drain the chick peas; force through food mill or beat in blender. Add Tahina Sauce, previously prepared, and additional lemon and garlic salt to taste. Serve as a dip with sesame crackers or as a sauce over cold vegetables, meat or fish. Makes about 2 cups.

# Garbanzo Salad

Chick peas are frequently served as appetizers in all the Mediterranean port cities. In Greece, roasted salted chick peas are sold from peddlers' carts along with salted almonds and pistachio nuts. Garbanzo salad is my favorite of them all.

The name for chick peas is different in every country: it is ceci in Italy, garbanzo in Spain, grão in Portugal, hummus in the Near East, revithia in Greece and pois chiches in France.

| | |
|---|---|
| ½ teaspoon salt | ¼ cup minced parsley |
| 1 or 2 garlic cloves, crushed | ¼ cup chopped pimiento |
| 1-pound can chick peas, drained | ¼ to ⅓ cup olive oil |
| 1 small onion, minced | 2 tablespoons vinegar, or to taste |

Crush garlic and salt together; add remaining ingredients; blend well. Marinate at room temperature several hours before serving. Makes 6 to 8 appetizer servings.

# Eggplant

This vegetable originated in China and was brought to the Mediterranean for the first time by Arab traders in about the tenth century. Today it's as hard to imagine Mediterranean kitchens without eggplants as without tomatoes and potatoes. The Arabs call it batinjaan; the Spanish altered this to berejena, and the French name, aubergine, undoubtedly originated as "the berejeen." The English word eggplant goes back to a time when the fruits were small, not much larger than eggs, and some were even whitish-gray in color. Small eggplants, pink or mauve in color, are often served raw in Lebanon and Israel, pickled as an hors d'oeuvre. The big purple vegetable we know as the eggplant in America is an evolution of the species.

Until I became acquainted with the Mediterranean way of preparing eggplant, I was never enthusiastic about the vegetable. Now eggplant is one of my favorite vegetables, and it goes with olive oil like bread goes with butter. Besides the following relishes or appetizers, many other eggplant recipes will be found in the chapter on vegetables.

In my opinion, the purplish peel of the eggplant is the best part, but not everyone agrees with me. Mediterranean cooks recommend sprinkling eggplant with salt and letting it stand 15 minutes to ½ hour before trying to extract the bitter juices. When eggplant is very fresh this may not be necessary; the bitterness becomes more pronounced when the vegetable is older.

# Batinjaan Imfasak
*(eggplant-yogurt dip)*

| | |
|---|---|
| 1 large eggplant | 2 cloves garlic |
| Salt | ½ cup yogurt, or sour cream |
| ½ - ¾ cup olive oil | Chopped parsley |

Peel and slice eggplant very thin. Sprinkle every slice with salt from shaker; let stand ½ hour; then drain, pressing to remove liquid. Fry in hot olive oil until slices are lightly browned on each side. At the same time, add garlic cloves to the oil; and, when golden, press into oil with tines of fork. The eggplant will absorb garlic flavor as it fries. When all the eggplant has been cooked, combine with yogurt or sour cream and parsley; beat to blend to a purée. If a stronger garlic flavor is desired, crush additional garlic in a bowl; add to the purée. Add more salt to taste. Makes about 2 cups.

# Eggplant Chips

Small oblong eggplants, unpeeled, are sometimes thinly sliced and fried in olive oil until browned on each side, then salted and served hot as hors d'oeuvres, like potato chips. Zucchini squash is also delicious served this way.

# Green Caviar
(*eggplant salad*)

In all the Balkan countries and throughout the Near East, this salad is frequently served as an hors d'oeuvre, but it can just as well be offered as a dip. It is especially good with sesame crackers.

The small oblong eggplants of the Mediterranean always seem to me more flavorful than our American giants; unfortunately, the little ones seldom appear in our markets. In any case, it's important that the eggplants have been picked fully ripe; if picked when somewhat green, they have less flavor and are likely to be bitter.

1 large or 4 tiny eggplants
3 or 4 cloves garlic
 Salt to taste
⅓ - ½ cup olive oil
1 small onion, grated or minced

Lemon juice or vinegar to taste
¼ cup minced parsley
 Black olives for garnish

The best way to make this salad is to grill the unpeeled whole eggplant over charcoal; the next best way is to grill it over a gas flame. But if neither of these methods is available, the eggplant can be put under the broiler unit or baked in the oven. Grill, turning occasionally, until skin is very wrinkled and somewhat charred. Allow to cool, then peel off the skin. If there are a large number of seeds, remove as many as possible. Drain the pulp. One large eggplant may produce only 1 to 1½ cups pulp.

Crush garlic, work in salt (about ½ teaspoon), then olive oil. Combine with eggplant pulp, lemon juice or vinegar, onion and parsley; beat until smooth. Serve with additional parsley over top; add black olives as garnish. When served as an hors d'oeuvre the salad is served over lettuce. It can also be used as a dip. Makes 1½ to 2 cups.

# HORS D'OEUVRES VARIÉS

There's no doubt that the French have a special touch when it comes to preparing hors d'oeuvres: that certain delicacy of flavor that is piquant without ever becoming overpowering. Also, the selection offered from an hors d'oeuvre cart always seems to be well balanced: two or three kinds of seafood, such as mackerel fillets in a white wine sauce, plump sardines dressed only with lemon, perhaps fish salad, nearly always a few shrimp. Usually there will be Salade Russe in some form, and at least two pickled vegetables. Sliced cooked potatoes dressed simply with oil and vinegar offset cold sliced *saucisson*. And tiny crisp radishes, sliced tomatoes and shredded carrots round out the flavor-texture balance.

The following recipes could all be included in hors d'oeuvres variés, even though not all are French.

## Champignons à la Grecque
(*pickled mushrooms*)

"Greek style" is what the French call mushrooms pickled in this manner, though I've never encountered their like in Greece.

|  |  |  |  |
|---|---|---|---|
| 2 | pounds button mushrooms | 1 | bay leaf; or ½ teaspoon thyme |
| ½ | lemon |  | |
|  | Water | 2 | whole cloves |
| 1 | cup wine vinegar | ⅔ | cup olive oil |
| ½ | teaspoon salt |  | Minced parsley |
| 12 | whole peppercorns |  | |

Select very white fresh mushrooms; trim ends only; do not peel. Squeeze lemon into a bowl half filled with water; drop mushrooms into the water as they are trimmed. Make sure mushrooms are thoroughly cleaned—soil often clings to them. Meantime, combine vinegar with 2 cups fresh water, salt, dried herbs, cloves and 6 of the peppercorns. Bring to a boil; add mushrooms; and cook 1 minute. Cool mushrooms in liquid. Remove mushrooms with slotted spoon to jar or bowl. Strain vinegar mixture; add ¾ cup of vinegar mixture to ¾ cup olive oil; pour over mushrooms. Add

6 remaining peppercorns. Refrigerate. To serve, sprinkle with minced parsley. Makes about 4 cups.

# Celeri Vinaigrette à la Crème
*(celery root hors d'oeuvres)*

| | | |
|---|---|---|
| 1 | large celery root, cut in slivers | Salt, pepper |
| 1 | egg yolk | Lemon juice to taste |
| ¼ | cup sour cream | Minced parsley or chives |
| ½ | cup olive oil | Sugar to taste, if desired |

If celery root is not available, this can be made with Pascal celery, cut in thin slivers and cooked until barely tender, then drained. However, the true French version is made with celery root, a big brownish knob of a vegetable with leaves faintly resembling badly wilted celery leaves. Peel the knob; cut the root into slivers; then cook in boiling salted water about 5 minutes; drain. The root should still be crisp. To make the dressing, beat egg yolk in blender until thickened; add the sour cream; beat until smooth. Then, with the blender in motion, add olive oil in a thin stream. The mixture should thicken somewhat, but will be the consistency of heavy cream, not as thick as mayonnaise. Add seasonings and lemon juice. The sauce should be tart, but just a bit of sugar gives a smoother flavor. Toss celery or celery root with sauce; serve as part of hors d'oeuvres variés. Makes about 6 servings.

# Salade Russe

In its most elemental form, Salade Russe is simply diced carrots and peas held together by mayonnaise, and with this beginning, you can go in almost any direction. Other vegetables may be added, such as cooked potatoes, cooked diced turnips, minced raw celery, minced raw green pepper or canned pimiento. For best flavor, the vegetables should be cooked separately in salted water, and, ideally, the mayonnaise should be homemade. Some people marinate each vegetable first in well-seasoned Vinaigrette Sauce (see Sauces and Seasonings chapter), then toss together with mayonnaise.

## Turkish Cucumber-Walnut Salad

Walnuts are used in many unusual ways in Turkey, and this salad mixture is one. All the ingredients should be chopped, but not too finely.

| | |
|---|---|
| 2 medium cucumbers, peeled and chopped | ½ cup chopped walnuts |
| Salt, pepper | 2 tablespoons chopped green peppers |
| 1 teaspoon lemon juice | 1 tablespoon chopped fresh mint; or ½ teaspoon dried mint, crushed |
| 2 garlic cloves | |
| ¼ cup olive oil | |
| 1 tablespoon vinegar | |

First sprinkle chopped cucumber with salt, pepper, lemon juice. Let stand ½ hour; then drain well. Crush garlic cloves; add olive oil and vinegar. Combine drained cucumber, walnuts, green pepper, mint and the garlic-flavored oil and marinate 1 hour before serving. Serve on lettuce. Makes about 6 servings. (Instead of oil and vinegar, try adding ¼ cup yogurt and 1 teaspoon sugar as dressing.)

## Salpichon de Mariscos
*(shrimp hors d'oeuvres)*

| | |
|---|---|
| 2 jars tiny Danish or Norwegian shrimp | 1 cup cooked peas |
| 2 small onions, sliced paper thin | ¼ cup diced pimiento |
| | ¼ cup olive oil |
| 1 carrot, cooked 5 minutes and diced | ½ cup wine vinegar |
| | Salt to taste |

Drain shrimp; combine with remaining ingredients; marinate an hour or more before serving. A delicious hors d'oeuvre, and with the vegetables added, not expensive. Makes about 10 appetizer servings.

# Artichokes à la Turque

Cook frozen artichoke hearts in olive oil (no water), using, for each 10-ounce package, ¼ cup olive oil, ¼ teaspoon salt, ¼ teaspoon thyme or oregano, ¼ teaspoon crushed coriander (or use chopped fresh coriander or chopped parsley) and a whole garlic clove. Saucepan must be tightly covered, with the heat kept low. Cook about 10 minutes or until fork-tender. Turn off heat; remove and discard garlic; add lemon juice or vinegar to taste. Serve cold, topped with minced parsley.

# Salade Niçoise

One can find almost as many different recipes for this famous salad of Nice as for Salade Russe. This, too, is a salad of mixed cooked vegetables, most often including green beans and potatoes plus black olives (the one ingredient *always* included). Since such vague directions only confuse many cooks, here is what I find to be an interesting combination.

| | |
|---|---|
| 3 medium potatoes, cooked and diced | ½ cup black olives (Italian or Greek) |
| 1 cup Vinaigrette Sauce (see Sauces and Seasonings chapter); or oil-vinegar French dressing | Anchovy fillets<br>Capers |
| 2 cups cooked French green beans | 2 tomatoes, quartered or sliced |
| 2 or 3 hard-cooked eggs | 1 can white meat tuna, drained (optional) |

While potatoes are still warm, cover with about ¼ cup of the Vinaigrette Sauce; toss to blend. Do the same separately with the green beans. Both should be prepared some time ahead. Arrange the salad in the following manner on a platter, or on individual serving dishes if this is to be a first course or a main course at lunch: a mound of potato salad, a mound of green beans, over-lapping tomato slices or tomato quarters, well moistened with Vinaigrette Sauce, and quarters of hard-cooked eggs. Anchovy fillets are arranged like wheel spokes between other ingredients. If tuna is added, it should be in chunks, moistened with the sauce. Black olives are dotted around the plate, and capers sprinkled over the top. Sometimes small whole beets, or sliced pickled beets, are also added to the arrangement. Makes enough for 6 to 8 persons.

# PASTRIES AND HOT SNACKS

Every country has its own meat- or cheese-filled pastries, some so similar that only the names, or the pastry used, are different. In Greece, phyllo, or fila pastry (much like strudel) is generally used; a very thin pancake, unlike a French crepe because it contains no egg, is used in Tunisia and Algiers. The Turkish *börek* is made with pastry dough rolled very thin. Most of these Mediterranean pastries are fried in deep fat, but they can be baked in the oven, if brushed with melted butter or oil before baking. The dough used in making Sambousik in Lebanon is very much like our pie crust dough.

*Brik*, or *brek*, is the most unusual of all. The first time I had it was in a hotel dining room in Carthage, and when I ordered it, I had no idea what to expect. Presently there was put before me a crisply fried turnover almost the size of the plate, and when I cut into it with my fork, it was to taste a superb filling of meat blended with yogurt, fresh coriander and pepper. With another bite, out came a golden stream of egg yolk. This was called on the menu, Brik a la Viande, meaning there was meat in the filling. The more common name is Brik a l'Oeuf, for a raw egg is always enclosed in the pancake.

I'm sad to report that I haven't yet mastered the technique of making this at home. In Tunis, pancakes especially for the purpose —huge (about 10 inches), very thin and soft—are sold in the bakeshops and public markets. I tried duplicating them with pancake mix, but was unable to make a pancake large enough to both enclose the egg and keep it soft inside while frying.

Fortunately I had more luck with a similar appetizer made in Algiers, called *betzel*. The same paper-thin pancakes are used, but not the unbeaten raw egg, so that it was possible to fold over and enclose the filling more easily.

The names börek in Turkey, bourekakia in Greece, and brek (or brik) in Tunisia indicate that all may have been the same originally, and have gained their differences in the hands of imaginative cooks over the centuries.

# Betzel
(*Algerian rolled pancake*)

| | |
|---|---|
| 1½ cups pancake mix | Dash of nutmeg |
| 1½ cups water | Salt, pepper to taste |
| ¼ pound ground beef or lamb | Chopped fresh coriander or parsley (optional) |
| ¼ cup chopped onion | 1 egg, beaten; or |
| 1 tablespoon olive oil | 2 tablespoons yogurt |
| ½ teaspoon cumin | |

Combine pancake mix and water to make a very thin batter. Lightly grease skillet or griddle and pour ¼ cup batter onto it, tilting the skillet so batter spreads out into a large thin pancake (8 or 9 inches). Cook on one side only until firm; turn out. Cover each pancake with waxed paper; continue until all the batter has been used. This mixture should make about 12 pancakes.

Sauté meat and onion in oil; season with cumin, nutmeg, salt and pepper, and also coriander, if available, or parsley. Stir in beaten egg and yogurt. Place a tablespoon of filling in each pancake; fold pancake in half; then fold open edges back toward the middle of the pancake, tucking in the ends. Lower gently into deep hot fat; or, brush generously with oil or melted butter on all sides and bake in a preheated hot oven until crisply browned. Serve hot. Makes 12.

# Börek
*(Turkish pastries)*

The pastry used in making these may be packaged pie crust mix rolled out very thin and cut into circles 3 to 3½ inches in diameter; or puff paste rolled out into flat circles; or phyllo pastry (available in sheets at Greek-American groceries), brushed generously with melted butter.

The filling may be a chicken mixture, a lamb mixture or cheese blended with a beaten egg. But the most distinctively Turkish are the chicken pastries.

# Tavuklu Börek
*(chicken pastries)*

For 12 pastries, use 1 raw chicken breast, boned and chopped, or ¾ to 1 cup chopped cooked chicken; ¼ cup chopped walnuts or grated coconut; 1 teaspoon minced parsley; about 2 tablespoons yogurt or sour cream; 1 egg, beaten; and a little minced onion. Blend ingredients very well. Place a teaspoon of mixture in center of each circle; fold over, moistening and sealing edges. Brush with melted butter; place an inch apart on a baking sheet and bake in a hot oven (425° F.) until golden, about 25 minutes. The pastries may also be deep-fried in olive oil.

# Tyropitakia
*(Greek cheese pastries)*

For the pastry, as in making börek, use pie crust mix, puff paste, or phyllo pastry.

**Cheese filling.** For 12 pastries, use ½ pound feta cheese, or an 8 ounce package pot cheese; 1 egg, beaten; 2 or 3 tablespoons yogurt or sour cream. Beat to blend well. Place a teaspoonful of mixture in each pastry circle; moisten edges; fold over into triangles. Brush each with melted butter, place 1 inch apart on baking sheet, and bake in hot oven until golden.

# Sambousik
*(Lebanese meat pastries)*

For the pastry, use pie crust mix or a standard recipe for pie crust dough, but instead of water, add a beaten egg. Roll out very thin and cut into circles, as for Turkish börek.

**Meat filling.** For 12 pastries sauté ½ pound ground meat (lamb or beef) in 2 or 3 tablespoons olive oil with 2 chopped onions, 2 tablespoons minced fresh coriander (if available—otherwise use fresh parsley) and about ¼ cup pine nuts. Season to taste with salt, pepper and ¼ teaspoon cinnamon or nutmeg. Place a teaspoonful of filling in each pastry circle; moisten edges; fold over to seal. Fry in deep fat until golden; or brush generously with melted butter or oil and bake in a hot oven. Serve hot or warm.

# Sfeeha
*(Syrian meat pastries)*

The same filling ingredients are used as for Sambousik, except a little yogurt is added to the mixture. For seasoning, thyme may be used instead of coriander, or pistachio nuts may be added instead of pine nuts. Instead of being folded over, the pastry is pinched together like a cocked hat with the meat filling exposed on top. Sfeeha are baked in a very hot oven.

# Empanaditas de Ternera
*(Spanish veal pastries)*

**Pastry.** Use regular pie dough or pie crust mix. Roll out very thin; cut into 3½-inch circles.

**Filling.** Use ground veal or ground meat loaf mixture; sauté minced onions and chopped pimiento in olive oil; add the meat; cook until lightly colored; season with salt, nutmeg and paprika.

Put a teaspoonful of the filling in each pastry circle; moisten edges; and fold over to seal. Bake in a hot oven until golden crisp.

For other appetizers see *Pizzas and Related Snacks* in the "Cereals and Breads" chapter.

With skill and varied art the sauce
I will compound, in such a tasty way that all
The guests will plunge their very teeth
Into the dish for joy and eagerness;
And the recipes and different modes of dressing
I am prepared to teach the world for nothing
If men are only wise enough to learn.

— Athenaeus, *The Deipnosophists*

Martial returned a gift of a wild boar because he could not afford the sauce to go with it, made of "mountains of pepper" and Falernian wine.

—H. Warner Allen, *A History of Wine*

# Sauces and Seasonings

The "seven original sages of the kitchen," according to loquacious Athenaeus, author of *The Deipnosophists*, were Orion, who invented the white sauce; Lampriades, originator of the brown sauce; Nereus of Corinth, who "made conger eel a dish fit for the gods"; Agres of Rhodes, who first taught others how to fillet fish; Atlantus, who made the most perfect cordial; and Euthymus, who cooked vegetables so exquisitely he was nicknamed Lentillus.

It's odd that none of the seven sages named by this great gastronomic author of antiquity were specialists in meat cookery, though the explanation was probably that the sauce was considered of more importance than the meat itself. At least, this is true of Apicius' cookery book, whose section on "Quadrupeds" is concerned primarily with recipes for sauces and stuffings for the various kinds of meat that graced Roman tables.

One thing is certain: skillful seasoning was considered the true measure of a cook by the Greeks of old, as it is today by their spiritual heirs, the French chefs who boast of having two hundred different sauces in their repertories.

As great as the demand for exotic spices would become in Western Europe during the Middle Ages, there was never any dearth of condiments in the Mediterranean area. Among the herbs that were indigenous, and whose use was mentioned in the earliest literature, were mustard, cumin, mint, oregano, coriander, caraway, bay leaf and thyme. Crushed cumin seeds give a spiciness almost as piquant as that of black pepper. Parsley, too, is peppery, as is cress when used chopped as an herb. Pliny the elder said that in his time there was scarcely a dish brought to the table that didn't have a little parsley in it. The fragrance of bay leaves (laurel) was so admired by the Greeks that they made garlands of it as crowns for their Olympic heroes. Fennel was often added to the olive brine; sesame seeds crusted loaves of bread and pastries. Even cardamom seeds, sometimes called "grains of paradise," were known in biblical times. We know that saffron was used by the Minoans in Crete as well as by the Egyptians.

How has it happened that fresh coriander is still so little known in American kitchens, when it has been a staple in nearly all the Mediterranean countries for as far back as anyone knows? I learned about fresh coriander, which is completely different in flavor from crushed coriander seeds, only about seven years ago, when I was asked to write a piece on the cooking of Peru. Interviewing a Peruvian woman, I was told emphatically that I couldn't write about her country's cuisine unless I included recipes containing this herb, which in appearance looks so much like parsley but which has a taste unlike any other seasoning in the world. From her I learned that fresh coriander, or culantro as it's called in Spanish, is sold in most Spanish-American markets as well as in oriental groceries, where it is sometimes called "Chinese parsley." Since then I've been told that coriander can be found in many gourmet shops in California, where its use is spreading rapidly. There is no other herb with a flavor quite like this. Fortunately the uncrushed seeds sold in spice racks can be planted in pots to grow the fresh herb, which is an essential ingredient in many Mediterranean recipes.

As for garlic, this controversial herb has been both praised and condemned since the beginning of time, but few cooks are willing to do without it. The pungent aroma of garlic is as much a part of a Mediterranean kitchen as is olive oil, and the two are so frequently paired that it's hard to think of one without the other. It takes a passionate protagonist of garlic to admire the hefty Skordalia of Greece or the Aïoli of France (called Alioli in Spain), but when garlic is blended with herbs as well as oil the effect is not quite so devastating, as in Italy's Pesto Genovese, Spain's Salsa Verde and the Aïllade of Languedoc.

Perhaps the original sauce, that one that preceded all the rest, was what is now known to most of the world by the French name vinaigrette: two-thirds oil, one-third vinegar, with salt and other seasonings to taste. (Only in the United States is this called "French dressing.") But this is not the only sauce with a French name whose origins go back to a time before France existed as a nation. Orion's "white sauce" was probably more nearly like what the French now call Velouté than like Bechamel Sauce; this, at least, can be concluded from the recipe for white sauce given in Apicius: a base of chicken broth blended with white wine, with egg white rather than flour for binding.

As for mayonnaise, it was being whipped up on the island of Minorca long before the Duc de Richelieu first tasted the creamy emulsification of egg and olive oil that he named after the island's capital city, Mahon, when he brought the recipe back with him to France.

Even the pride of the French kitchen, the long-simmering bouillon, which is used as stock for so many important sauces, was introduced to France by the Florentine chefs of Catherine di Medici; and Sauce Espagnole, the most renowned of all French professional "basic sauces," was brought to Paris from Madrid by the chefs of the Empress Eugénie.

The word sauce itself comes from the Latin *salsus*, meaning salted. In fact, the art of saucery is the same as the art of seasoning, and it's less important to know thirty or forty separate sauce recipes as it is to learn how to season foods so that natural flavors are enhanced.

Vinaigrette, Bechamel, and tomato sauces are to be found today in every Mediterranean cuisine, but there are also certain geographical specialties: in the Near East (the Levantine coast), yogurt sauces and those with a base of sesame oil (tahina) are the favorites; cinnamon and black pepper are also frequently combined as seasonings. Anchovy sauces are used more in Italy and France than elsewhere; cumin is more characteristic of North African, Spanish and Portuguese cooking. The most distinctive of all Greek sauces is *avgholemono*, or egg-lemon sauce, creamy-smooth and delightfully tart. Truffles and capers are most favored by the

French and Italians; pine nuts and almonds show up in the sauces of every Mediterranean country; and the Turks use walnuts in many surprising ways.

# Sauce Vinaigrette

Combine ⅔ cup oil with ¼ cup vinegar, ½ teaspoon salt and other herbs or seasonings as desired. These could include minced onion, minced parsley, capers, a pinch of thyme, very thin slivers of lemon peel or minced hard-cooked egg. Use as a dressing for fish, with hot or cold vegetables and with tossed salads. Also an excellent marinade for tenderizing meats.

# Oil-Lemon Sauce

Use 1 part lemon juice to 4 parts olive oil plus salt to taste and, if liked, a dash of cayenne. Used mostly with seafood.

# Aïoli

Crush in a mortar 3 or 4 garlic cloves and ¼ teaspoon salt. In blender or small narrow bowl beat an egg yolk until thickened and light in color; add crushed garlic; then add olive oil (1 cupful) in a thin steady stream with blender in motion (or beating constantly by hand) until sauce is the thickness of mayonnaise. Add lemon juice to taste. Serve with seafood, boiled potatoes, broiled lamb or pork. Makes 1 cup.

# Skordalia

Mash 3 or 4 garlic cloves with a teaspoon of salt. Tear a slice of white bread into cubes; cover with ¼ cup olive oil; mash oil into bread. In a blender place garlic salt, bread, oil and 1 egg; beat until smooth, slowly adding an additional ½ cup olive oil, keeping blender in motion; toward the end add the juice of 1 lemon. Makes 1 cup. Use as a sauce with fish, shrimp, potatoes or cooked greens. Crushed almonds, or crushed or chopped pistachio nuts, are often added to Skordalia.

# Pesto Genovese

Pound in a mortar 3 garlic cloves, about ½ cup chopped fresh basil and the same amount of chopped parsley, until a smooth paste is formed. Add 1 cup olive oil in a thin stream, beating constantly, until the consistency of thick cream. Sometimes 1 or 2 anchovy fillets are crushed with the garlic; sometimes anchovy is omitted and grated Romano cheese is added. Season to taste with salt and pepper. Serve as a sauce over fish, or with hot spaghetti, or add to vegetable soup.

# Aïllade

As for Pesto Genovese, garlic is pounded in a mortar with fresh chopped basil, sometimes with chopped shallots or chives. Then add olive oil slowly, at first drop by drop, beating until thick. Season to taste with salt and pepper.

Aïllade à la Toulousaine is made with crushed walnuts, garlic and chives, with oil added. Pound a few walnuts to a paste with garlic and chives; or beat in blender. Add olive oil in thin stream, beating until thickened. Season to taste with salt and parsley. Sometimes roasted tomatoes (grilled until the skin is black, then peeled) are mashed with garlic, and the walnuts omitted. The mixture may be spread on bread, then toasted for a snack. Otherwise serve as a sauce for cooked potatoes, spaghetti, meat or fish (hot or cold).

# Salsa Verde

There are many sauces called by this name in Spain. The easiest is made by crushing a full cup of minced parsley in a mortar or a blender; then add ½ cup olive oil a little at a time. At the end, add 1 tablespoon lemon juice. Add salt to taste, about ¼ teaspoon. Makes ½ to ¾ cup of a thick sauce, delicious over any fish, fried, baked, broiled or poached, or with shrimp or lobster.

# Bechamel, or White Sauce

Every cook should know this sauce. In a saucepan melt 2 or 3 tablespoons butter (depending on thickness desired); stir in same amount of flour and ¼ teaspoon salt. Cook over low heat until mixture bubbles; then slowly stir in 1 cup milk and beat with whisk until smooth. Black pepper may be added, if desired. Sometimes an egg is added, in which case add some of hot sauce to beaten egg; then combine with rest of sauce; continue cooking over lowest heat, stirring constantly, for a few minutes longer. Makes 1 cup sauce. Double all ingredients for 2 cups sauce; triple for 3.

# Velouté Sauce

Start out as for Bechamel, but for the liquid use chicken broth or fish stock instead of milk; add 2 tablespoons heavy cream for each cup of liquid.

# Avgholemono Sauce

Beat 2 egg yolks until very thick; add 2 tablespoons lemon juice, beating until smooth. Heat ½ cup clear chicken broth; beat the broth into the egg-lemon mixture a little at a time, in a blender, if you have one, until a thick sauce is formed. If the sauce is not as thick as desired, place mixture over heat; stir constantly until thickened and smooth. Makes ¾ cup sauce the consistency of mayonnaise. Delicious with cooked potatoes, broccoli, artichokes, meatballs, fish, chicken or almost everything. Double all ingredients to make 1½ cups sauce.

# Yogurt Sauce

|  |  |
|---|---|
| 2 cups (1 pint) yogurt | 1 teaspoon dried dill weed |
| ½ tablespoon flour or | or crushed dried mint |
| cornstarch | Salt, pepper |
| A little water | 1 egg, beaten (optional) |

Force yogurt through a fine sieve. Make a paste of the flour with water; then stir into yogurt. Add dill or mint. Separately beat egg, if used. Place yogurt in top of double boiler over warm water; stir constantly until the consistency of Bechamel Sauce. Add warm yogurt to egg; then return to saucepan and beat until smooth. Serve with meatballs or green vegetables. Makes 2 cups.

# Yogurt Dressing for Fruit Salad

Beat together 1 cup yogurt, 1 tablespoon honey, a few drops lemon juice, the grated rind of ½ lemon and salt to taste. Makes 1 cup.

# Mayonnaise

If you have a blender, place in it one whole egg, ½ teaspoon dry mustard and ½ teaspoon salt. Beat until smooth (no foam): then gradually start adding oil in a thin stream—use 1 cup altogether—with blender at low speed. As the mixture thickens, add a little vinegar or fresh lemon juice (1 to 2 tablespoons). Beat until very thick. This makes 1¼ cups sauce.

If you do not have a blender, use 1 or 2 egg yolks; beat the oil in drop by drop at first, then in a thin stream, adding 1 cup oil. A whisk is better than an egg beater for this. Hand-beaten mayonnaise may not get as thick as mayonnaise made with a blender. It takes a practiced wrist to thicken it; but don't despair, the flavor is just as good. If mayonnaise separates, start again with another egg yolk and beat in curdled mayonnaise until smooth.

# Sauce Andalouse

To mayonnaise, add about a teaspoon tomato paste, some minced pimiento and minced parsley. A good sauce over cold vegetables or with sandwiches. For a hot Sauce Andalouse, add tomato paste, pimiento and parsley to Bechamel Sauce.

# Sauce Maltaise

In blender place 2 egg yolks (3 if a thicker sauce is desired) with 1 tablespoon lemon juice, 1 tablespoon orange juice and the grated rind of 1 orange. Beat until thickened; add 1 tablespoon *hot* water. Then gradually (with blender in motion) add ½ cup (8 tablespoons) melted butter while butter is still warm. Beat until thick as mayonnaise. Serve this way, or add a tablespoon of sweet or sour cream. Delicious with partridge, pheasant, turkey or ham. Makes ¾ cup.

# Joinville Sauce

Joinville was a Crusader who accompanied St. Louis IX to the Holy Land; his account of the pilgrimage is one of the earliest books written in vernacular French. Like mayonnaise, this sauce, which bears Joinville's name, may well have been created by a native cook in Acre or Caesarea, on the shores of Palestine. The sauce is always served with poached fish, such as sole, turbot, whiting or halibut.

In a professional kitchen, fish broth would be used, simmered with the trimmings of fresh mushrooms. For the home kitchen, the use of canned shrimp and canned mushrooms will simplify preparation.

1 jar (3½ ounces) Danish or Norwegian baby shrimp
3 tablespoons butter
1 can (3 ounces) button mushrooms
2 tablespoons flour
½ teaspoon paprika
1 cup broth
½ cup cream
2 egg yolks
Salt to taste

Drain the shrimp, saving the liquor. Mash the shrimp to a paste with 1 tablespoon of the butter. Combine the shrimp liquor with the liquor from the mushrooms, keeping drained mushrooms aside until later. Melt the remaining 2 tablespoons of butter; stir in flour and paprika and let mixture bubble 2 or 3 minutes. Add water to the combined shrimp and mushroom liquor to make 1 cup. Add cream. Slowly stir this into butter-flour mixture. When thickened, beat a little at a time into egg yolks; then beat in the shrimp paste. Taste for seasoning; add salt if needed. Stir in mushrooms. Makes about 1½ cups.

# Bigarrade Sauce

This should properly be made with the skin and juice of bitter or wild oranges, and no doubt it originated during the period when bitter oranges were first brought to the Mediterranean from the Orient by Arab traders. Or, it may have originated in Seville when that city was still under Moorish rule. If bitter oranges are not available, use a combination of orange and lemon. The best-known use of the sauce is with roast duck; but it's equally delicious with ham, roast pork or roast chicken. The pan drippings listed as an ingredient are those from the roast meat or poultry.

2 bitter oranges; or 1 large sweet juicy orange and ½ lemon Well-browned pan drippings
1 can beef gravy; or 1 cup beef gravy made with mix
½ cup white wine
2 tablespoons Madeira, port or Curaçao
1 tablespoon butter

First, squeeze the juice from the bitter oranges (or from the sweet orange and ½ lemon); strain the juice; put aside. Then carefully cut away the outer peel of the fruit, none of the white pithy part. With a small sharp knife, cut the rind into thin strips. Place in a pan; cover with boiling water; let stand 5 minutes; then drain and put aside. Blend beef gravy with white wine, Madeira and reserved fruit juice; simmer uncovered until reduced and thickened. When meat or poultry has been removed from roasting pan, skim off all fat from drippings. When roasting duck, pour fat and drippings into a narrow bowl and chill in freezer 5 minutes so that all fat rising to top can easily be separated from brown essence or glaze at bottom. Combine fat-free glaze, or drippings, with the thin strips of orange peel and the gravy-wine-juice mixture. Simmer, stirring, until sauce is smooth and well blended. Makes about 1½ cups sauce.

# Sauce Espagnole

The following is a much simplified version of the sauce that in great kitchens, under the direction of master chefs, takes several days to prepare.

| | |
|---|---|
| 1 small onion, chopped | 2 tablespoons butter |
| 1 small carrot, grated | 1 tablespoon flour |
| 1 tablespoon minced parsley | 1 tablespoon tomato paste |
| ¼ teaspoon thyme | 1 cup beef broth (clear) |
| ½ bay leaf, crumbled | 1 can or cup beef gravy |
| | ½ cup red wine |

Simmer onion, carrot, parsley, thyme and bay leaf in butter until onion is soft. Stir in flour; cook 2 minutes. Add tomato paste; blend well; then add remaining ingredients and simmer over low heat until sauce has cooked down to desired consistency. For a smoother sauce, force through food mill or sieve. Use with any meat; add to pan drippings from a roast for an extra-delicious gravy; or use to reheat leftover roast meat. Makes about 2 cups.

# Mirepoix

This is not a sauce in itself, but the first step in making many

French sauces. Simmer minced vegetables—carrot, onion, leeks, celery and chopped fresh herbs (the "bouquet garni" herbs, parsley, thyme and bay leaf)—in butter until very tender. Make this the basis of a gravy, adding broth or pan drippings; or use as a bed on which chicken or fish are placed during baking.

# Sofrito

Like the Mirepoix in French cooking, a Sofrito is the first step in making many Spanish sauces. Slowly cook chopped onion, minced or crushed garlic, chopped tomato and chopped parsley in olive oil until very soft. Other vegetables may also be added: carrot, green or sweet red peppers, leeks or celery.

# Sauce Provençale

| | |
|---|---|
| 1 medium onion, chopped | 1 cup beef broth (clear) |
| 1 or 2 garlic cloves | Few sprigs basil, chopped |
| ¼ cup olive oil | 1 tablespoon chopped |
| 1 large can tomatoes, strained | parsley |

Simmer onion and garlic in oil until soft and golden; crush garlic into pan with tines of fork. Add strained tomato, beef broth, basil and parsley; cook down to desired consistency. Season to taste. Serve over rice, add to various chicken dishes or reheat leftover meat in the sauce. Makes 2 to 2½ cups.

He who rightly cares for his own eating
Will not be a bad cook . . .
Often taste your dishes
While you are boiling them. Do they want salt?
Add some. Is any other seasoning needed?
Add it, and taste again, 'til you've arrived
At harmony of flavor; like a man
Who tunes a lyre till it rightly sounds.

—Athenaeus, *The Deipnosophists*

The French cuisine owes its superiority to that of other nations because of the excellence of its bouillon, which requires seven hours of continuous cooking, *faire sourire*, only smiling. . . .

—Ellwanger, *The Pleasures of the Table*

# Soups and Stews

The pottage of lentils, which hungry Esau craved so desperately that he sold his birthright for a taste of it, is probably the oldest written mention of stew. But, undoubtedly, other stews had been simmering on other Mediterranean hearth fires for many centuries before the biblical tale was recorded—from the time, in fact, when the first pot or cauldron was invented. Dried legumes were known to make good eating in prehistoric Jericho; bean and lentil stews have always been and always will be family favorites.

The great thing about both soups and stews is that you don't need to follow formal recipes. Not really. French cookbooks often make the preparation of a bouillon sound formidable, but the truth is that the most important ingredients are time, patience, sensitive taste buds and the courage to improvise.

There are, of course, certain guidelines to follow. In the Mediterranean, as elsewhere, both soups and stews can be divided between those that first require sautéeing meat (if used) or onions in fat, and those in which all ingredients are simply tossed into the pot and cooked until done. On Mediterranean family tables, the soup of the first course is often the broth in which the meat or chicken of the main course has cooked. This is true of the French Pot au Feu and of many soups with a chicken base. But bouillon cubes are by now considered as indispensable in Mediterranean kitchens as the salt box, and the old-time long-simmering method of making soup or stock has become increasingly rare.

Nevertheless, for those soups in which the flavor of the broth itself is of paramount importance, the cook "who rightly cares" will feel it's worth the trouble of following the old-time method. If the cook uses such chicken parts as necks, backs and even feet, the cost can be minimal.

When a recipe specifies first cooking onions (and perhaps other vegetables as well) in olive oil or other fat, be sure to cook the onions slowly until very soft and very golden. In a few recipes, the onions should brown slightly (as in Esau's Pottage) for a more pungent flavor, but never, never let them burn, not even around the edges. If this happens, each particle of burned onion must be carefully removed. A little detail like this can make all the difference in the flavor of the broth.

# Chicken Broth

Throw chicken necks into a pot; cover with water; add salt (a teaspoon to a quart of water), a quartered onion, a cubed carrot, some celery leaves, some parsley and just a pinch of thyme. Simmer 45 minutes, skimming occasionally. Cool slightly; strain through a fine sieve. Add more salt to taste if needed. That's all there is to it.

# Consommé

Do the same as for chicken broth, but instead of salt, add a beef bouillon cube for each cupful of water, and, in addition to the foregoing soup herbs, add an entire celery stalk, a bay leaf and, if possible, a peeled white turnip. The broth will be even better if you happen to have a ham or pork bone or just a little minced raw pork (cut off from a roast waiting to be cooked) to add to the pot. Simmer 1 to 1½ hours, skimming every now and then.

Skimming is important. This takes away the unsightly impurities that even a fine strainer may let through. When meat broth is being made with a regular soup bone or marrow bone, the broth must gently simmer, or "smile," for at least 3 hours, and in this case skimming becomes doubly important.

# Avgholemono Soup
(*Greek egg-lemon soup*)

Excellent chicken broth is essential in this recipe, so prepare the broth first. To 1 quart strained chicken broth, add 1/3 cup uncooked rice; bring to a boil; cook 20 to 25 minutes until rice is very soft. Turn off heat. In a bowl, beat 3 egg yolks; add a little of the hot broth until eggs are well blended; then return egg mixture to rest of soup. Cook over very low heat, stirring constantly, until soup is slightly thickened. Remove from heat; add 3 tablespoons lemon juice, 1 tablespoon at a time. Cover; let stand 5 minutes before serving. Makes 6 servings. This is a first course soup. Follow it with a big Greek salad and a fruit dessert for a beautiful luncheon.

# Jewish Chicken Soup with Kreplach

"Mom's chicken soup" must be homemade, exquisitely flavored. Add Kreplach (for recipe, check Index) to the boiling broth; cook 15 to 20 minutes longer. Sprinkle minced parsley over the top of each serving.

# French Onion Soup

Slice 4 or 5 onions; simmer in 3 or 4 tablespoons butter until very soft and golden. Add 6 cups well-flavored beef broth or consommé; continue cooking 20 to 25 minutes. Cut French bread at an angle into 1-inch slices; toast lightly under broiler. Place a piece of toast in each soup bowl; add soup. Cover top of each bowl with a generous amount of freshly grated Parmesan cheese. Place bowls under broiler, 4 inches from the heat, until top is lightly browned.

Obviously, this requires heat-proof bowls or individual casseroles. If you don't have such casseroles, you will have to settle for untoasted grated cheese on top, which isn't nearly as good. Makes 6 servings. Follow with a green salad with Roquefort dressing, and serve pastry for dessert.

# Spanish Onion Soup

Slice 2 large Spanish onions or 4 medium yellow onions; cook gently in ½ cup olive oil until very soft and golden. Add 6 cups well-flavored beef broth or consommé; season with powdered cloves and nutmeg (or mace); and add 1 teaspoon wine vinegar. Bring to a boil; lower heat; simmer 15 to 20 minutes. Break 6 eggs, one at a time, into a small bowl. (If any yolks break into the white, put these eggs aside for other cooking use). Then slip each egg into the soup and continue cooking, over low heat, until eggs are poached. Put a slice of toast in each serving dish; spoon a poached egg onto the toast; then add soup. Grated cheese may be served separately if desired. Makes 6 servings, hearty enough for a luncheon entrée.

# Spanish Potato Soup

Slice 2 or 3 onions; gently cook in ¼ cup olive oil until very soft; sprinkle with salt as they cook. Add 6 cups (1½ quarts) chicken broth and ¼ cup dry or medium sherry; bring to a boil. Add 6 peeled and diced raw potatoes; cook until potatoes are very soft. Coarsely mash potatoes in broth (do not purée); serve garnished with parsley or chopped cooked bacon. Makes 6 to 8 hearty luncheon servings.

# French Leek and Potato Soup

Cook together 5 or 6 peeled and diced raw potatoes with 3 leeks, sliced crosswise (white part only) in 5 cups salted water *or* chicken broth, until both vegetables are very tender. Force through food mill to purée; add ¼ cup heavy cream; reheat without boiling. Serve with chopped chives for garnish. (Chill this and it becomes Vichyssoise.) Makes 6-8 servings.

# Sopa de Ajo
*(garlic soup)*·

This soup is popular in both Spain and southern France and if the soup is properly made, the garlic flavor is not as overwhelming as it sounds. Peel 6 or 8 garlic cloves, leaving them whole or split in half. Dice 6 slices of white bread. Place both garlic and bread in hot olive oil in a skillet or heavy kettle, turning as they become golden. Do not allow to burn. Remove with slotted spoon. Mash softened garlic and fried bread together in mortar with pestle; work in some minced parsley (about ¼ cup) and then a cup of tomato juice. Return to stove in a kettle; add 4 to 5 cups well-flavored beef bouillon or consommé; bring to a boil; cook 10 minutes. Then, as for Spanish Onion Soup, lower 6 eggs, one at a time, into simmering (not boiling) broth and cook until they are poached (yolks firm, whites completely white). Makes 6 servings.

# Turkish Chicken and Cucumber Soup

| | |
|---|---|
| 2 tablespoons butter or margarine | ¼ teaspoon ginger |
| 2 large cucumbers, peeled, seeded and chopped | 1 tablespoon chopped fresh mint; or 1 teaspoon dried mint, crushed |
| 5 cups clear chicken broth | ¼ teaspoon thyme |
| 1 green onion or shallot, thinly sliced | 1 cup yogurt or sour cream |

Gently cook chopped cucumber and onion or shallot in butter until golden and soft. Add ginger; then slowly add chicken broth and seasonings. Simmer 15 minutes. Turn off heat. Add some of hot broth to yogurt or sour cream; then combine the two. Serve hot but do not allow to boil. Makes 6 to 8 servings for a first course soup.

# Badem Çorbası
(*Turkish almond soup*)

Many Mediterranean soups are thickened with crushed almonds. The Phoenicians are the ones credited with having planted almond trees through the western Mediterranean, so, who knows, maybe they were the first to put almonds in their soups. Interestingly, almost the same recipes turn up in countries that are far apart. This recipe for Badem Çorbası has its counterpart in a Portuguese soup called simply Sopa de Amendoas, the only difference being that sweet cream rather than sour cream or yogurt is used in the Portuguese soup. In Sicily, a very similar soup is called Minestra Alla Siciliana, though it is made with milk rather than with cream and contains no coriander.

| | |
|---|---|
| 1  cup blanched almonds | ½  cup heavy sweet cream, |
| 1  small onion, grated | or sour cream |
| 6  cups clear chicken broth | 2  or 3 egg yolks |
| Seasonings to taste | Grated rind ½ lemon |
| 2  tablespoons chopped fresh | |
| coriander; or 1 teaspoon | |
| crushed coriander seeds | |

Homemade chicken broth is important for the success of this soup; so, too, are almonds blanched at home just before using, rather than already-blanched almonds purchased in a can. Blanch almonds; toast lightly; let cool until crisp; then crush in an electric blender, if you have one. Otherwise a mortar and pestle can be used. Add grated onion to almonds; mash or beat to a paste; then put mixture into strained chicken broth with coriander and any other seasonings desired. Simmer 15 minutes. Beat cream and egg yolks together; add some of hot broth; then return the egg mixture to rest of soup and stir constantly over low heat until thickened. Add grated lemon rind just before serving. One cup yogurt may be used instead of the sour cream. First, force yogurt through a fine sieve; then beat a teaspoon of cornstarch into the yogurt to prevent curdling when it is placed over heat. Makes 6 to 8 servings.

# Sopa Castilla La Vieja
(*Spanish almond soup*)

Either chicken broth or beef broth may be used for this delicious soup. Add ½ cup crushed blanched almonds to 1½ quarts (6 cups) broth, along with 2 tablespoons olive oil or butter. Bring to a boil; simmer 10 minutes. Place in individual earthenware bowls; top each serving with toasted or fried croutons and grated Parmesan cheese. Place bowls under broiler until cheese is melted. Makes 6 to 8 servings.

# Okrochka
(*cold cucumber and shrimp soup*)

This delicious soup is always served cold, an excellent hot-weather luncheon choice.

| | |
|---|---|
| 3 cups chicken broth (canned may be used) | 1 tablespoon fresh dill, minced; or 1 teaspoon dried dill weed |
| 1 cup (½ pint) yogurt or buttermilk | Grated rind of ½ lemon |
| 1 jar (3½ ounces) Danish or Norwegian baby shrimp, drained | Salt, pepper, nutmeg to taste |
| ½ cup diced chicken | 2 hard-cooked eggs, chopped |
| 1 medium cucumber, peeled and grated | 1 tablespoon minced chives or parsley; or both |

Beat together chicken broth and yogurt or buttermilk; add remaining ingredients except eggs and parsley or chives. Chill until serving time; then serve in soup bowls with eggs and parsley or chives sprinkled over top of each. Makes 6 servings.

# ALL-VEGETABLE SOUPS

Many quite lovely soups can be made with vegetables alone, without a hint of chicken or beef broth, though in most of these soups you may use bouillon cubes instead of salt for a richer flavor if you like. When there's no meat, always add either butter or oil to the broth. This enhances the vegetable flavor and makes the texture smoother, too.

# Minestrone

The word minestra in Italian means simply "soup"; Minestrone is a "strong soup," hearty with beans, rice or macaroni and just about any vegetable you may want to add. Minestrone can also be enriched with beef broth or bouillon cubes, but this is not necessary. No two recipes for minestrone are alike, and that's as it should be.

| | |
|---|---|
| 1  large onion, sliced | 1-pound can peeled |
| 1  minced garlic clove, | tomatoes |
|    if desired | 2  quarts water or stock |
| 2  stalks celery, diced | Salt and pepper to taste |
| 1  tablespoon chopped | 1-pound can kidney or white |
|    parsley | marrow beans |
| 1  carrot, scraped and diced | ½  cup uncooked rice; or |
| ¼  cup olive oil | 1 cup elbow macaroni |
| 1  or 2 small white turnips, | 1  cup chopped spinach, kale |
|    peeled and diced | or green cabbage |
| | Grated Parmesan cheese |

Simmer the onion, garlic, celery, parsley and carrot in olive oil until onion is soft and golden. Add turnips, tomato and water or stock. Bring to a boil; adjust seasonings to taste. Add beans and rice or macaroni; cook 20 minutes. During last 5 minutes add spinach, kale or cabbage. Serve in soup plates topped with cheese. A meal in itself. Makes 8 to 10 servings. Good served as a leftover.

# Portuguese Spinach Soup

Cook 2 small to medium potatoes, peeled and quartered, and a few slices of onion in 5 cups salted water until potato is very soft. Force through a food mill. This makes a thin gruel. Return gruel to saucepan; add 1 or 2 tablespoons olive oil and 2 cups spinach

leaves, coarsely chopped; bring to a boil; cook just unti
is limp. Serve in bowls, garnished, if liked, with sieved eg
grated cheese over top. Watercress may be used in this recipe
instead of spinach. Makes 5 or 6 servings.

# Sopa de Lentejas Madrileña
*(lentil soup Madrid style)*

Lentils are considered vegetables in most Mediterranean countries; technically they are seeds, as are other dried legumes. Call
them what you will, lentils can be turned into very flavorful,
hearty dishes, the soups differing from stews only in the amount
of liquid in the pot in proportion to other ingredients. The
following Spanish soup is a favorite of mine. It is meaty in flavor,
even though there's not a bit of meat in it. Lentils never need
be presoaked, but they drink up a lot of water, so keep an eye
on the pot to be sure they don't go dry.

| | |
|---|---|
| 1  medium to large onion, chopped | 1 - pound can tomatoes; or 2 small tomatoes, peeled and chopped |
| ½  green pepper, seeded and diced | 2  medium carrots, scraped and diced |
| 2 - 3 tablespoons chopped pimiento (optional) | Salt to taste |
| 2  tablespoons olive oil | 1  cup lentils |
| 1  tablespoon flour | 6 - 8  cups water |
| | ½  cup shredded Swiss cheese |

Simmer onion, pepper and pimiento in oil until very soft. Stir in
flour; cook until bubbling but do not brown. Add remaining
ingredients except cheese; simmer over very low heat for 2 hours,
stirring occasionally. Add more water if necessary. Place cheese
in each soup bowl; add the soup; stir together. Makes 6 to 8
hearty servings.

# Garbanzo Soup

| | |
|---|---|
| 1  pound chick peas, presoaked | 2  medium to large onions, chopped |

½ pound lean pork or leftover cooked pork, diced
1 pimiento, chopped
1 tablespoon chopped
  parsley
¼ cup olive oil
½ pound chorizo; or 1 cup
  diced ham

Ham bone (optional)
Salt to taste
Water to cover
1 pound spinach, washed
  (optional)
1 hard-cooked egg, chopped

Drain soaked peas. Cook onions, pork, pimiento and parsley in olive oil until onions are soft. Add chorizo, if available, or chopped ham, and ham bone; place in pot with chick peas; add water and salt; cook slowly until chick peas are tender, about 2 hours. Soak spinach until water is clear; trim off stems. When chick peas are cooked, add spinach; cook 4 or 5 minutes longer. Serve topped with chopped egg for garnish. Makes 6 generous servings.

# Cocido

Cocido is the great national dish of Spain—more so than paella, even though the latter is better known to the rest of the world. Almost anything can be added to this meal-in-a-pot stew, but the more meat products the better. Don't worry about making too much. It's wonderful the second or even third day.

½ pound chick peas, soaked
1 pound hind shank of beef
1 small chicken, cut up
1 or 2 onions, quartered
  Water
  Salt
½ pound ham, diced; or
  sliced chorizo

2 carrots, scraped and
  quartered
4 leeks, sliced
1-pound can tomatoes
2 or 3 sweet potatoes or
  white potatoes, quartered
½ cup minced parsley
2 tablespoons sherry or
  brandy

Soak chick peas the day before; also precook the hind shank of beef, with the quartered onions, and neck, back and wing tips of chicken in salted water to cover. When meat is so tender it is falling from the bones, remove; cut up the edible meat; discard the bone. Strain the broth; chill. Next day, remove fat from top; place broth in large kettle with drained chick peas, chopped beef and the diced ham or chorizo; add the remaining pieces of chicken, cut very small. Add carrots, leeks, tomatoes and potatoes. Simmer until chick . peas and chicken are very tender, keeping liquid an inch above solid ingredients at all times. In last 5 to 10 minutes add parsley, sherry or brandy. Makes about 10 servings.

# Gazpacho Sevillana

Everybody now thinks of gazpacho as a chilled uncooked "salad soup" made principally of tomatoes. But actually, gazpacho can be almost anything you want, hot or cold, and there's no anticipating its ingredients.

Where and when the name originated, no one seems to know, but a soup by this name was certainly being made centuries before the tomato was first introduced to Spain.

One very hot midsummer day in the inland town of Villena, not far from Valencia, I had been invited to lunch by the *alcaide* (mayor) to taste the famous gazpacho of the region. The heat was so intense that to walk along the street was like being in a furnace. Nothing seemed more attractive than an icy soup for lunch. But what were we served? A tureen of steaming hot broth was brought to the table, and in it floated what looked like squares of pasta. The *alcaide* explained somewhat apologetically that traditionally the gazpacho should have been made with rabbit, but in these modern times, chicken was often used instead. The pasta floating in the broth he called torta, and the chef brought some to show me what it was like: simple wheat flour and water dough pounded flat and baked in the oven until dry, like the earliest hearthbreads. I have a feeling that this gazpacho of Villena was the original one, since all the earliest histories describe Spain as being a land overrun with rabbits, and what better way to rid the fields of the pests than to put them in the soup pot?

Sometime after this, when reading a book called *The Bible in Spain*, written about 1830 by an English missionary, I came across a description of Andalusians preparing their gazpacho: the author told how they made a paste of garlic, bread and olive oil, then thinned it with broth—much like the more primitive form of Sopa de Ajo still made by very poor Spanish peasants.

I've had gazpacho in Barcelona that was green in color, made, as I recall, with green peppers and parsley and perhaps other green herbs, but not with tomato. And I've come across gazpacho recipes in Spanish cookbooks calling for grapes for garnish instead of minced onion. In North Africa, where many of the Moors fled when they were finally expelled from Spain, gazpacho is often a clear broth in which forcemeat balls float: one recipe I found in an Algerian cookbook calls for rabbit, chicken, pigeon and pork for the forcemeat, and the broth in which the meatballs are served is seasoned with bay leaf and saffron.

After this summary, it's easy to see that there is no one authentic gazpacho recipe. And having delivered this bit of gastronomic history, I will present my favorite of all gazpacho recipes, one served at a memorable dinner in Seville at the home of Don José Ybarra, whose family has for generations been producing one of the finest of all Spanish olive oils.

1 or 2 garlic cloves, crushed
2 slices white bread, broken (crusts removed)
½ cup water
¼ cup olive oil
1 teaspoon salt
2 pounds ripe peeled tomatoes; or, largest size can plum tomatoes, sieved

¼ cup onions, minced
¼ cup chopped pimiento
2 tablespoons sherry vinegar
2 to 3 cups cold water
Assorted garnishes: chopped eggs, minced cucumber, minced green pepper, minced onion

The night before (if possible) crush garlic in a bowl; add bread, water and olive oil; marinate overnight or at least 4 hours; then crush into a paste. To this paste add the sieved tomatoes, onion and pimiento; beat, one-third at a time, in a blender. (In Andalusia, the ripe tomatoes are crushed with a big wooden pestle in a long wooden bowl until thoroughly puréed, but when I tried doing this myself, the results weren't nearly as good as with a blender. It must take long practice to learn.) Chill mixture in refrigerator until time to serve. Add vinegar and ice-cold water to desired consistency. Serve in soup bowls. Pass garnishes in separate bowls. Makes 6 to 8 servings.

# POT AU FEU

"Pot on the fire" means in most French households a big soup kettle on the back of the stove that simmers away gently for hours. Traditionally, it starts with a good-sized piece of boiling beef, the bottom round or rump which, after it has cooked to tenderness and has lent its juice to the soup, will be served as the second course, the entrée.

Into the pot may be thrown any or all those vegetables that make a truly fine soup: onion, leeks, carrots, turnips and celery. Then add the traditional French soup herbs: parsley, bay leaf, thyme, just a few tiny leaves of marjoram. Other meats or meat bones may be added: a veal knuckle (sliced by the butcher) is a particular asset. For special occasions, an entire chicken or perhaps a joint of duck or turkey may also go into the pot. In Languedoc (the province adjoining Spain in the south), a slab of bacon, diced, is considered an essential ingredient. In some households, pork or veal sausages may also be added.

Whatever the other ingredients, the beef needs a good 4 hours of simmering. Other meats are added according to the time required for cooking: a whole or cut up chicken in the last hour. Sometimes only the giblets of chicken or turkey are served with the Pot au Feu. They may be diced and sautéed separately to be served as garnishes.

When all meat is cooked, it is removed from the kettle and kept warm in the oven. The broth must then be strained (all the flavor will have cooked out of the soup vegetables) and seasoning must be adjusted. The broth may be served as a clear soup, or, if vegetables are wanted, fresh vegetables cut julienne may be added and cooked au pointe. The broth is never thickened.

When the meat appears as the main course, a horseradish sauce, made by blending heavy sweet cream with freshly grated horseradish, is served with it, along with potatoes (cooked separately) and assorted pickles. This is good, substantial French family fare. Everything is cooked to perfection. Just one thing mars it: appearance. A boiled dinner (and this is what Pot au Feu really is) is not as beautiful to behold as meat that comes from the oven crisply browned. Minced parsley and other colorful garnishes will help to embellish its looks, and just a little melted butter brushed over the meat before bringing it to the table will also add immeasurably to its mouth-watering appeal.

# Osso Buco
*(Italian veal knuckle stew)*

The knuckle of the veal does not contain much meat; it's the marrow inside that gives the broth of this famous stew its fine flavor. To ensure that all the marrow is extracted, the knuckle needs to be sawed into 2-inch lengths by the butcher. One knuckle will serve 2 persons; for 6 servings, 3 veal knuckles will be needed—and to hold all this, you need a big kettle or pot.

Dredge the sawed-up pieces of knuckle with salted flour; brown in olive oil, or a mixture of half olive oil, half butter, in a skillet. Remove to kettle or pot. Add to the same fat about ½ cup chopped onion, 1 or 2 garlic cloves, minced or crushed, a bit of sage, some rosemary and chopped parsley. Simmer until onion is soft. Deglaze the pan with white wine (1 cup), stirring over heat until all browned particles are dissolved; then add onion mixture to the pot with the meat. Cover with 2 cups of chicken broth (made with concentrate or bouillon cubes); blend in a tablespoon of tomato paste. Bring to a boil; lower heat; and cover pot. Simmer 2 or 3 hours, until meat begins to separate from the bones. Shortly before serving, add thin slivers of lemon peel, cut carefully so no white is on the outer peel, and additional chopped parsley to the broth. Taste for seasoning: more salt may be needed. The flavor is delicate, and it's the lemon "zest" that makes it special. Hot buttered fettucini and a green salad are the traditional accompaniments.

# Hirino me Selinorizes
*(pork stew with celery)*

It would be easy to believe that the famous French veal stew, Blanquette de Veau, is a direct descendant of this Greek pork stew with celery. The two are strikingly alike—even to the flavor of the meat. Pork and veal are both white meats, both delicate in flavor, and could be interchanged in this recipe or the following one without many people knowing the difference.

2 to 3 pounds lean pork, cubed
6 tablespoons butter
2 medium onions, sliced
Salt to taste; or chicken bouillon cube
2 tablespoons flour

½ cup dry white wine
1 cup water
1 tablespoon minced parsley
1 celery knob, peeled and diced; or 1 entire bunch celery, diced
4 egg yolks
4 tablespoons lemon juice

Brown the pork in butter; remove from pan. Add onions; cook until soft and golden. Stir in salt (1½ to 2 teaspoons) and flour; blend well; cook until lightly browned. Add wine slowly, then water; cook and stir until smooth. Add parsley and replace meat. Cover pot tightly; cook over lowest heat 1½ hours. Add diced celery root or celery; place over meat; cover pan again; continue cooking another ½ hour or until meat and celery are tender. Beat egg yolks until thick; beat in some of hot broth and the lemon juice (1 tablespoon at a time). Pour this mixture over celery and meat; stir to blend with remaining broth. Turn off heat; leave covered 5 minutes before serving. Makes 6 to 8 servings.

# Blanquette de Veau
(*French veal stew*)

3 pounds boned veal from breast or shoulder, cubed
½ cup white wine
1 carrot, scraped and quartered
1 leek, sliced (white part only)
½ cup celery, diced
Sprig of parsley
Pinch of thyme
16 button mushrooms, trimmed

3 cups water
Salt, about 2 teaspoons
16 to 20 small white onions
2 tablespoons butter, melted
2 tablespoons flour
2 egg yolks
2 tablespoons heavy cream
Juice ½ lemon
Grated lemon rind
Minced parsley for garnish

Marinate meat in white wine 1 hour. Remove meat, but save wine. Place meat, carrot, leek (or 2 small sliced white onions could be used instead), celery, parsley, thyme and mushroom trimmings in pot; add water and salt. Cook 1½ hours; skim occasionally. Remove meat; put aside. Strain broth and measure; add reserved wine and water, enough to make 3 cups. Parboil onions in salted water 20 minutes or until tender; drain. Sauté mushrooms in butter until lightly browned; remove; add to onions. Stir flour into the butter; cook until it bubbles. Slowly add strained stock; bring to a boil; lower heat; cook 5 minutes, stirring until very smooth. Add meat; cook until meat is very tender. Add onions and mushrooms. (All this can be done ahead of time.)

Beat egg yolks until thick; stir in cream. Reheat veal in its sauce; then beat 1 cup of hot sauce into egg mixture a little at a time. Stir in lemon juice; add this sauce to remaining broth in pot. Add onions and mushrooms and transfer to a large shallow casserole. Sprinkle grated lemon rind and minced parsley over top. Makes 8 to 10 servings.


# Rojoes a Minhota
(*Portuguese pork stew with cumin*)

Cumin is a most fascinating and little-appreciated spice. It's been in use in the Mediterranean countries since the first stews were invented. The Celts in northern Spain and Portugal were using it when the first Greek historians visited them and described their lifestyles. Apicius used cumin freely in his Roman recipes. The Egyptians were fond of it, and it's still widely used through-out North Africa.

| | |
|---|---|
| 3 pounds pork, cubed | 1 teaspoon crushed cumin |
| 2 cups very dry white wine | 2 tablespoons pork fat |
| 1 bay leaf | 3 teaspoons salt |
| 1 teaspoon paprika | 2 cups water |
| 3 garlic cloves, thinly sliced | ¼ cup white port or brandy |
| ¼ teaspoon powdered cloves | |

The pork should not be too lean: it needs fat for a richer and more flavorful broth. Marinate the meat at least 24 hours in the wine, bay leaf, paprika and garlic. Remove from marinade; pat dry; sprinkle with mixture of cloves and cumin. Place pieces of the pork fat in a heavy pot; heat until fat is drawn out; then add the cubes of trimmed pork and brown over high heat. Sprinkle with salt; add 1 cup of the marinade and 2 cups of water. Simmer, covered, for 1½ or 2 hours, until meat is very tender. During last 15 minutes, add port or brandy. Serve with potatoes. Makes 7 or 8 servings.

# Greek Lamb Stew with Okra

2 pounds boneless lamb for stew; or 3½ pounds lamb with bone
¼ cup olive oil
¼ cup chopped onion
2 cups tomato juice
¼ teaspoon thyme
Salt to taste
1 pound fresh okra, trimmed; or 1 package frozen whole okra, defrosted
1 teaspoon lemon juice

Brown the meat in olive oil; push to one side or remove from pan. Add onion; cook until golden. Add tomato juice, thyme and salt. Cook slowly, covered, until meat is tender, 1½ to 2 hours. Add okra and lemon juice in last 10 minutes. Serve with rice. Snap beans can be substituted for okra. Makes 4 or 5 servings.

# Cochifrito

2 pounds boneless lamb; or 3½ pounds lamb with bone, cut for stew
Seasoned flour
3 to 4 tablespoons olive oil
1 garlic clove
1 onion, sliced or chopped
1 teaspoon paprika
2 tablespoons chopped parsley
1 tablespoon lemon juice
Water to cover
1 package frozen artichoke hearts, thawed

Dredge meat in flour seasoned with salt and pepper; brown in olive oil with garlic. When garlic is soft, press into oil with tines of fork. Add onion, paprika, parsley and lemon juice; cook until onion is soft; then add water. Cook covered until lamb is tender, 1½ to 2 hours. Add artichoke hearts during last 10 minutes. Sprinkle with additional lemon juice when serving. Serve with rice. Makes 4 or 5 servings.

# Dobrada a Minhota

Tripe has been the subject of poetry and nostalgia since ancient times. Homer praised its excellence, as did Athenaeus, and Rabelais asserted that it was a huge dish of tripe on which the mother of Gargantua feasted just before she gave birth to her prodigious offspring.

In American markets, honeycomb tripe (the most desirable part) is usually sold precooked and tenderized, which eliminates not only several hours of parboiling but also the messy job of scraping and trimming that once was required.

Even when purchased precooked, tripe needs an hour of gentle simmering, with herbs and other ingredients, to enhance its flavor and delicacy. The most famous of French recipes, that for Tripes à la mode de Caen (a Normandy dish), calls for 24 hours of slow baking in an earthenware pot, sealed tight shut with flour paste.

My personal favorite is this Portuguese dish prepared in the province of the Minho, which is spicy with cumin and very thick with beans.

|  |  |
|---|---|
| 2 pounds honeycomb tripe, precooked | 1 chicken leg, ham bone or veal knuckle |
| ¼ pound slab bacon, diced | 1 pound dried white beans, presoaked |
| 1 tablespoon olive oil | 1 quart tripe stock or beef stock |
| 3 or 4 onions, chopped | Salt, pepper to taste |
| 2 teaspoons cumin | |
| 2 teaspoons paprika | |
| ¼ pound chorizo or ham | |

Precook tripe with herbs and an onion until tender; strain and save the stock. (To make this stock, beef bouillon cubes may be used instead of salt in the water.) Cut tripe into squares.

Brown diced bacon in olive oil; sauté onion in drawn-out fat, adding cumin and paprika. When onion is soft, add remaining ingredients. Simmer, keeping well covered with liquid, until beans are tender, about 2 hours. Remove bones before serving. Sprinkle top with minced parsley. Makes 8 to 10 hearty servings.

This Bouillabaisse a noble dish is —
A sort of soup, or broth, or brew,
Or hotchpotch of all sorts of fishes . . .

— William Makepeace Thackeray

Among the Romans, fish was looked upon as tainted unless it expired in the hands of the guests.

— Hackwood, *Good Cheer*

However great the dish that holds the turbot, the turbot is still greater than the dish.

— Martial, *Epigrams*

# Fruits of the Sea

The first time I ever tasted bouillabaisse was in New York City, where it had been prepared by a French friend who came from Béziers, an ancient city on the Mediterranean coast not far from the Spanish border. Elie had a magic touch with everything he prepared, and much of what I know about the cooking of southern France—and Catalán cooking, too, since Béziers is close to Spain,—I learned from him. His bouillabaisse was so superb that when I made my first visit to France a year or so after that, I determined that I must visit Marseilles for the express purpose of sampling this marvelous fish stew in its native city, to learn what it was like when made with those special kinds of fish available only in the Mediterranean, ingredients Elie insisted would make it still better.

Arriving at the station in Marseilles, I promptly hired a taxi, instructing the driver to take me to the best restaurant in the city for bouillabaisse. But the steaming dish soon placed before me proved disappointing. It wasn't nearly as good as Elie's. When I next saw him in New York, and told him this, he asked sternly, "How soon after you were seated in the restaurant did they serve you?"

"Oh . . . very quickly. The service was excellent. . ."

"Ah, that explains it! A true bouillabaisse must be cooked to order—it must cook no more than 20 minutes, and then be served right away! What they gave you was leftover bouillabaisse, from someone else's order. They do this to tourists; they think tourists won't know the difference. You should have sent it back."

Later I would try bouillabaisse in other places, in Cannes, Nice and in Paris. Each was different from all the others. I studied recipes in French cookbooks, but no two were alike. Amusingly, each expert—and most of my French cookbooks have been authored by renowned chefs—had his own standard of what a bouillabaisse should be, and scathingly denounced the way others might do it. Some recipes call for as many as six cloves of garlic; others assert that not a whiff of garlic should go into bouillabaisse. One authority states categorically that a bouillabaisse should never be made with mussels; another puts not only mussels, but clams, lobsters, crab and even sea urchins into the pot. Most modern recipes, but not those recipes of older vintage, call for lobster. Even the question of proper seasonings is debated. Most experts agree that saffron is essential, yet one much-respected French chef dared aver that saffron was not all that important. Fennel, bay leaf, thyme and even a bit of orange zest are other condiments favored by some cooks, but by no means used by all.

What is bouillabaisse, then? And who invented it? Basically it's a "hotchpotch of all sorts of fish," as Thackeray defined it well, and whether it's a soup or a stew depends on how one interprets those two words. The French poet Joseph Mery asserted that the dish was invented by Venus—a tongue-in-cheek history that no one takes seriously. The Greeks have long maintained that bouillabaisse is simply a variation of their far older fish stew, Kaccavia, and that it was Phocaean Greeks who brought the recipe to the shores of France shortly after they founded Marseilles back in 600 B.C. But that was a long, long time ago, and since nearly every country bordering the Mediterranean has a very similar fish soup or stew, by another name, it's more than likely that bouillabaisse simply evolved, and its excellence is due to that careful attention to detail that marks the best of French cooking.

After trying numerous ways of preparing bouillabaisse, I always come back to Elie's as the best, and even after tasting it made with fish available only in the Mediterranean, such as rouget, dourade and baudroie, I'm convinced that it's not the type of fish that matters as much as its freshness, and that important business of serving the stew the moment it's ready.

Elie is the one who insists a good fish stock (*court bouillon*) should be made in advance, though a number of eminent authorities merely add water to the pot. I find it also worth the trouble to make a tomato sauce separately, though, again, a number of recipes for the "true" bouillabaisse of Marseilles instruct readers to put layers of onion and tomato in the bottom of the pot, adding the seasonings and fish, then water, and simply bringing it to a boil. But if the sauce is made ahead, one can taste it critically, adjust the seasonings if necessary, and have a greater feeling of confidence in the final results.

As for the fish to be used, you should have at least three kinds (one recipe calls for 12!): one red-fleshed, such as red snapper; one white-fleshed; one firm or fat; another soft and lean. But it's even possible to make a stew resembling bouillabaisse with just one kind of fish, if that's what a family angler happens to bring home. Maybe it won't be a true bouillabaisse, but it can be mighty good.

Can frozen fish be used in any of the following fish soups or stews? A purist would say no; yet I've noted that even in French supermarkets frozen fish is for sale these days and even, horrifying as it may seem, frozen portions of bouillabaisse. What *is* poor France coming to! And this must be said: frozen fish will taste infinitely better cooked in a sauce such as has been described in any of the previous recipes than it would taste if merely fried or baked. And so, for family meals, why not try cooking frozen cod or haddock, or even perch, in a well-flavored tomato sauce, one spiced with orange zest, parsley and a pinch of fennel—perhaps even with a hint of saffron? And with a little white wine or sherry spooned into the broth, it could make a truly wonderful Zuppa, or Caldeirada or Kaccavia, even if one doesn't dare call it a Bouillabaisse.

# Elie's Bouillabaisse

There are 4 important steps: (1) shop around for the freshest and most interesting combination of fish and shellfish; (2) make the court bouillon; (3) prepare the tomato sauce; and (4) only after everyone has arrived and is waiting in eager anticipation, reheat the broth and add the fish and shellfish.

### 1. The Fish
To serve 10 persons (and this might as well be for a party), you will need at least 4 pounds of assorted fish; plus a pound of shrimp in the shell or 12 ounces of already shelled shrimp; 5 small lobster tails, each cut in half; and, if available, a few mussels or clams in the shells.

The best red-fleshed fish is red snapper; red mullet is also good, if available. Porgy is good, and even fresh tuna may be used. For the white-fleshed fish you have a choice of whiting, conger eel, haddock or cod; for the tender lean fish, pompano, halibut or sole. Sea bass is also good, as is fresh perch or even catfish.

Clean the fish; cut in chunks; remove bones as much as possible without tearing the fish to pieces. Sprinkle fish with salt from a shaker. Save all trimmings for the stock.

Scrub and soak mussels or clams to be sure all sand is removed. Shell shrimp, keeping tails intact. Save the shells for the stock. Remove thin upper shell of lobster tails; gently pull flesh partly away from hard outer shell so that meat will be easier to pull from the shell when cooked.

### 2. Court bouillon
Into a kettle, throw all the trimmings, shrimp shells, bones, fish heads, etc. (If you bought the fish minus heads, see if the fish man has any fresh ones he'll give you). Add 2 quarts water, 1½ teaspoons salt, bay leaf, thyme, parsley and a few celery leaves; also put in an onion stuck with 2 cloves. Bring to a boil; cook hard 20 minutes, no more. Strain through a fine sieve or cheesecloth. Measure; you should have 6 cups. Boil to reduce to this amount; or add water to make 6 cups if necessary.

### 3. Tomato Sauce

| | |
|---|---|
| 1 cup chopped onion | ½ teaspoon saffron, or to taste |
| 2 garlic cloves, minced | Pinch of powdered fennel |
| 2 tablespoons parsley | 2 tablespoons chopped |
| ½ cup olive oil | parsley |
| 1 pound can best quality tomatoes, chopped | Grated orange peel (optional) |
| | Salt to taste |

Cook onions, garlic and parsley in olive oil until soft. Add tomatoes; cook 5 minutes. Add seasonings; simmer 10 to 15 minutes. Taste to see if it pleases you. Combine with strained court bouillon.

### 4. The final step

Bring the combined broth and bouillon to a boil; add the larger, firmer pieces of fish and the lobster. Lower heat; simmer (do not boil hard) 6 or 7 minutes. Add the smaller and more tender pieces of fish. Cook 4 or 5 minutes longer. Add shrimp or crab and mussels or clams; cook until shrimp are pink and mussel shells have opened. Serve immediately. A slice of French bread may be placed in each bowl before soup is added; or sprinkle croutons over the top. Some cooks add a tablespoon of butter to bind the broth.

# La Bourride

| | |
|---|---|
| 2 to 3 pounds assorted fish | 6 leeks, sliced (white part |
| Court bouillon (see Elie's | only) |
| Bouillabaisse) | 1 stalk celery, diced |
| 1 cup Aïoli Sauce | 4 or 5 potatoes, thickly sliced |
| ¼ cup olive oil | 2 tablespoons mixed herbs: |
| 2 to 4 garlic cloves, to taste | parsley, thyme, bay leaf |
| 6 tomatoes, sliced | ¼ teaspoon saffron |
| | Salt |

Select fish for contrast of flavor and texture, as in making bouillabaisse. Cut in portions, sprinkle with salt. Put bones, trimmings and fish heads in a kettle; add 2 quarts water and seasonings to prepare a court bouillon. Also prepare Aïoli Sauce (see recipe in Sauces and Seasonings chapter).

In a heavy pot or top-of-stove casserole, place olive oil; add garlic; cook until soft; then crush garlic into the oil. Add tomatoes, leeks, celery and 1 tablespoon of the mixed herbs. Sprinkle vegetables lightly with salt. Add potatoes; sprinkle these with salt. Add the fish. Add remaining herbs and the saffron to the still-hot court bouillon; bring court bouillon again to a boil; strain boiling hot over the fish. Cook fish over low heat, uncovered, without stirring, until fish flakes easily. Remove fish to heatproof platter or serving dish; keep warm. Remove potatoes to a second dish. Strain the cooking liquid; adjust seasonings. Add ¼ cup Aïoli Sauce to the broth; beat with whisk until smooth. Serve this hot as a first course soup. Serve the fish and potatoes as a second course, accompanied by the remaining Aïoli Sauce. (For a short-cut Aïoli Sauce, crush together 3 or 4 garlic cloves and ¼ cup chopped parsley to a paste; beat in 1 cup commercial mayonnaise and a few drops lemon juice.) Makes 6 servings.

# Kaccavia
(*Greek fish stew*)

| | |
|---|---|
| 3  pounds assorted fish | 2  cups fish stock |
| Salt | 2  small carrots, cubed |
| Juice of ½ lemon | 1  stalk celery, diced |
| Fried bread croutons | 4  whole peppercorns |
| ½  cup olive oil | 1  bay leaf |
| 2  medium onions, sliced | 3  tablespoons minced |
| 1  garlic clove, crushed | parsley |
| 4  tomatoes, peeled and | Thin slices of lemon peel |
| chopped | ½  cup dry wine |
| 2  medium potatoes, peeled | |
| and quartered | |

As for bouillabaisse, fish varieties should be chosen for contrast in texture and flavor and should be thick enough to cut in chunks. Sprinkle with salt and lemon juice. Make a stock with fish heads, bones, excess skin, herbs (parsley and thyme), 4 cups water, salt and a tablespoon of butter to bind it. Cook ½ hour; strain. Reduce to 2 cups by boiling. Also in advance, fry cubes of stale bread in olive oil until crisp to make croutons; remove and drain on absorbent papers. In the same oil, cook onion, garlic and tomatoes, until onion is soft. Add fish stock, remaining vegetables and seasonings, including lemon peel and wine. Bring to a boil. Add the fish; cook 15 minutes or until it flakes easily. Taste for seasoning; add more salt if needed. Serve topped with croutons. Makes 6 servings.

# Caldeirada
*(Portuguese fish stew)*

This savory mixture may be made with a single kind of fish, a mixture of fish and shellfish, or with shellfish only (such as shrimp and mussels). The version that follows is typical of the Lisbon area. Some say it should contain at least six kinds of seafood, but three or four will do.

| | |
|---|---|
| 3  to 4 pounds assorted fish | ½  cup olive oil |
| Salt | A pinch of cumin or ginger |
| 1  large can (1 pound 12 ounces) tomatoes, strained | 2  tablespoons parsley |
| | 2  cups water |
| 2  or 3 onions, chopped | 4  or 5 potatoes, peeled and quartered |
| 1  or 2 garlic cloves, minced | Dash of Tabasco (optional) |

Sprinkle fish with salt an hour before cooking; cut into good-sized chunks. Prepare the sauce by putting into the pot tomato, onion, garlic, olive oil and cumin or ginger; simmer until well blended and reduced. Add parsley and water; when boiling, add the potatoes; cook 10 minutes. Taste sauce; add salt as needed and Tabasco if desired. Add the fish; reduce heat; simmer until largest pieces of fish are fork-tender, 15 to 20 minutes longer. Serve with additional parsley sprinkled over the top. Makes 6 servings.

# Zarzuela

This dish is not technically a stew: only enough liquid is added to cook the combined fish and shellfish. It is always served in the pan, cooked to order ready for the table after everyone is assembled.

| | |
|---|---|
| 1  pound shrimp in the shell; or 12 ounces shelled shrimp | 1  pound halibut or fillet of sole, cut in chunks |
| | ¼  cup olive oil |
| 1  cup water | 2  tablespoons brandy |
| 1  quart mussels or clams in shell; or 1 can chopped sea clams | 1  medium onion, chopped |
| | 1  pimiento, diced |
| | 2  garlic cloves, crushed |

| | |
|---|---|
| 3 tablespoons crushed blanched almonds | 1 teaspoon salt |
| | ½ cup white wine |
| 2 tomatoes, peeled and chopped | ½ teaspoon saffron |
| | 1 tablespoon minced parsley |

If the shrimp are purchased in shells, remove shells, keeping tails intact. Make a broth by simmering shells in water; strain and save broth. Scrub mussels or clams and soak until water is clear. (This much can be prepared ahead of time.) Gently sauté cut-up fish in olive oil until delicately browned; add brandy to pan; set afire. When fire has burned out, add onion, pimiento, garlic and almonds; cook until onions are golden. Add tomatoes, salt and wine (and canned clams if used instead of fresh); simmer 5 minutes. Dissolve saffron in the heated shrimp broth. Bring to a boil; cook over lowered heat until mussels open and shrimp have turned bright pink. Serve at once. Makes 4 to 6 servings.

# Mariscada
*(Spanish seafood casserole)*

| | |
|---|---|
| 6 4-ounce lobster tails | 4 to 6 shallots or green onions, chopped |
| 1 pound clams in shell; or 1 can chopped sea clams | ½ cup minced Italian parsley |
| 1 pound large shrimp, shelled | 2 tablespoons flour |
| ½ cup olive oil | 2 eggs |
| 2 or 3 garlic cloves, cut in half | 1 cup milk or light cream |
| | 1 cup dry white wine |
| ½ teaspoon powdered ginger | Salt to taste |

Split lobster tails down the back vertically. If tails are frozen, hold under hot running water a moment or two and then pull flesh partially away from shell. Thoroughly scrub clam shells (if fresh clams are used). Pour olive oil into a heavy skillet. Add garlic and ginger. Remove when garlic is golden and soft; reserve. Add all the shellfish and the shallots to the oil; cover; cook 7 to 10 minutes or until clam shells open. Meanwhile, crush the softened garlic with minced parsley to a paste; blend in ½ teaspoon salt and the flour; then beat in eggs, milk and wine. When shrimp are bright pink, quickly stir this sauce into the oil in the pan. The eggs will give the sauce a slightly curdled appearance, like Chinese lobster sauce, but that's the way it's supposed to be. Serve with rice. Makes 6 to 8 servings.

# SHELLFISH ASSORTMENT

Most of the time at Mediterranean restaurants shrimp, lobster, crayfish and other crustaceans are served plain, already cooked, in their shells, accompanied by mayonnaise or another sauce. Or they may appear as part of an assortment of grilled shellfish, served hot, to be pulled apart with the fingers and dipped in sauce. (Finger bowls, each containing a slice of lemon, appear at each place for rinsing greasy fingers.) The shellfish assortment usually includes, besides shrimp and crayfish, mussels, clams, baby squid and sometimes sea urchins, sea snails or small crabs. In Marseilles, the sauce served with such an assortment would be Aïoli. In Greece it might be Oil-Lemon Sauce, or Avgholemono; in Spain, Salsa Verde or Romesco; in Italy, Pesto Genovese or Bagna Cauda; in Portugal, fiery-hot Piri-Piri, a simple sauce made by sautéeing the shellfish in hot olive oil, or a mixture of oil and butter, then seasoning sparingly with salt and generously with several dashes of piri-piri sauce, a Portuguese condiment similar to Tabasco.

"Shrimp" is a word I use for want of a better; it includes crustaceans of several varieties differing in size from smaller-than-bite-size *crevettes* to huge prawns. In color the shells range from gray to crimson red. Of a different species are the orange-ribbed crayfish (*cigalas*, they are called in Spain) whose flesh is as sweet as our Maine lobsters and far more desirable than the *langosta* or *langouste* (rock lobster) of the Mediterranean, which tends to be coarse and a little tough. All these fish are served whole, heads and tails as well as the shells. Many Europeans think the inside of the shrimp's head is a delicious bit, like the coral of the lobster, but I've always suspected that one reason for serving shrimp with the head still on is because it looks like a bigger portion that way.

When not served in their shells or dipped in batter and fried (see the recipe for Fried Scampi in the Appetizers chapter), shrimp are delicious braised, as in one of the following variations.

# Shrimp a la Marinera

| | |
|---|---|
| 1½ pounds shelled shrimp | 2 tomatoes, peeled, seeded |
| 1 small to medium onion, | and chopped |
| minced | 1 carrot, thinly sliced |
| 1 or 2 garlic cloves, crushed | ¼ cup chopped green pepper |
| 4 tablespoons olive oil; or | ½ cup white wine |
| 2 tablespoons each olive | 1 tablespoon brandy |
| oil and butter | (optional) |
| ¼ cup minced parsley | Seasonings to taste |
| ¾ teaspoon salt | |

If shrimp are frozen when purchased, defrost completely before cooking. Cook onion, garlic and parsley in oil (or oil and butter) until soft. Sprinkle with salt. Add tomato, carrot and green pepper; cook 5 minutes longer. Add the shrimp, wine, brandy if desired and salt to taste. Simmer until shrimp turn pink, about 3 minutes. Serve with rice as an entrée. Makes 4 servings.

# Calamares Fritas

*Calamari* (squid) are popular throughout the Mediterranean, and when tender, can be a truly delicious morsel. The larger ones contain an ink sac, which must be very carefully removed, though in Spain, Italy, and Greece, the black "ink" is considered an attractive addition to the sauce. *Calamari en sua tinta* is frequently offered at Spanish bars as a tapa. A liking for squid is much like a liking for tripe: it's hard to convince those who have never tasted either, and who find the appearance revolting, that the delicate flavor is something to be treasured. Each to his own taste; I've long since given up trying to force my likes on others. But for myself, I have come to rate well-cooked tender squid as highly as shrimp, especially when the squid is sliced, dipped in batter and fried until golden, or simmered in a fragrant sauce.

Octopus is a still different variety, and requires long hours of parboiling to tenderize before it can be added to a stew or pickled. About octopus my feelings are less passionate.

1 medium squid
¼ cup flour
¼ teaspoon salt
1 teaspoon paprika

1 tablespoon water
1 small bottle club soda
Olive or salad oil for frying
Lemon wedges

The most important part of preparing squid for cooking is to clean it so that every bit of the outer skin and every bit of the black ink is removed. (The ink sac is rarely present in the smaller species, which the English call cuttlefish and the Portuguese call lulas.) This is no more difficult than trussing a chicken, for the outer skin peels off easily. To remove the ink sac, turn the main body of the squid inside out. First pull the gristle out; then pull the squid inside out as you would pull a belt that had been stitched along one side, so that the seam will be on the inside.

When the squid has been thoroughly cleaned, the remaining white part is cut in slices and the cleaned tentacles are chopped, then dipped in the following batter.

Combine flour, salt and paprika; add enough water to make a thick paste; then thin with soda water to make a paste the consistency of heavy cream. Heat oil in heavy skillet to depth of ½ inch; drop the floured pieces of squid in hot oil until crisp on each side. Or, use the batter given in the recipe for Fried Scampi (see Appetizers) or a batter of 1 beaten egg and 2 tablespoons each, flour and water.

Serve squid immediately, sprinkled with fresh lemon juice. One pound squid makes enough for 3 or 4 servings.


# Moules au Poulette

Mussels and clams are abundant and still quite reasonable in price (depending on the season), and the Mediterranean ways of dressing them up are no less than splendid.

I recall with particular relish the tender sweet Moules au Poulette served in the elegant dining room of the Hotel Reine Didon in Carthage. The room was entirely walled with glass, permitting a magnificent view of the bay where the Phoenician princess Dido landed with her handmaidens in 814 B.C. to found the ancient city of Carthage. One could fully appreciate, when gazing over the beauty of the harbor and dining on shellfish fresh from the waters of the surrounding sea, why Dido would want to tarry here. The dish is French, as is the cuisine in most Tunisian hotels, but it was because the mussels themselves were so sweet and fresh that the sauce was so beautiful.

| | |
|---|---|
| 2 quarts mussels | 1 cup white wine |
| 2 tablespoons chopped shallot; or one small white onion, chopped | 2 tablespoons flour |
| | ¼ cup cream |
| | 2 egg yolks |
| 1 sprig parsley | Juice ½ lemon |
| Few leaves of thyme | 2 tablespoons minced parsley |
| 1 bay leaf | |
| Butter (6 tablespoons altogether) | |

First scrub mussels; remove beards; soak in several changes of water until water is clear. Place the shallot, parsley sprig, thyme, bay leaf and 2 tablespoons of the butter in a large kettle or pot. Over this place the scrubbed drained mussels. Add the wine. Cover tightly; bring to a boil; cook 5 minutes or until mussels are opened. (Do not add salt to the pot: the mussels have enough salt inside their shells.) Remove the mussels; discard one shell of each, so that the mussel remains on the second shell. If any mussels have gone to the bottom of the pot, rescue them and add to the sauce later. Strain the cooking liquid through cheesecloth. Let stand ½ hour so that any sand will go to bottom. Then pour off from the top 1½ cups broth. (All this should be done ahead.)

Melt 2 tablespoons butter in a casserole; stir in 2 tablespoons flour; then slowly add the reserved broth and the mussels in their half shells. Bring to the boil; simmer 5 minutes. Beat cream and egg yolks together; add to the egg mixture a little of the hot broth; then add this to rest of broth over lowered heat (or above hot water) and stir in lemon juice and parsley. Stir constantly until thickened and smooth. Serve at once. Do not allow sauce to come even close to the boil or it may curdle; use a whisk for stirring. Makes 4 to 6 servings.

# Ameijoas a Cataplana

The cataplana is a strange-looking utensil of Moroccan origin, used only in Morocco and in the Algarve district of Portugal. Those used in North Africa look like huge unopened scallop shells—and it's quite possible that originally, in the distant past, real scallop shells were so used, for at one time there were molluscs many times the size of those now available. The Portuguese cataplana is deeper and rounder than the Moroccan, though it, too, consists of two parts that clamp together like a closed scallop shell.

All sorts of mixtures may be cooked in the cataplana, but invariably, one ingredient is clams (ameijoas), which provide both the liquid and the salt needed for the dish. No other liquid is added. Probably this cookery method was born of necessity in the desert. When water was precious, ways had to be devised to cook without it.

The typical dish of the Algarve contains not only clams, but also spicy chorizo sausage, or the sun-cured ham called presunto (much like the Italian prosciutto). Diced lean pork is also sometimes added, or even chicken. It's surprising to find pork products in a dish of Moroccan origin, since most Moroccans are Moslems, and good Moslems are forbidden to eat pork, but this may have been the influence of the successive Portuguese, Spanish and French occupants of North Africa, who certainly left other culinary traces behind as well.

The following is the recipe of my Portuguese friend Antonio, who has spent considerable time in French Morocco and says his version borrows from both Moroccan and Portuguese recipes for cataplana. The dish can be made in any pot with a tight-fitting cover (a porcelain-lined iron pot with cover is fine), but the cover must fit very tightly, and it must be roomy enough to hold the clams in their shells with ample "breathing space" besides.

| | |
|---|---|
| 3 pounds clams in shells | ½ cup heavy cream |
| 2 onions, minced | ½ pound chorizo sausage, sliced; or ¼ pound prosciutto; or 1 cup diced, cooked tenderized ham |
| 1 or 2 garlic cloves, minced | |
| 2 tomatoes, peeled and chopped | |
| 1 tablespoon chopped fresh coriander (if available) | 3 ounces shrimp (optional) |
| 1 or 2 tablespoons chopped parsley | 1 cup diced cooked pork or leftover cut-up chicken |
| ¼ cup olive oil | Dash of Tabasco |

Scrub the clams and rinse through several waters, or soak in sea water. In the bottom half of the cataplana, or in any heavy pot, cook the onions, garlic, tomatoes and herbs in olive oil until soft. Add the Tabasco, cream and the meat and shrimp; place the clams over all. The clams should not come above the lower half of the cataplana, or more than half the way up the inside of the pot. Cover; clamp shut. Bring to a boil until steam can be seen escaping from the cover; then turn heat low and cook 25 minutes. The clam shells should all be open. If they are not, it probably was because the pan was too full, so try cooking for another 5 minutes. Any clams whose shells still don't open should be discarded. Serve from the cataplana or pot, accompanied by rice. Makes 5 servings.

Sole is one of the most popular of all fish everywhere, and since it is easy to fillet, it lends itself to all manner of manipulation. Often, in Mediterranean kitchens, it is combined with shrimp or lobster; the flavors complement one another beautifully. In fact, in the following two recipes, shrimp, lobster or crab may be used interchangeably; only a small amount is needed in each case.

# Filete Langosta Relleno
*(lobster-stuffed rolled sole)*

| | |
|---|---|
| 6  fillets of sole | ¼  cup minced parsley |
| 1  cup soft bread crumbs | 1  tablespoon minced onion; |
| 1  lobster tail (about 4 | or 1 teaspoon instant dried |
| ounces), chopped; or ¼ | onion |
| cup shrimp or crabmeat | Pinch of oregano |
| 2  tablespoons oil | 1  cup tomato sauce |
| ¼  teaspoon salt | |

Trim fillets evenly. Combine all remaining ingredients except tomato sauce; place a spoonful of filling over each fillet and roll up. Place each fillet in a separate piece of aluminum foil, with overlapped side of fillet on bottom. Spoon tomato sauce over each. (If canned tomato sauce is used, add a little olive oil and some chopped chives.) Seal foil tightly by crimping edges. Bake in a large shallow baking pan, or two pans, with oven preheated to hot (400° F.) for 30 minutes. Makes 6 servings.


# Linguado Imperador
(*shrimp-stuffed fried sole*)

| | |
|---|---|
| 2 pounds small fillets of sole | 2 tablespoons cream |
| Salt, lemon juice | Dash of nutmeg |
| 1 jar (3½ ounces) baby shrimp | 2 eggs, beaten |
| | 2 tablespoons flour |
| 2 tablespoons butter | ¼ teaspoon salt |
| 2 tablespoons flour | ½ cup fine dry crumbs |
| ¾ cup broth | Oil for frying |

Lay out the fillets and cut so that they form even portions. Sprinkle with salt and lemon juice; let stand ½ hour. Drain canned shrimp (I find the Danish or Norwegian shrimp the best for this); measure liquid and add water to make ¾ cup. Melt butter; stir in flour; slowly stir in shrimp liquid, then the cream. Cook until thickened. Add shrimp and trimmings of sole. Spoon a little of the shrimp mixture in center of each fillet; roll up, keeping all sauce inside. Dip each rolled sole in mixture of egg, flour and salt; roll in crumbs. Chill until ready to cook; then fry in deep oil preheated to 375°F., or until a cube of bread browns in 60 seconds, turning brown evenly on all sides. Serve hot with lemon wedges. Makes 6 servings.


# Loup Grille au Fenouil
(*grilled sea bass with fennel*)

In Marseilles, one of the most costly items offered on restaurant menus is Loup de Mer Grille au Fenouil, "sea wolf" broiled over layers of fennel. When a customer orders this fine dish in one of the best restaurants facing the Vieux Port, the waiter brings him the uncooked fish so that he may examine it for freshness. The customer is shown the bright red gills of the head and the bulging shine of the eyes, to be convinced that the fish about to be prepared for him is from the previous night's catch, if not brought in that morning.

Given such fresh fish, nothing much needs to be done but cook it gently. It's a fine trick to know about in the summer, especially for those spending a vacation near the ocean. Almost any freshly caught fish can be so cooked. First clean the fish, scaling and removing the entrails (and the head, too, if you insist); then sprinkle the fish inside and out with salt and marinate it in olive oil until time to cook. Then, when the charcoal fire is ready—a low fire, not too hot—place sprigs of fresh fennel (if you can find it) over the grill. Or, sprinkle dried fennel weed over the fish itself. Drain the fish of its oil and pat off excess oil with paper towel; then place fish on the grill. Broil only until skin is lightly colored and fish is firm to the touch. Serve with lemon and drawn butter.

If neither fresh nor dried fennel weed is available, add the merest bit of powdered fennel, crushed anise or crushed tarragon to the fish before cooking. Or use—if available—sprigs of fresh tarragon. The licoricelike flavor of anise and tarragon are similar to that of fennel.

# Nut-Stuffed Fish, Turkish Style

| | |
|---|---|
| 1  whole fish, 3-4 pounds dressed for stuffing | 1  tablespoon chopped fresh coriander; or 1 teaspoon crushed coriander seeds |
| 3  tablespoons olive oil | |
| ½  cup pine nuts or chopped walnuts | ¼  cup seedless raisins or currants |
| 2  small onions, minced | Salt, pepper |
| 2  tablespoons chopped parsley | Flour |
| | 1  cup white wine |

The center bone of the fish should be removed and the fins cut from the back. Sprinkle with salt and lemon juice inside and out; let stand ½ hour while preparing the stuffing. Heat olive oil; add the nuts; brown lightly; add onions, parsley and coriander; cook until onions are golden. Add raisins or currants. Season to taste with salt and pepper. Put mixture inside fish; fasten with picks. Cut slashes in top of fish, 1 inch apart, down to center bone. Place in shallow pan; brush generously with oil; or lay slabs of butter or margarine over top. Pour wine around fish. Bake in moderate (350° F.) oven until fish is firm when touched, about 40 minutes. Baste occasionally with pan drippings. Makes 4 or 5 servings.

# Dourade à la Provençale

Dourade à la Provençale (French) has its counterpart in Psari Plaki (Greek) and Peixe Assado (Portuguese). In each, a whole fish is baked in a sauce of tomato, onions, herbs and white wine. There are slight differences: in Provence and in Greece, olive oil is used in the sauce; in Portugal, it is butter or margarine. The herbs used differ, too, of course, but as this is another of those concoctions which may be varied according to the whim of the cook, the regional differences are not hard and fast.

|   |   |   |   |
|---|---|---|---|
| 1 | 3- or 4-pound fish suitable for baking | 1 | lemon, thinly sliced |
| 1½ | teaspoons salt | ¼ | teaspoon thyme |
| ½ | cup olive oil | ¼ | teaspoon fennel |
| 2 | large onions, thinly sliced | 1 | bay leaf, crushed |
| 2 | leeks, white part, sliced | 2 | tablespoons minced parsley |
| 4 | or 5 tomatoes, peeled and sliced | 1 | cup white wine |

In France, the fish called dourade is used, but one could also use almost any firm thick fish, such as red snapper, sea bass, or whiting. Cut deep slashes across the top of the dressed fish, down to the center bone, about 1 inch apart. (If the fish is caught by a family angler, be sure to leave the head on—it adds greatly to the flavor of the sauce.) Sprinkle with salt ½ hour before baking. Pour half the oil in a shallow casserole; place a layer of onion mixed with leeks in the bottom. Place the fish over the onion and insert the slices of lemon in the slashes; then, between the lemon slices, lay the slices of tomato cut to fit. Sprinkle with the herbs. Add remaining oil, wine and olives. Place remaining tomatoes around fish. Bake in a moderate (350°F.) oven for an hour to an hour and a half, until flesh is firm and well browned and slits have spread wide apart. Baste several times with liquid in pan. Makes 4 or 5 servings.

# Peixe Assado

Prepare as in Dourade à la Provençale, but instead of olive oil, use butter or margarine; omit fennel. Instead of (or in addition to) parsley, add chopped fresh coriander, if available. Lemon may be omitted, with only tomato slices placed over the top of the fish or inserted in the slits. Add enough liquid to come more than halfway up sides of fish. Dot top with butter.

Frozen fish, such as haddock, perch or halibut, may be baked in the same sort of sauce. Make sure the fish is completely covered with sauce. Add water if tomatoes do not produce enough liquid as they bake. Chopped chives are also good in this sauce.

# Baked Fish en Papillote

To bake fish *en papillote* is a very old technique, one described by Athenaeus, except that in his time, the fish was "swathed" in vine leaves and thrust under the ashes of the fire. In these modern times, either aluminum foil or parchment paper (available in gourmet shops) is more convenient, and it's easier to bake the fish in an oven instead of under hot ashes—though in summer, when the charcoal grill is on the patio, the latter is not a bad idea.

|   |   |
|---|---|
| 3 pounds fillets of sea bass or halibut | 1 tablespoon grated onion, chives or shallot |
| 2 tablespoons olive or salad oil | 2 tablespoons butter |
| 1 teaspoon salt | 2 tablespoons white wine or Madeira<br>Joinville Sauce |

Cut fish in 6 serving portions. Sprinkle with salt. Have ready six separate parchment bags, or six large pieces of foil. Brush inside with oil. Spread onion, shallot or chives over top of each slice of fish; dot each slice with butter and moisten with wine. Place inside parchment so that butter is on top, or wrap with foil. Bake in preheated hot oven for 20 minutes or until fish flakes easily. Remove the fish from its packets when serving. Joinville Sauce is perfect with this (see recipe in chapter on Sauces and Seasonings). Makes 6 servings.

# Croustade de Saumon

This excellent fish pastry was offered as a first course at the Hiely-Lucullus Restaurant in the city of Avignon, where I enjoyed the most memorable of all the meals on my round-the-Mediterranean trip. The Hiely restaurant rates two stars in the Michelin Guide; I would give it more. The selections from which one could choose for the three-course luncheon were all so tempting I greedily ordered two first courses—and by the time the superb dessert was placed before me, I was too full to enjoy it properly. No doubt fresh salmon was used in the Lucullus recipe, but canned salmon was used in the test and it proved delicious. You may need to add water to make 1 cup liquid for the sauce.

While this dish was served as a first course at Hiely's, for a less Lucullan occasion it is quite grand enough to serve as an entrée, and to distinguished company at that.

| | |
|---|---|
| 2 1-pound cans finest red salmon | 3 tablespoons flour |
| Bouquet garni of thyme, bay leaf, parsley | 1 cup stock (from salmon) |
| | Pinch of nutmeg |
| 1 teaspoon instant minced onion | ½ cup heavy cream |
| | ½ cup shredded Natural Gruyere or Swiss cheese |
| Pinch of cloves | ½ cup fine crumbs blended with melted butter |
| Salt, water | |
| 3 tablespoons butter | Baked pastry shells |

Drain salmon, saving liquid. Pick over fish, removing dark skin and bones; flake. Combine reserved liquid and water to make 1 cup broth; heat with instant onion, cloves and herbs; then strain. Melt butter; stir in flour; cook until it bubbles; then slowly stir in strained liquid, nutmeg and cream; stir until smooth.

Add salmon to this; taste for seasoning. Place salmon in pastry shells; sprinkle shredded cheese over top; sprinkle buttered crumbs over cheese. Bake in moderate oven (350° F.) until top is golden and cheese melted. Makes 6 servings.

**Pastry shells.** Prepare frozen patty shells, baking according to package directions. Or, use regular pie crust dough for a 2-crust pie, rolled out to fit a single 10-inch round Pyrex baking pan (1 inch high). After trimming edge, use leftover scraps to cut into shapes and place, loosely, over top of salmon.

# Bacalao Vizcaina

Bacalau, salted dried codfish, is popular in all the countries bordering the northern shores of the Mediterranean. The Portuguese, who introduced the first salted cod to the world at the turn of the sixteenth century, claim to have more than 100 ways of preparing bacalau, their favorite food, and when the cod fleet sets sail for the banks of Labrador each spring, it's such a special occasion that the Bishop of Lisbon blesses the fleet. Yet after having tasted at least 15 different Portuguese bacalau dishes, I must confess the one I prefer to all others as an entrée (different from the little fried Pasteis de Bacalau or croquettes whose recipe is given in the Appetizers chapter) is the Spanish dish called Bacalao Vizcaina, baked in a rich tomato sauce flavored with saffron.

There's no doubt that bacalau (or bacalao, baccala or bakalarios) is an acquired taste. I, too, used to be less than enthusiastic about it. But I've come to like it so much that when I haven't had any for some time, I get hungry thinking about it. Like so many other foods, it all depends on how it's prepared.

One mistake many American cooks make is soaking the dried cod too long, or putting it through too many changes of water. It should still be rather salty, that's what gives bacalau its special flavor. Otherwise, you might as well use tasteless frozen cod—which you can do, if you prefer a blander dish.

| | |
|---|---|
| 1  to 1½ pounds salt cod | 1  large can (1 pound |
| ½  cup olive oil | 12 ounces) tomatoes |
| 3  to 4 onions, thickly sliced | 2  tablespoons minced |
| 1  or 2 garlic cloves, crushed | parsley |

1 can pimientos, drained
  and diced

¼ teaspoon saffron
3 or 4 potatoes, thickly sliced

Soak salt cod overnight or for at least 12 hours. Drain; add fresh water; bring just to a boil; cook 5 minutes. Remove from water and throw out water; cut cod into small cubes and remove skin and bones. Cook onions in olive oil in large deep skillet or heavy pot until onions are soft. Add garlic, tomatoes, parsley, pimiento and saffron; simmer 20 minutes. Add cod and potatoes, pushing down so they are covered with sauce. Do *not* add salt. Simmer over very low heat for 2 hours. During first hour cook uncovered, shaking pan occasionally to thicken sauce and prevent sticking. After sauce has thickened and is smooth, cover skillet or pot and continue cooking another hour, but keep heat very, very low. Makes 6 to 8 servings.

# Baccala alla Vincenta

1½ pounds salt cod, presoaked
¼ cup olive oil
2 large onions, sliced

¼ cup chopped parsley
4 or 5 potatoes, sliced
2 cups milk
  Butter

Soak cod overnight; drain; add fresh water; bring to a boil; cook 10 minutes. Drain again; remove bones and skin and cut into pieces. Moisten bottom of casserole with oil; add layers of cod, onions and potatoes, moistening with additional oil. Do not add salt. Sprinkle parsley and dots of butter over top. Add milk. Bake until milk is absorbed and cod and potatoes are tender. Makes 6 to 8 servings.

**With Frozen Cod.** Defrost cod; cut in serving portions. Proceed as when using fresh cod (fish need not be soaked or precooked), sprinkling salt over each layer.

# Brandade de Morue

Frenchmen can become eloquent over Brandade de Morue, the way of treating salt cod in the south of France. Even the great

Escoffier added his praises, though he put the fluffy mixture into rich puff pastry and garnished it with truffles. The preparation is more complicated than that of Bacalao Vizcaina and for the novice may prove tricky, but for those seeking the unusual, it's a technique worth mastering.

1½   pounds salt cod, presoaked
  2   garlic cloves, crushed
      (optional)
  1   tablespoon lemon juice
  5   tablespoons olive oil,
      heated to lukewarm

  5   tablespoons heavy cream,
      heated to lukewarm
  2   tablespoons minced
      parsley
      Dash of cayenne
  2   cups mashed potatoes
      (optional)

Drain soaked cod; add fresh cold water; simmer 15 to 20 minutes or until cod is quite tender. Discard water; shred cod, removing bones and skin. Pound shredded fish in a mortar or beat in blender until smooth. Add garlic, if desired. Place in chafing dish, over water, or in a pan that can be placed in another pot with water in bottom. Water below should be simmering but not boiling. Beat lemon juice into cod; then alternately add olive oil and cream a tablespoon at a time, beating briskly after each addition. Finally add parsley and cayenne. If potatoes are to be added prepare separately but do not add salt. Beat until mixture is very fluffy and smooth. Serve garnished with parsley or with shrimp or quartered hard cooked eggs. Grilled tomatoes, topped with chopped chives and parsley, are a delicious accompaniment. Makes 6 to 8 servings.

Meats such as godlike kings rejoice to taste.

—Homer, *The Iliad*

Just at the close of winter when spring has cleared the sky,
Oh, then the lambs are fat, then are wines most mellow.

—Virgil, *Georgics*

I will place this carefully fed pig
Within the crackling oven; and, I ask,
What nicer dish can e'er be given to man!

—Aeschylus

# Meats

Ulysses was an expert at laying a fire; Achilles turned the spit; while Patroclus drew the wine—so Homer described their preparation for dinner on the field of battle during the Trojan War. Roasting meat over an open fire was probably for many centuries the only way it was cooked, except for those bits and pieces and bones thrown into a stew pot. And when people hadn't the time or the need to roast an entire sheep, an ox or a wild boar, they cut off chunks or pieces to spear on a sword or skewer, like the shish kebab that Persian horsemen are said to have invented as a quick way of getting their meat cooked while on the march. Cooking meat over an open fire out of doors is still the favorite method in most of the countries bordering the Mediterranean.

The pig was domesticated in the Near East as early as 7000 BC, as archaeological findings have proved. Then, strangely, the eating of pork was forbidden for religious reasons by the ancient Egyptians and the Babylonians long before Moses named swine flesh unclean, and a thousand years before the followers of Mohammed were ordered to abstain from the eating of any pork product.

The usual explanation is that there was a practical sanitary reason for such an edict: pork spoils more quickly than other meats, especially in a hot climate. Yet in other regions with the same subtropical climate, pork is still, to this day, a favorite meat. Suckling pig is feast food in Greece, Italy, Spain and Portugal.

Suckling pig was such a popular meat with the Romans that a law had to be passed limiting the number of the piglets that could be killed. But no such ban applied to wild boar. At a Macedonian banquet described by Athenaeus, each one of the 300 guests at a wedding feast was served an entire stuffed boar, though the guests were encouraged to carry home whatever they could not finish on the spot. (Imagine the job of building enough fires to roast 300 stuffed boars!)

Today lamb is the meat served more frequently than any other in all Mediterranean countries, and the lamb of the Mediterranean is so succulent and tender that it's delicious in whatever way it's cooked. In Greece and Cyprus they explain the wonderful flavor of the lamb as due to the wild oregano on which the sheep graze in mountain pastures, preseasoning the meat. Cabrito (baby goat) is the next most commonly served meat in the countries of the Near East and North Africa, with a flavor so similar to that of mutton that most people can't tell the difference. There's a practical reason for these two meats being more abundantly available than any others: both sheep and goats climb happily to high mountain peaks and are content to graze on whatever sparse grasses they can find. Cattle, on the other hand, require verdant rich pasture land, of which there is a critical shortage in the Mediterranean area. Mediterranean beef is generally inferior to ours. But the veal is usually excellent, far more tender and delicate than American veal, because, due to the shortage of pasture, calves are butchered at a younger age.

In every Mediterranean country, the charcoal burner is put to good use throughout the year. At Eastertime in Greece, so many suckling lambs are turning on forked spits over charcoal, outside every country taverna and in the courtyards of simple restaurants as well as home gardens, that the very air is heavy with the smoky fragrance of sizzling meat. Kebabs, chops, sausages, meatballs and chicken livers all are broiled over charcoal, cooked to order and served on bread to soak up the still dribbling meat juices.

In the Near East, where shish kebab was invented, the ways of preparing meats for the grill are infinite. Every bit of meat is used in one way or another: it is minced into patties or forced into sausage skins if too small to be laced on skewers; or the trimmings are used in stews or casseroles.

One night in Tel Aviv, trying to find that part of the city that the guidebooks described as "picturesque Old Jaffa," I stumbled upon a street within sight of the water's edge where several portable charcoal braziers were set up right on the sidewalk. Here one could choose from among half a dozen kinds of meat already sizzling on the grids or waiting to be cooked to order: skewers containing chicken livers, or bits of heart, or lamb or goat kidneys, hamburger-shaped meat patties, sausages and, of course, chunky kebabs. At the side were as many or more kinds of relishes or sauces, and for the "buns," there was the flat Arabian bread that is slit through the center to form a pocket, into which a selection of ingredients could be piled.

# KEBABS

The word kebabs, which in the American parlance has come to mean chunks of any kind of meat cooked on a skewer, means in the Arab countries simply meat (almost invariably lamb) cut in cubes. But the meat also may be braised in a sauce or stewed instead of being cooked on skewers. Shish originally meant a sword. Now it means any kind of skewer, long or short. Shashlik is Armenian for shish kebab. The Greek word souvlakia means literally "skewer," as does the Italian spiedini. Swarma is the name for shish kebab in Hebrew. En brochette in French means "on the skewer."

Almost everywhere lamb is used in making shish kebab (by whatever name it is locally called); only in Greece is pork used as an alternate. In America, though, where beef is more tender than lamb, there's no reason why beef shouldn't be substituted for lamb in most of the lamb recipes that follow. Veal, too, if marinated in advance, can be delicious broiled over charcoal.

Some cooks insist that tender young lamb needs no other seasoning but salt and pepper before it is placed on skewers, and I'm inclined to agree with this, when it's Mediterranean lamb. But since American lamb is often stronger in flavor (the lambs are butchered at a more advanced age—up to a year old), marinating can both improve flavor and tenderize. Some cooks insist that no vegetables be placed on the skewers next to the meat, yet other recipes call for all sorts of vegetables, not only onion (the most used) but mushroom caps, green pepper squares, eggplant, zucchini, tomatoes and yellow summer squash. The Greeks slip bay leaves between the meat cubes and vegetables, which adds delightful flavor. When meat alone is placed on skewers, the cubes should be spaced apart so that all sides will cook. This is especially true with cubes of pork.

# Shish Kebab

Cut lamb, from leg or shoulder, into 1½-inch cubes. Save trimmings or small pieces for stews or casserole dishes. Grate, or crush in blender, 1 large onion; blend with 2 tablespoons olive oil. Marinate the lamb in this mixture for at least 3 hours, turning several times. (The onion helps tenderize the meat.) Place on skewers ½ inch apart; broil until sizzling on all sides. Serve over rice or bread, accompanied by sauce of yogurt mixed with chopped cucumber, chopped onion and a little dried mint.

# Yogurt-Marinated Shish Kebab

Instead of the onion-oil mixture, marinate the lamb cubes in yogurt or buttermilk enough to cover the meat; turn several times. Before cooking, the meat will not look pretty, but the culture in the yogurt makes the meat butter-tender and the outside will become very brown and crisp. Serve with lemon wedges so that lemon can be sprinkled over the meat.

# Lahm Mashwi
(*Lebanese shish kebab*)

Cut meat into cubes; rub with coarsely crushed or freshly grated black pepper and salt, or with a mixture of 1 teaspoon each, coarse black pepper, cinnamon and salt. Leave this way several hours or overnight. Thread on skewers; brush with olive oil; place small whole onions or thick onion slices between meat cubes, if desired. Broil until meat is sizzling on all sides. Serve over toast, with Tahina or Hummus as a sauce. Or, serve Eggplant-Yogurt Dip as a sauce (see recipes in Appetizers chapter). Beef cubes rubbed with the same black pepper-cinnamon mixture taste *very* exotic when served as shish kebab.

# Arni Souvlakia
(*Greek shish kebab*)

Rub cubes of lamb with mixture of salt, pepper, crushed marjoram or oregano, lemon juice and a little oil. Thread loosely on skewers, with bay leaves between. Broil until sizzling. Serve on a bed of chopped parsley or watercress, with lemon wedges (sprinkle lemon over meat at table).

# Hirino Souvlakia

Use 1-inch cubes of lean pork instead of lamb. Rub with same mixture, but sage may be used instead of oregano. Tomato halves, or cherry tomatoes, may be placed between the meat cubes; or, tomato halves may be broiled separately on the same grid. Be sure to serve lemon wedges with the meat—grilled pork especially is improved with lemon.

# Veal en Brochette

Cut 2 pounds veal from shoulder, leg or breast into 1 to 1½ inch cubes. Marinate overnight in mixture of 1 cup olive oil, 1 teaspoon paprika, ¼ cup red wine vinegar, 1 teaspoon salt, a sliced onion, a bay leaf and a pinch of thyme. In the same marinade, place 2 thickly sliced zucchini (each about 6 inches long). Next day, remove meat and zucchini slices and thread alternately on skewers. Cherry tomatoes and thick onion slices may also be placed on the skewers alternately with the zucchini. Broil slowly, 6 inches from heat, until nicely browned, turning frequently.

# Kafta ala Shish

This beautiful combination was served at the Saloum Restaurant in midtown Beirut. On the plate with the kafta were served tiny little radishes, watercress and fanned gherkin pickles.

| | | |
|---|---|---|
| 1 | pound ground lean lamb | ½ cup olive oil |
| 1 | teaspoon salt | 1 medium eggplant |
| ½ | teaspoon pepper | Salt |
| ½ | teaspoon cinnamon | ½ cup pine nuts |
| ½ | cup minced parsley | |

The meat should be very lean: ask the butcher to put it through the grinder at least twice. Then place ground meat in a bowl or large mortar with the salt, pepper, cinnamon and parsley and mash with a pestle until it is like a paste. (This could be done in a blender, but the meat tends to stick to the blades and is hard to get off.) The meat must be very smooth. Form into balls the size and shape of an egg, but a little more elongated. Brush the outside with a little olive oil.

Cut the eggplant into cubes or slices; sprinkle with salt; let stand 15 minutes. Cover with the olive oil; marinate ½ to 1 hour; drain; pat off excess oil with paper towel. Impale meatballs on skewers alternately with eggplant cubes. Broil until meat is brown and sizzling on all sides and eggplant is soft. Remove from skewers; serve topped with pine nuts sautéed in the marinating oil. Makes 4 servings.

# Seftalia

One evening in Nicosia, I dined at a simple little restaurant whose sign proclaimed it a "Kebab House." Colored lights strung from tree to tree lit up the gathering dusk. The wine was served from a pitcher, simple but good red native wine, and the tables were of the crudest four-square design. But the tender little grilled pork sausages called seftalia that I ordered were completely delicious.

The pork meat had been ground and mashed until very soft, seasoned with parsley, garlic, minced onion, a pinch of nutmeg, salt and pepper. The meat was held inside sausage skins, but I found that if ground twice, then mashed with a pestle until pastelike, the meat will stick to the skewers without benefit of skin. Brush with oil and grill over charcoal until well done. Serve with lemon wedges, sliced tomato, a little pile of chopped onion and watercress.

# Kaytan Kebabi

Coconut is the surprise ingredient in this beautiful Turkish recipe.

| | |
|---|---|
| 1½ pounds veal from leg or shoulder | ¼ cup white wine, or 2 tablespoons wine vinegar |
| 1 large onion, grated or crushed | 2 tablespoons butter, melted |
| 1 teaspoon salt | 1 tablespoon grated coconut |
| ¼ teaspoon freshly ground pepper | ¼ teaspoon cinnamon |
| 2 tablespoons olive oil | 2 tablespoons chopped parsley |
| | 2 green onions, minced |

Cut veal into strips 3 inches long by ½ inch wide. Marinate for 12 hours in mixture of grated or crushed onion (onion can be crushed easily in a blender), salt, pepper, olive oil and wine or wine vinegar. Remove from marinade; weave strips on small skewers, 1 to a skewer. Grill above charcoal, or under a broiler, 5 to 6 inches from heat, just until nicely browned. Just before removing from fire, baste with the combined melted butter, coconut, cinnamon and parsley. Serve over rice, with minced green onions as garnish. Makes 4 to 6 servings.

(The same ingredients can be prepared like a ragout: cut veal in chunks; marinate in same seasonings, onion and wine. Then sauté in oil; add coconut, parsley, a cup of tomato purée and ½ cup wine; simmer until meat is tender. This is called Dana Tas Etli Kebabi.)

# Salsa Tiberio

The Emperor Tiberius, who was among the more gluttonous of Rome's rulers, is said to have favored the following as a basting sauce for meats turning on the spit. It is even better as a marinade. Use for beef, mutton or pork to be barbecued or roasted.

| | |
|---|---|
| 1 cup dry white wine | 2 garlic cloves, thinly sliced |
| 1 cup olive oil | ¼ cup wine vinegar |
| 1 tablespoon honey | ¼ teaspoon crushed hot |
| ½ cup chopped onion |     red pepper |
| | ½ teaspoon salt |

Combine all ingredients; pour over meat to be grilled over the barbecue fire or oven-roasted. Makes 2½ cups, enough for 4 pounds of meat.

# ROAST LAMB

Roast lamb is even better when turned on a spit over charcoal than when cooked in the oven. Leg of lamb also is delicious when charcoal broiled. To prevent meat from drying out over the heat of an open fire, it's wise to marinate it in an oil and vinegar or wine and oil mixture for several hours in advance. Using a meat thermometer, roast to 150° for rare meat.

# Gigot

This is the French way of preparing roast leg of lamb, with garlic cloves inserted in the meat near the bone. When roasted in an oven, dried white beans, presoaked the night before, are added to the roasting pan, to capture all the pan juices.

A Provençal recipe for Gigot calls for a dozen cloves of garlic plus an equal number of anchovy fillets, rinsed of excess salt. Both garlic and anchovy are inserted in the meat, which then, if it is to be cooked on a spit, is brushed generously with olive oil.

Those Frenchmen who are not natives of Provence and everyone else (except possibly Basques) would find this enough garlic to keep the werewolves and everyone else from the door. In my estimation a thin sliver or two of garlic is enough. In fact, there are other ways of flavoring lamb for roasting that I personally much prefer.

# Italian Style Roast Lamb

Marinate the lamb leg or shoulder in red wine 24 hours in advance. Remove from marinade; crush rosemary or basil over the meat; dust meat with salt. Roast in a preheated oven to rare (140° F. on a meat thermometer). To give it a browner "crust," brush with a little oil halfway through.

# Spanish Style Roast Lamb

Rub the meat with a mixture of crushed cumin and oregano; brush with oil; dust with salt before roasting.

# Arabian Style Roast Lamb

Cut incisions in meat; rub coarsely crushed black pepper into the meat, or a mixture of ½ teaspoon pepper, ¼ teaspoon ginger and 1 teaspoon salt. Brush with oil just before placing in oven or over charcoal.

# Stuffed Roast Lamb

Stuffed lamb or kid is the traditional Easter meat in the Near East, and for non-Christians who do not observe Easter, it's the feast food at weddings and other great celebrations. Just in case you happen to see a baby lamb hanging in the butcher shop next

Easter, you might be interested to know that to stuff a 16 to 20 pound lamb you will need 4 cups of uncooked rice, 2 cups of mixed nuts (almonds, pistachio nuts, pine nuts), salt, pepper and some chopped parsley (or fresh coriander if you know where to get it).

A similar stuffing, in smaller quantity, can be put inside a boned lamb shoulder. Have the butcher cut a pocket in the boned shoulder; place inside it ¾ cup uncooked rice, ½ cup almonds or pine nuts, 1 teaspoon salt, pepper, ¼ teaspoon cinnamon (if desired) and a little parsley. Moisten the rice mixture with ½ cup water. Stuff loosely (rice will swell); sew with butcher's cord or truss the edges of the meat to close; sprinkle outside with salt; roast in moderate oven until the meat is nicely browned, allowing 25 minutes to the pound for "pink" meat, 30 to 35 minutes per pound if you prefer lamb well done.

# Ballotine d' Agneau

Ballotine d'Agneau is a French version of stuffed lamb shoulder that is the spécialté de la maison at the Jules Cesar Hotel in Arles. There the ballotine is baked inside rich puff paste, though the classic French recipe for a ballotine does not require pastry.

|   |   |   |   |
|---|---|---|---|
| | Boned shoulder of lamb, about 4 pounds | ½ | teaspoon thyme |
| 1 | pound ground lamb, or a mixture of lamb and pork | | Salt, pepper, to taste |
| 2 | onions, chopped | 1 | egg, beaten |
| 2 | tablespoons chopped parsley | 2 | tablespoons oil |
| 2 | to 3 tablespoons fresh lard or butter | 1 | cup red wine |
| | | 1 | tablespoon meat glaze or Kitchen Bouquet |

Ask the butcher to bone the lamb and trim it so that it can be stuffed and rolled. The trimmings should be put through the grinder, with enough additional meat to make 1 pound altogether. Sauté the onion and parsley in lard or butter until soft; add the ground meat; stir until it loses its pink color. Add thyme, salt and pepper. Blend in the beaten egg. Place stuffing in meat so that there is a 1 inch border all around; roll up and tie with butcher's cord, making it as compact and evenly shaped as possible. Sprinkle meat with salt. Heat the oil in a large skillet; sear the meat on all sides until nicely browned. Place in a roasting pan. To the drippings from the skillet, add the wine and meat glaze or Kitchen Bouquet and boil up, stirring to loosen all bits in the bottom; boil until reduced to half; pour over the meat. Bake in a moderate oven until meat thermometer inserted in center of stuffing registers 140° F. for pink or 160° F. for medium or well done. When done, remove to a platter and make a sauce of the pan drippings. Makes 12 to 16 servings.

# VEAL

## Spanish Roast Veal with Orange Sauce

|   |   |   |   |
|---|---|---|---|
| | Rump of veal, 4-6 pounds | ⅓ | cup orange juice |
| 3 | tablespoons flour | | Grated rind 1 orange |
| 1 | teaspoon salt | ¼ | teaspoon cinnamon |
| 2 | tablespoons olive oil | ½ | cup medium sweet sherry |
| 1 | medium onion, chopped | 1 | cup water, or broth |
| 1 | garlic clove, minced (optional) | | |

Rub meat with mixture of flour and salt. Heat oil in large skillet and sear meat on outside. Remove meat to deep roasting pan. Add onion and garlic to oil; cook until very soft. Add remaining ingredients except water; bring to a boil; lower heat; cook 1 minute. Pour sauce over meat in pan. Roast at 325° F. (moderate) for 2 hours or until meat thermometer registers 170° F. Add water after first hour. Remove meat to platter. Skim off excess fat from pan drippings; add water or broth made with chicken stock concentrate. Bring to a boil; cook; stirring, until reduced. If plain water was used instead of broth, add salt to taste.

## Pot Roast of Veal

Use the same ingredients as above, but have the meat boned and rolled into a compact shape by butcher. Sear in the oil in a

Dutch oven or similar heavy pot; add remaining ingredients; cook, tightly covered, for 2 hours, or until very tender.

# Muscoletti
*(roast veal Italian style)*

| | |
|---|---|
| 3 pounds boned shoulder of veal | ½ teaspoon thyme |
| 1 cup dry white wine | 2 bay leaves |
| 2 tablespoons lemon juice | ½ teaspoon dry mustard |
| Grated peel 1 lemon | Salt |
| 1 onion, sliced | 2 tablespoons olive oil |
| | 1 cup water |

Marinate the meat in the wine, lemon juice, grated peel, onion, herbs and mustard for at least 5 hours. Remove from marinade; pat dry; sprinkle with salt. Roll and tie with butcher's cord into a compact, even shape. Place in a deep roasting pan or casserole; brush top generously with oil. Roast uncovered in a slow to moderate oven (325° F.), for 2½ hours or until meat thermometer registers 170° F. Turn once. Baste with marinade during last hour. Remove meat when done; stir a tablespoon of flour into pan drippings; cook 5 minutes on top of stove. Add any remaining marinade and 1 cup water; boil until reduced to one-half, stirring occasionally. Serve sauce with the meat. Makes 8 servings.

# Lombo de Porco

This is the Portuguese way of roasting a boned loin of pork, the tenderloin section. First shape meat into a neat compact roll and tie with butcher's cord to hold it in shape. Next, make a paste of 4 or 5 garlic cloves mashed with a teaspoon of salt, a teaspoon of paprika and 4 tablespoons butter. Rub this paste all over meat. Place in a roasting pan; add ½ cup water. Roast about 2 hours in a slow to moderate oven (325°); baste occasionally with pan drippings. Let cool 15 to 20 minutes after removing from oven. Cut off cord. Arrange very thin lemon slices over top. Cut meat into very thin slices at table. In summer, or for buffets, this is often served cold. In this case, after meat is cooked, make incisions at

1-inch intervals and insert lemon slices in the incisions; do not slice until completely cold. Makes 6 to 8 servings.

# Drunken Pig

Put either a whole loin of pork or a boned and tied pork shoulder in a deep roasting-pan or casserole. Sprinkle meat with salt; then cover with an entire bottle of very cheap red wine (or 4 cups if it's taken from a gallon jug). A clove of garlic may be inserted near the bone or inside the roll, if you like. Roast slowly, basting occasionally with wine. The red wine does something really wonderful to the pork and makes the meat snowy-white. Allow 30 to 35 minutes to the pound.

# MEATBALLS

# Kibbe

This mixture of bulgur and lamb, which is the national dish of Lebanon and Syria, is far more delicious than it sounds. The crust gets very crunchy-crisp, the inside remaining soft. In Lebanon, a stone mortar and pestle are used to mash the meat slowly and rhythmically to a paste, though those who lack such a utensil can achieve much the same thing if the meat is put through the grinder at least three times, then mashed at home with a wooden pestle or a wooden rolling pin. A blender can also be put to good use.

Bulgur, the cracked wheat that is essential in this dish, can be bought not only in Armenian, Greek and other groceries carrying imported foods, but also in many health food stores, for it is now produced in the United States.

For 2 pounds of lean lamb, you need 1½ cups of *fine* (not coarse) bulgur, 2 or 3 large onions, salt and pepper. Ask the butcher to put meat through grinder three times. At home, put the meat in a bowl and mash it vigorously with a pestle; or put it on a pastry board and roll vigorously with rolling pin.

Place bulgur in a bowl; cover with water. With hands, lift the wheat from the water and press it together to push out excess water; then knead with your fingers into a compact shape.

Chop, grind and mash the onions in blender; add meat; beat until smooth. Add salt (2 teaspoons) and plenty of freshly ground black pepper; work into meat with fingers. Add bulgur; beat and knead mixture until very smooth, adding a tablespoon of ice water to make it like a paste. Moisten palms with water, too, to prevent sticking.

The mixture can be served uncooked, shaped into meatballs, as an appetizer. Or, it may be flattened into patties and grilled over charcoal or under a broiler. But more often it has a stuffing such as the following:

| | |
|---|---|
| ¼  cup pine nuts | ½  teaspoon salt |
| ½  pound lean lamb, ground | ¼  teaspoon pepper |
| 3  tablespoons olive oil | |

Sauté pine nuts and meat in olive oil until lightly browned. Add seasonings; stuff meat in one of two following ways.

**Kibbe bi Ssanieh.** Divide kibbe mixture in half. Place ½ in oiled 9 x 17 x 2-inch baking pan; press out flat. Arrange stuffing over this layer; cover with remaining mixture. Score top into diamond shapes with a sharp knife. Brush melted butter (1 cup) over top. Bake in preheated hot oven (400° F.) until top is crispy brown. Serves 8.

**Kibbe bi Laban.** This variation is made by forming the kibbe into balls the size of an egg. Push a deep pocket into each and fill with the stuffing; close the egg-shaped balls so that the stuffing is inside. Fry in oil or butter or margarine until crisply browned on outside. Serve with Yogurt Sauce (see recipe in Sauces and Seasonings chapter). Makes 8 party servings.

# Kafta Sno-Bar

The word *kafta* means meat ground very fine, sometimes mashed to a paste.

1½ pounds ground lamb
2 medium potatoes
1½ teaspoons salt
½ teaspoon mint
1 egg, beaten

¼ teaspoon freshly ground
or crushed pepper
¼ cup pine nuts
1 tablespoon butter
1 cup water or tomato sauce

When buying lamb, ask butcher to put it through the grinder two or three times. Cook potatoes; mash with fork until smooth. Mash meat until smooth. Work in salt, mint, pepper and beaten egg. (If you have a food grinder, put mixture through the grinder. Otherwise, beat hard with a wooden spoon, then work mixture with fingers until very smooth.) Shape into 12 thin patties. Sauté pine nuts in butter; place a few pine nuts in center of each patty; then enclose the nuts with meat, shaping into a ball. Place balls in roasting pan, in oven preheated to 350° F. (moderate). Add water or tomato sauce, as preferred. Bake 30 minutes or until balls are nicely browned; baste once during this time. Makes 6 servings (2 balls to a serving).

# Kafta bi Ssanieh

As for Kafta Sno-bar, have meat (lamb or beef) put through grinder two or three times; then mash fine with seasonings: salt, mint, ¼ teaspoon each cinnamon and black pepper and 2 tablespoons grated onion. Work in 1 beaten egg, using fingers. Mixture must be very smooth. Make a "steak" with the meat mixture, spreading out evenly in a roasting pan. Cover with 1 cup tomato juice or tomato sauce. Bake in hot preheated oven for 20 to 25 minutes until top is crusty.

# Albondigas

¼ pound chorizo sausage*
1¼ pounds ground beef or
lamb
¾ teaspoon salt
2 tablespoons grated onion

1 egg, beaten
½ cup fine crumbs
2 tablespoons olive oil
1 cup tomato sauce; or
1 cup red wine

*If chorizo is not available, use instead 1½ pounds ground beef or lamb, add a crushed garlic clove and ½ teaspoon paprika to mixture.

Remove skin from chorizo sausage; crumble meat fine with fingers; blend with beef or lamb. Work in salt, onion, egg and crumbs. Shape into 1-inch meatballs. Sauté in oil until nicely browned. Add tomato sauce or wine; simmer balls in sauce or wine for 10 to 12 minutes. Makes 4 or 5 servings.

## Côtes de Veau Haches à la Provençale

| | | |
|---|---|---|
| 1½ | pounds veal, ground* | |
| 1½ | teaspoons salt | |
| | Dash of pepper | |
| | Dash of grated nutmeg | |
| 1 | cup soft white crumbs | |
| ¼ | cup milk | |
| 1 | egg, beaten | |

| | |
|---|---|
| 1 | tablespoon butter |
| 1 | tablespoon olive oil |
| 1 | garlic clove |
| 2 | tablespoons minced onion |
| ½ | cup white wine |
| ½ | cup tomato sauce |
| 1 | tablespoon minced parsley |

To meat add salt, pepper, nutmeg, the crumbs soaked with the milk and the beaten egg. Work with fingers until well blended and smooth. Shape into thick patties or like a chop without the bone. Smooth surface with the blade of a silver knife. Sauté in mixture of butter and oil until browned on each side; remove. To fat of pan, add garlic clove and minced onion; when garlic is soft, crush into fat to release juices; then remove and discard. Add wine to pan, "deglaze" the browned bits; add tomato sauce and parsley. Simmer 5 minutes; replace chops; simmer 10 minutes longer. Makes 6 servings.

## CUTLETS

## Côtes de Veau à la Languedocienne

Sauté loin veal chops (1 for each serving) in chicken fat or in olive oil. When browned on both sides, remove temporarily; add

*Ground meat loaf mixture, frequently on sale in supermarkets, may be used instead of all veal, if desired.

2 to 3 tablespoons chopped onion, ¼ cup diced ham and 1 or 2 minced garlic cloves. Cook until onion is soft; add ½ cup white wine and ½ cup water (or ¼ cup Madeira or sherry and ¾ cup water). Replace chops; cover pan; simmer until fork-tender. Add more liquid if it cooks down too much. When chops are tender, add a dozen pimiento-stuffed green olives to sauce. Season sauce to taste with salt and pepper.

## Côtes de Porc à la Provençale

Sauté 4 loin pork chops in a small amount of olive oil until nicely browned on each side; remove. Add to pan a medium onion, chopped, 1 or 2 garlic cloves, minced or crushed, and 2 tablespoons chopped parsley. Sprinkle with 1 teaspoon salt. Simmer until onion is soft. Add 1 cup tomato sauce, 12 black olives and a teaspoon of capers. Simmer 5 minutes; replace chops; cook until chops are tender. Taste for seasoning; add salt and pepper if needed. Serves 4.

## Scallopini al Marsala

Pound each scallopini with the edge of a plate or with a meat mallet especially for the purpose, working in a mixture—for 8 scallopini—of 2 tablespoons flour, ½ teaspoon salt and ½ teaspoon paprika. Sauté in a mixture of equal parts olive oil and butter until lightly browned on one side only. Turn. Add to the pan ¼ cup Marsala wine and ¼ cup water. Simmer until meat is tender. Spoon the sauce over the meat to serve. Garnish with watercress. Cream sherry may be used in place of Marsala for much the same results. Allow 2 scallopini per person.

## Scallopini Zingara

For 12 scallopini, pound into them a mixture of 3 tablespoons flour, ¾ teaspoon salt and ¾ teaspoon paprika. Sauté in butter and oil until lightly browned on each side. Remove to a shallow casserole as they are cooked. To same pan, add ¼ cup each chopped mushrooms, chopped pimiento or green pepper, a little grated or minced onion, a little shredded carrot and a little chopped ham or bacon. Cook until lightly colored; sprinkle with salt. Spoon mixture over the scallopini. To pan drippings, add ¼ cup sweet sherry or Marsala and a cup of water; boil until reduced and deglazed. Thicken sauce with a teaspoon of cornstarch thinned with water to consistency of cream; add to pan drippings; simmer until smooth and just slightly thickened. Pour over the scallopini. Place thin slices of mozzarella cheese over the top. (This can be prepared ahead.) Shortly before serving, put casserole in preheated oven or under broiler until cheese is melted. Makes 6 servings.

# Saltimbocca

For 8 scallopini, you need 8 very thin slices of ham, preferably prosciutto. Top each scallopini with a slice of ham; pound the two together with a meat mallet or edge of plate, working into the veal side a mixture of 1 teaspoon grated lemon rind, ½ teaspoon sage and ¼ teaspoon salt. Roll up, with ham inside; fasten together with picks. Sauté in butter until browned on all sides. Serve immediately. The name means "pop in the mouth." Makes 4 servings.

Poultry is for the cook what canvas is for the painter. . . .
It is served up boiled, roasted, fried, hot or cold, whole or
in parts, with or without sauce, boned, grilled, stuffed,
always with the same success.

—Brillat-Savarin, *The Physiology of Taste*


Those who eat sparrows are rendered exceedingly
prone to amorous indulgences.

—Athenaeus


The cock did not at first enjoy culinary reputation in
Rome until that tyrant of the kitchen, C. Fannius, the Con-
sul, thought that hens, owing to the enormous consump-
tion of them, would soon become extinct, so he ordered
that Romans should dispense with fattening and eating
this delicious bird. But the law said nothing about cocks,
a silence which saved Roman gastronomy, for the capon
was invented.

—Hackwood, *Good Cheer*

# Birds

**W**hen you cook a crane," Apicius advises in his immortal cookbook, "see to it that the head does not touch the water but is outside it."

Cranes, swans, ostriches, figpeckers, pigeons, turtledoves, ortolans, every sort of field bird and water bird went into the pot or oven in Roman kitchens. Ostrich brains and hummingbird tongues were served up in pies to such ostentatious gluttons as the emperor Heliogabalus. Others devised ways to make a cooked bird look ready to fly off the platter. Cooked peacocks were invariably put back into their feathers and gilded before being brought to the banquet table. In a recipe for flamingo, Apicius explains: "Pluck, wash, and truss the flamingo, put it into a sauce-pan with water, dill, and a little vinegar. Half-way through cooking, add a bouquet of leek and coriander. When it is nearly done add defrutum to give it color. . . ." The sauce to be served over it was seasoned with assafoetida, caraway, Jericho dates and numerous other strange ingredients. The author concludes, "The same recipe may also be used for cooking parrot."

Even today, all sorts of game birds are served in Mediterranean homes, some brought home by hunters, others purchased in markets where they may be seen hanging in all their plumage.

121

Domestic poultry, turkeys, ducks and chickens often are sold live in cages, killed and dressed to order. One day I looked out the window of my apartment near Lisbon to see a flock of turkeys being driven up the street, right in the heart of a busy shopping section, the driver keeping them out of the way of speeding cars with two long bamboo poles.

Turkey in a comparatively short time has become the most-prized holiday bird all over the world, replacing goose for Christmas. Its name is different in every country: in Turkey, it's hindi, in Portugal, peru, in Spain, pavo, in Lebanon, habash, in Greece, galopoulo, in France, dindon, in Italy, tacchino. Innumerable ways of stuffing the bird are observed. In the Near East, it's usually a rice stuffing containing nuts and fruit. The French do it with truffles. The Spanish make the stuffing almost a one-dish meal.

The Portuguese have a wonderful way of preseasoning a live turkey: they get it very drunk on cheap brandy just before killing it. The meat becomes extraordinarily tender, perhaps because the bird is so soused and relaxed he feels no pain.

# CHICKEN

Chicken on the spit is sold everywhere ready-cooked if wanted that way. The American way of raising chickens in batteries ready for the market in six weeks is now almost universal, though in Mediterranean country places, and even in urban areas where homes have sufficient enclosed garden space, a few hens are allowed to roam, pecking for their food—kept primarily to provide fresh eggs for the family.

Spit-broiled or roast chicken is usually seasoned simply with salt and paprika and brushed with oil before cooking, but these regional seasonings are interesting:

# Chicken Piri-Piri

The Portuguese rub the chicken with a mixture of lemon juice, salt, pepper and Piri-Piri sauce, a liquid red pepper seasoning similar to Tabasco, before roasting or sautéeing.

# Chicken Ajillo

The Spanish rub the chicken with a cut clove of garlic, in addition to paprika and salt. The meat may be cut up and sautéed in oil, cut in quarters and broiled over charcoal or roasted whole in a hot oven.

# Kota Riganati

The Greeks season chicken this way. A whole chicken is brushed inside and out with a mixture of ½ cup melted butter, ¼ cup lemon juice, salt, pepper and a teaspoon of oregano. A garlic clove or a small whole onion is placed inside the cavity. As it roasts, the chicken is basted with white wine.

# Chicken à l'Orange

For oven roasting, place half an orange (a bitter orange if you happen to have a wild orange tree in your yard), in the cavity of the chicken, along with a sprig or parsley and a bay leaf. Brush the outside with oil and sprinkle with salt. The orange flavor penetrates the chicken deliciously. Add orange juice to pan drippings for sauce.

# Chicken Spatchcock

This is an Italian specialty, especially recommended for charcoal broiling. The chickens should be tender small broilers. Split each chicken in half; pound with a mallet to flatten; then rub with lemon juice. Place in a large shallow pan; cover with a marinade of olive oil, chopped parsley, grated onion, a generous amount of powdered ginger, salt and pepper. Leave in marinade several hours—it's the ginger flavor that makes this special. Broil until golden, brushing occasionally with the marinade.

# Israeli Stuffed Chicken

Ginger is also the surprise in this recipe. For the stuffing, first brown 2 onions (sliced or chopped) in chicken fat and boil 4 potatoes. Mash cooked onions and cooked potatoes to a purée; season with salt and pepper. Put mixture in breast cavity of 4- or 5-pound roasting chicken; truss. Rub outside of chicken with mixture of ½ teaspoon salt, ¼ teaspoon pepper and ¼ teaspoon powdered ginger. Place in roasting pan; roast in moderate oven until leg moves easily. Add 1 cup water to pan after chicken begins to brown.

# Yogurt-Marinated Chicken

Add a chopped onion and a teaspoon of salt to a pint of yogurt; spoon over whole chicken if meat is to be roasted, or chicken halves or quarters if it is to be broiled. Buttermilk may be used for the marinade instead of yogurt with almost the same results. Marinate several hours. For a 6-pound roasting chicken, a rice stuffing is typical: combine 2 cups *cooked* rice, 1 cup cooked or frozen peas, ½ cup pine nuts or chopped toasted almonds and, if liked, a little chopped ham. Season to taste; stuff chicken with mixture.

# Chicken Cacciatore

At least one recipe for chicken braised in a flavorful tomato sauce is to be found in the cuisine of every Mediterranean country. Usually wine, chicken broth, or both are added so that the sauce is not as strong in tomato as in most American recipes. Seasonings differ from country to country, though the cooking method is pretty much the same. It is always advisable to make chicken broth by cooking the neck, giblets and wing tips in salted water at the same time as the more tender pieces are being sautéed.

Dust cut-up chicken pieces with salted flour (½ teaspoon salt to ½ cup flour plus freshly ground black pepper). Sauté in hot oil until crisply browned on all sides. Place a clove of garlic in the oil at the same time; when it is golden (do not let it burn), crush garlic with tines of a fork to release the juice; then discard. As chicken is browning, make broth with the giblets and neck by cooking in salted water. Remove chicken pieces from skillet as they are cooked—they will brown better if the pan is not crowded. Then, to the same oil, add about a cup of chopped onion, ½ chopped green pepper, a fistful of chopped parsley and 3 or 4 peeled and chopped tomatoes. (When tomatoes are not locally in season, add a 1-pound can of plum tomatoes instead, chopping the tomatoes in small pieces.) Simmer 10 minutes; add a cup of dry wine, either red or white, and ½ cup chicken broth. Replace chicken in sauce. Continue cooking for 30 minutes over very low heat. Some cooks prefer to use 3 tablespoons of tomato paste instead of the fresh or canned tomatoes. Chopped bacon may be cooked with the onion, if liked. A little oregano may be added to the sauce. Others add rosemary, thyme, basil or mint. Make it your own way. Serve with spaghetti.

# Chicken Marengo

Napoleon's chef is said to have invented this dish while the Battle of Marengo was raging, but it is not unlike the preceding Chicken Cacciatore. First dust cut-up chicken pieces with salted flour; make broth with neck, giblets and wing tips; then brown the floured chicken in olive oil (always olive oil, no other). When chicken pieces are browned, remove; add to the oil ½ cup chopped onion, a garlic clove or two (crushed) and ¼ pound sliced fresh mushrooms. Simmer until vegetables are golden; add a tablespoon of tomato paste and 1 cup canned tomatoes, forced through a sieve, or 1 cup tomato juice. Then add ½ cup Marsala wine or medium sweet sherry. Replace chicken in sauce; simmer until very tender and sauce is reduced and thickened, 30 to 40 minutes. Serve with rice, sprinkled with chopped parsley.

(Escoffier says that the dish should be garnished with shrimp or lobster and triangles of bread fried in olive oil, an added touch I do not find necessary.)

# Frango Estufado

Heavy cream added to the sauce makes this Portuguese dish wickedly rich.

| | |
|---|---|
| 1 chicken, cut up | 1 cup mushroom caps |
| 3 tablespoons flour | 2 tomatoes, cut in thick |
| 1½ teaspoons salt | slices |
| ¼ teaspoon pepper | ¼ cup minced fresh |
| 2 tablespoons olive oil | coriander or parsley |
| 3 tablespoons butter | 2 or 3 tablespoons butter |
| 1 large onion, chopped | or margarine |
| 1 garlic clove, minced | ¼ cup white wine |
| 1 green pepper, seeded, | ¾ cup chicken broth |
| cut in squares | ½ cup green or black olives |
| | ½ cup heavy cream |

Dust chicken pieces with flour mixed with salt and pepper. Make broth with neck and giblets cooked in salted water for 30 minutes. Brown chicken pieces in hot oil and butter, removing to shallow casserole as they are cooked. Add onion and garlic to the same oil; cook until soft. Add green pepper and mushrooms; cook about 2 minutes. Spoon vegetables around chicken pieces in casserole. Place tomato slices over top of chicken and sprinkle coriander or parsley over tomato, then sprinkle with salt. Dot tomato with butter. Add wine and chicken broth. Bake uncovered in moderate oven (350° F.) for 1 hour or until chicken is tender. Add olives and cream during last 15 minutes. Serve with rice or mashed potatoes. Makes 4 to 6 rich hearty servings.

# Poulet Tajine

The *tajine* is an earthenware utensil used in North Africa. The bottom part is like a round shallow casserole, the upper part rises into a peak or what looks like a closed chimney top. Its virtue is that it can be used on a very primitive fire. But those of us blessed with stoves whose burners can be controlled may cook this dish in a heavy porcelain skillet with cover, or any top-of-stove casserole.

There are many different recipes called Poulet Tajine, which is like saying "Chicken Casserole." One is quite similar to the Portuguese Frango Estufado except that there is no cream in the sauce and a bit of saffron is added. The most unusual of all the Tajine recipes I've come across, however, is the following.

1 cut-up chicken
¼ cup olive oil
2 large onions, chopped
　Salt, pepper

¼ cup crushed almonds
15 to 18 pitted prunes,
　presoaked
½ cup water
　Pinch of cayenne

Dust chicken pieces with salt; sauté in the olive oil, removing from pan as they are browned. Add the onions; sprinkle with salt and pepper; cook slowly until soft. Add almonds; cook 5 minutes longer. Place chicken and prunes over the onions; add water and cayenne. Cover. Cook very slowly until chicken is tender, 30 to 40 minutes.

# Pollo con Naranjas
(*Spanish chicken in orange sauce*)

1 chicken, cut up
2 tablespoons flour
1 teaspoon salt
4 tablespoons olive oil;
　or 2 tablespoons each
　butter and oil
1 small onion, chopped

½ cup raisins
¼ cup crushed almonds
¼ teaspoon cinnamon
⅛ teaspoon cloves
1 cup orange juice
1 cup chicken broth

Dust chicken pieces with flour and salt. Make broth with neck, giblets and wing tips. Fry chicken pieces in olive oil or mixture of oil and butter; remove as they brown. Cook onion until soft; add remaining ingredients, including strained chicken broth. Replace chicken; continue to cook until chicken is very tender, 30 to 40 minutes longer. Serve with rice. Makes 4 to 6 servings.

# Poulet aux Pêches

At the Hiely-Lucullus Restaurant in Avignon, this dish was made with *pintadeau*, the bird we call guinea hen; but since guinea hens are not often found for sale in American markets, I suggest chicken (which I personally prefer anyway) be used instead.

1 frying chicken, cut up
Salt, freshly ground pepper
Dash of nutmeg
4 tablespoons butter
4 tablespoons cognac
12 to 18 very small white
onions, peeled

¼ cup seedless raisins
1-pound can cling peaches
2 tablespoons peach syrup
1½ cups chicken stock
1 teaspoon cornstarch
2 tablespoons heavy cream

Rub chicken pieces with mixture of salt, pepper and nutmeg. Sauté in butter over high heat, removing pieces as they brown. Then replace all chicken pieces in pan; add cognac; set aflame. When flame has died out, add onions, raisins and syrup drained from canned peaches. Cover; simmer at reduced heat until chicken is tender. Remove chicken pieces to serving dish; add peach halves to pan; brown slightly. Place peach halves and onions around chicken pieces. Skim off excess fat in pan, add 1½ cups strained chicken stock (made with neck, giblets and wing tips, or with chicken stock concentrate and water). Boil over high heat until reduced by half. Thin cornstarch with a little water; then add to broth; cook until slightly thickened and smooth. Add cream; blend well. Spoon a little of the sauce over the chicken pieces; serve the rest in a sauce boat. Makes 4 servings.

# Chicken and Lobster Costa Brava

In Spain, chicken is frequently combined with shrimp or lobster, as in this superb Catalonian casserole.

3 7-ounce rock lobster tails
1 3½-pound chicken, cut up;
or 3 or 4 chicken breasts
4 tablespoons olive oil
¾ teaspoon salt
Dash of pepper
1 or 2 carrots, peeled and
grated

2 leeks or 6 scallions, minced
¾ cup dry sherry
½ cup brandy
1 tablespoon tomato paste
or catsup
½ cup clear chicken broth
½ cup canned beef gravy

Cut away the thin undershell of the lobster tails. Then, with kitchen shears, cut right through the hard shell, so that each lobster tail is in three pieces. Select only the most tender parts of the chicken; use the neck, back, wing tips and giblets for making chicken stock (cook in lightly-salted water, covered, ½ hour). First sauté the chicken in the hot olive oil until crisply browned on all sides; add the lobster; cook until the shell is bright red and the white flesh is translucent. Remove the lobster. Add the minced carrot and leeks or scallions; cook until soft, about 1 minute. Add the sherry; simmer 2 minutes. Add the brandy; set it aflame. Or simmer about 2 minutes until reduced. Add the tomato paste or catsup, the chicken broth and canned beef gravy and simmer over low heat until sauce is well blended and smooth. Replace lobster in the sauce; cover; cook 1 minute or until lobster is heated through. Serve in shallow casserole with hot cooked rice. Serves 4 to 6.

# STUFFINGS FOR BIRDS

Big-breasted turkeys like those Americans take for granted are now being bred throughout Europe, but the price is so much higher that turkey is considered a luxury. In some Mediterranean kitchens, the bird is first stuffed, then stewed, then placed in the oven for browning. This seems to me unwieldy and unnecessary, since today's turkeys are so tender. The Portuguese rub the turkey inside and out with the cut side of a lemon and sprinkle it with salt some hours before roasting. The French sprinkle it with brandy inside and out. But everyone has a special way of stuffing it, and to please a variety of tastes, why not use one stuffing in the breast, another in the neck cavity?

The making of any stuffing is a matter of seasoning "with the fingers." Generally you need about ¾ cup stuffing for each pound weight of turkey, but the larger the turkey, the more stuffing per pound is needed. Dried fruit will swell with cooking, as will rice (even if precooked). Onions, apples and meat shrink with cooking. Keep these points in mind when "mixing your own."

All the following are in quantities sufficient for both cavities of a 10- or 12-pound turkey. If two different stuffings are to be offered, one for each cavity, divide the following measures by half. If you have an excess of stuffing, wrap what's left in foil and bake in the same oven as the turkey.

# Israeli Fruit-Nut Stuffing

1 medium onion, minced
4 to 6 tablespoons oil or
   margarine
1 tablespoon chopped
   parsley
1 teaspoon cinnamon
   Freshly ground black
   pepper
3 cups mixed dried fruit,
   such as currants, raisins,
   chopped dates, prunes
   and apricots
½ cup chopped walnuts

½ cup salted almonds,
   chopped
   Few thin slices of lemon
   peel, chopped
¼ cup chopped candied
   orange peel or preserved
   ginger
1 cup chopped peeled
   apples
2 cups diced stale
   bread crumbs
½ teaspoon salt
1 tablespoon brandy
   (optional)

Sauté onion in oil until soft. Add parsley, cinnamon and pepper. Soak dried fruit in boiling water 5 minutes; drain. Combine all ingredients in a large bowl and mix well. Use to stuff both cavities of a 10- or 12-pound turkey (or divide measures by half to use only for the breast cavity). Makes approximately 8 cups.

# Spanish Pork and Olive Stuffing

2½ cups chopped onion
2 garlic cloves, minced
⅓ cup olive oil
1 tablespoon chopped
   parsley
2 green peppers, seeded
   and chopped
½ pound ground lean pork
1 cup chopped almonds,
   walnuts or pine nuts

2 teaspoons salt
1 cup chopped dried prunes
   or apricots
2 or 3 hard-cooked eggs,
   chopped (optional)
1 cup sliced pimiento-stuffed
   green olives
½ teaspoon marjoram
2 cups bread crumbs

Cook onion and garlic in oil until soft; add parsley and peppers; cook 1 minute; add pork and nuts; cook until lightly browned. Add mixture to bowl with remaining ingredients; mix well. Taste for seasoning; if desired add other herbs such as sage or thyme, or a pinch of ginger. Stuff both cavities of turkey with mixture; or divide by half, use only for breast and put another mixture in neck cavity. Makes about 8 cups.

# Greek Chestnut Stuffing

2 pounds chestnuts in shell
2 large onions, minced
6 tart apples, peeled and chopped
6 tablespoons butter or margarine
Minced turkey liver and giblets
1 teaspoon thyme
2 tablespoons chopped parsley
1 cup raisins or currants
Salt to taste
1 cup diced celery (optional)

Cut slit in each chestnut shell; boil 15 minutes or until slits spread open. While warm, remove shells and skin; chop chestnuts. Sauté onions and apples in butter until soft; add turkey liver and giblets. Combine with remaining ingredients and season to taste. (Bread crumbs are not needed, but when chestnuts are very expensive, as they are in the United States, you may use only 1 pound of chestnuts and add as much diced bread as necessary.)

# Lebanese Rice Stuffing

This stuffing is a mixture of ground meat (usually lamb), pine nuts, pistachio nuts, currants or raisins and other fruit and rice— it's a stuffing like that for stuffed roast lamb (See recipe in Meats chapter). The stuffing is traditionally seasoned with cinnamon, pepper and salt, sometimes with a bit of ginger as well.

Another Near Eastern stuffing consists of cooked bulgur with chopped dried apricots, apples and peeled, chopped cucumber (yes—and it's good with cucumber!). Add to this last mixture some chopped fresh coriander, and you have a very exotic combination.

# DUCK AND GAME

Duck, both wild and domestic, appears on European tables more frequently than ours. As in the United States, the most popular recipe is with Bigarrade Sauce (also known as Duck à l'Orange). Wild duck is even better than domestic duck with such a sauce. Another nice way to prepare wild duck is to fill the breast cavity with chopped apples and melted butter (the wild duck has almost no fat); marinate in red wine; and baste with a mixture of melted butter and orange juice.

## Duck Bigarrade

If you are using Long Island duckling, defrost completely (this may take two days if the duckling is solidly frozen). Then remove as much fat as possible from under the skin. Rub duckling with cut side of lemon; dust with salt. Stick half an orange inside the cavity; or use a fruit-nut stuffing like the one given for turkey. Truss duck; prick skin with fork. Place on rack in roasting pan, breast side down. Bake in a slow oven, 300-325° F., and periodically remove fat from pan with a big kitchen syringe into a narrow bowl, so that fat will rise to top. Halfway through roasting, turn duck so that the breast side is up. Baste with a little fresh orange juice.

When leg moves easily, duck is done. Prepare Bigarrade Sauce (see chapter on Sauces and Seasonings). Remove duck to serving platter; pour off all pan drippings into a narrow bowl; then remove and discard fat, keeping only the brown residue at bottom. Return this residue to the stove with the sauce and simmer until well blended. Serve duck garnished with orange slices, with sauce passed separately.

## Duck Niçoise

| | |
|---|---|
| 1 duckling, 4-5 pounds | 1 small garlic clove |
| ½ lemon | 1 tablespoon chopped |
| Salt, pepper | parsley |

1 teaspoon thyme
1 bay leaf
½ cup white wine
1 cup chicken broth

½ cup pitted green olives
1 small can (3- or 4-ounce)
    button mushrooms

Cut duck into quarters with poultry shears. Rub with cut side of lemon; then sprinkle with salt and pepper. Place skin side down in large skillet or electric skillet; cook over moderate heat with water or fat until fat is drawn from duck. Place garlic in pan; when soft, crush with fork into pan juices; then remove and discard garlic. Remove all fat with a syringe (or tilt pan so fat can be scooped out with ladle). Add parsley, thyme, bay leaf, wine and chicken broth to pan. Simmer over lowered heat until duck is tender when pierced with fork. Add olives and mushrooms with their liquor; cook 5 minutes longer. Remove duck to serving platter. Carefully skim off as much fat from broth as possible; adjust seasonings to taste. The best way to remove the fat from the broth is to place it in a small bowl and put the bowl in the freezer so the fat rises to the top. Serve duck with olives and mushrooms as garnish. Make a thickened sauce with fat-free pan drippings. Makes 3 or 4 servings.

# Pheasant Maltaise

The day before roasting, brush pheasants inside and out with brandy and dust with salt. Wrap in foil; leave in refrigerator 24 hours. Open foil; brush birds with melted butter or olive oil; close foil packets again. Roast in hot oven (450°F.) for 15 minutes; reduce heat to 275°F.; bake 45 minutes longer. Open foil; continue roasting until pheasants are browned and legs move easily. Serve with Sauce Maltaise (see chapter on Sauces and Seasonings). One pheasant serves 2 persons.

# Perdiz Felipe Segundo

Named after Spain's most illustrious king, Philip II, partridges stuffed in this manner are indeed regal fare. (Lacking partridges, you can place the same stuffing inside boned flattened whole chicken breasts, fastened shut with small skewers.)

| | |
|---|---|
| 4 partridges | 1 cup soft bread crumbs |
| Salt | 1 teaspoon paprika |
| ¼ cup chopped ham | ¼ cup olive oil |
| ¼ cup minced pork sausage | 1 cup seedless white grapes |
| 1 garlic clove, crushed | ½ cup orange juice |
| 1 tablespoon minced onion | |

Sprinkle birds with salt inside and out. Combine ham, sausage, garlic, onion, bread crumbs and paprika. Season mixture to taste with salt. Divide stuffing in 4 parts; place in cavities of birds; truss. Brush birds with oil; place in shallow roasting pan, surrounded by grapes. Bake at 350°F., until delicately browned, about 40 minutes. Baste with orange juice once or twice. When birds are done, make sauce with pan drippings. Serves 4.

# Pheasant Portuguese Style

Juniper berries often are used to flavor game, but this Portuguese recipe uses a shortcut—gin, which gets its flavor from juniper berries.

Cut a cleaned, dressed pheasant into quarters; sprinkle with salt and lay in a casserole. Cover it with a layer of sliced onion, a layer of thinly sliced carrot (or shredded carrot) and a layer of minced shallots. Over all pour 2 cups gin. Marinate for 2 days; then turn over the pieces of pheasant so that they lie on top of the vegetables. Just before placing in the oven, cover with a layer of sliced fresh mushrooms and dot generously with butter or margarine. Roast uncovered in a moderately hot oven for about 50 minutes or until nicely browned. Makes 2 to 4 servings, depending on the size of the bird.

I must run round and bawl for what I want;
You'll call for supper when you home return
And I have got no vinegar, nor anise,
Nor marjoram, nor fig-leaves, nor sweet oil,
Nor almonds, nor the lees of new-made wine,
Nor garlic, no, nor leeks nor onions,
No fire, no cumin seed, no salt, no eggs. . . .
Here I stand useless with but knife in hand,
Girt and prepared for action all in vain.

— Cook in a play by Alexis,
as quoted by Athenaeus


The discovery of a new dish confers more happiness on mankind than the discovery of a new star.

— Brillat-Savarin, *Aphorisms*

# Made Dishes

Archestratus, the writer and friend of Pericles, was the inventor of "made dishes," according to Athenaeus. But if Archestratus had not invented the hearty mixtures that today we call "casseroles," someone else would have.

Rice, beans, pastas, bulgur or semolina may serve as the base, with all sorts of savory ingredients added. Many such "made dishes" are economical for the family table; others, because they are composed of chopped or minced ingredients, are perfect for the buffet; and some are so elegant that they deserve the place of honor at an epicurean repast.

The intricate rice dish called polou in Persia has its counterpart in the pilaf of Turkey, the pilau of Greece, and the paella of Spain. In fact, there is such similarity one can only conclude that the latter is of Arab heritage.

Italy's risotto is a more simple dish; like the Greek pilaf, it may be either a side dish or an entrée. Often it is served topped with tomato sauce, as is also true in Greece.

Pastas are distinctly Italian. The Greeks have a few notable pasta dishes—pastichio, a kind of custard, is the most famous—and both ravioli and cannelloni are frequently served on Greek tables. The Spanish occasionally make use of macaroni in casseroles, as do the French. But nowhere are there such ranges of shapes and sizes, or such imaginative sauces used to dress pastas as in Italy.

Roman cooks were making pastas in Apicius' day when the flour paste was called *lagamum*. Utensils for cutting the shapes and for cooking lagamum were found in Pompeiian kitchens. The tale that Marco Polo brought back from China the secret of how to make the tubular pasta the world now knows as spaghetti must be apocryphal; nor can Italian ravioli be a copy of Chinese won-ton, despite their similarities. There is written reference to ravioli in Italian cookbooks before Marco Polo returned from Cathar. Kreplach, the Jewish filled paste triangles, are more likely to have inspired, or to have been inspired by, ravioli.

Cous-cous belongs only to North Africa, though it is occasionally prepared in the Near East, where bulgur is used instead of semolina as its base. Polenta, when prepared Hunter's Style (cacciatore) is not unlike cous-cous.

# PILAF, PAELLA AND OTHER RICE CASSEROLES

In Greece and Turkey, the word pilaf, pilau or pilav is used almost as a synonym for rice. When other ingredients are cooked with the rice, the dish becomes a shrimp pilaf, a lamb pilaf or whatever is the outstanding ingredient.

Rice was known in the Mediterranean in antiquity. Strabo said it was cultivated in Syria in his day. The Arabians are said to have introduced rice first into Sicily and later into southern Spain, but it was not widely used in Mediterranean kitchens until after 1400.

Besides the following meal-in-a-dish mixtures, other more simple rice recipes and basic cooking methods will be found included in the chapter on Cereals and Breads.

## Kuzulu Pilav
(*Turkish lamb pilaf*)

| | |
|---|---|
| 1½  cups Patna long grain rice | 1  pound lamb, cut in small pieces |

4 tablespoons fat (butter, or butter and oil)
½ pound chicken livers
2 shallots or 3 green onions, minced
1 medium yellow onion, minced
3 cups chicken broth
1½ teaspoons salt

1 tablespoon chopped fresh dill, or 1 teaspoon dill weed
⅓ cup thin slivers of orange peel
1 tablespoon chopped parsley
½ teaspoon cinnamon
1 cup presoaked pitted prunes, chopped

First soak rice in salted water, or rinse in several changes of water until water is clear. To prepare the pilaf, you need a very large (14 inches) skillet with cover or a 2½- to 3-quart casserole. Sauté meat in 2 tablespoons of the butter until nicely browned; remove. Add chopped chicken livers to fat; when browned, remove and add to lamb. Add remaining fat; sauté shallots and chopped yellow onion in it until soft. Thoroughly drain rice; add to onions; sauté lightly until every grain is coated with fat. Heat chicken broth (made with stock concentrate) to boiling; add salt, dill and orange peel. When boiling, pour over rice. Replace meat and liver and add remaining ingredients; stir to mix well. Cook over high heat for 5 minutes; reduce heat as low as possible, cover, and cook until all liquid has been absorbed, about 10 minutes more. Remove cover of pan; place a cloth napkin or towel over top; allow to "rest" in a warm place (a warming oven at 250°F. is perfect) for 40 minutes. Remove cloth; serve pilaf in skillet or casserole in which it cooked, with chopped parsley over the top. Makes 6 to 8 servings.

# Morg Polou
(*Persian chicken pilaf*)

The ingredients in this recipe are authentically Persian, though the method of preparation is somewhat simplified. The rice in a true Persian polou is cooked so that a crisp golden crust forms over the bottom, then it is turned out upside down with the crust on top, a technique not easy to master.

1 chicken, cut in small pieces
1½ cups rice

3 cups chicken broth
5 tablespoons butter

1 large onion, minced
¼ cup pine nuts
½ teaspoon thyme
½ teaspoon dill or fennel
2 teaspoons salt
¼ teaspoon cinnamon

¼ teaspoon pepper
½ cup chopped dried apricots
½ cup seedless raisins or
    dried currants
Chopped parsley

Soak rice in salted water for one to two hours; drain thoroughly. Cut chicken into 12 pieces, but use only more tender parts for the casserole. Cut breast into 4 pieces; separate thigh and drumsticks; then cut thighs in half. Cut away tips from wings; use only meatier portions of back. With remaining pieces and trimmings, make broth, saving out only the liver. Sauté chicken and chicken liver in 2 tablespoons butter until nicely browned; remove as cooked. Add onion and pine nuts to pan with 2 more tablespoons butter; cook until onion is soft. Add seasonings and the drained rice; stir until well coated with fat. Strain chicken broth; heat to boiling; pour over rice. Add chicken pieces and fruit; stir to mix well. Bring to a boil over high heat; cook 5 minutes; lower heat; cover; cook 10 minutes longer. Uncover; place cloth towel or napkin over top. Place in warming oven for 40 minutes. Remove cloth; brush remaining tablespoon of butter over top; sprinkle with chopped parsley. Makes 6 to 8 servings.

# Atzem Pilafi me Yarides
(*Greek shrimp pilaf*)

1 large onion, minced
1 or 2 garlic cloves, minced
¼ cup olive oil or butter
1 cup long grain rice
¼ teaspoon cinnamon
1 tablespoon minced fresh
    or frozen dill; or 1 tea-
    spoon dill weed

1 cup chicken broth
1 cup tomato juice
1 teaspoon sugar
¾ teaspoon salt
½ pound already-shelled
    shrimp, minced
1 tablespoon minced parsley
    Grated kefalotyri or
    Parmesan cheese

Sauté onion and garlic in oil or butter until soft. Add rice; stir to coat with oil. Add cinnamon and dill. Heat broth (made with concentrate), tomato juice, sugar and salt to boiling. Add to rice; cook 5 minutes; then add shrimp; stir to mix well; reduce heat as low as possible and cook covered 15 minutes longer, or until all liquid is absorbed and tunnels appear through rice. Sprinkle with parsley; pour a little melted butter over top. Serve cheese on the side, to be spooned over each helping. Makes 4 to 6 servings.

# Paella a la Valenciana

The authentic Paella a la Valenciana, I was told by the leading chef in Valencia, never contains seafood, only chicken and snails. But no one outside Valencia seems to know this. The following can be considered a basic paella recipe subject to infinite variations. Some Spanish cooks say chorizo should never be added to paella, others always add it. An Algerian variation (the dish is as popular there as in Spain) includes both squid and chorizo.

The Spanish way of cooking rice is to add uncooked rice to oil, stir to glaze the rice and then add twice the quantity of water, 2 cups water for 1 cup rice plus 1 teaspoon salt. Rice is always cooked *uncovered* over very low heat, and then covered with a cloth or napkin during the last 5 minutes.

The fun way to prepare paella is on a picnic. All you need is three iron pipes, of exactly the same length, and a big paella pan. Find a nice picnic spot, put the pipes in the ground in a place protected from wind and build a fire of twigs in the center. The paella pan rests on the three pipes. This is your stove. That's the way it's done in southeastern Spain. Of course, it's a bit of a nuisance carrying all the ingredients to the picnic spot; it would be an easier operation in the back yard.

| | |
|---|---|
| 1 small chicken, cut up | 1 pimiento, drained and |
| 1 pound lean pork, diced | chopped |
| ½ to ¾ cup olive oil | ½ teaspoon saffron |
| 1 teaspoon paprika | Salt |
| 2 garlic cloves | 1 quart chicken stock |
| 1 medium onion, minced | 2 cups long grain rice |
| 2 tablespoons minced parsley | |

| | |
|---|---|
| 1 pound large shrimp, shelled; or several lobster tails, cut in pieces | 1 cup frozen tiny peas |
| | 2 tablespoons sherry |
| | Lemon wedges |
| 16 mussels or clams in shells | |

In advance, make chicken broth with neck, giblets, wing tips and bonier parts of chicken cooked in 4 cups water with 2 teaspoons salt. The rest of the chicken should be cut in small pieces. To the hot broth as it simmers, add saffron. Strain; measure and add water to broth if needed to make 1 quart.

Prepare shrimp or lobster; remove shells of shrimp, keeping tail intact; or remove thin upper shell of lobster tails; then cut through hard outer shell to make pieces of about ½ inch each. Pull flesh partially away from shell for easier eating later. Scrub mussels or clams thoroughly, removing mussel beards; soak in several changes of water.

If you are using a paella pan, the entire operation can be carried out in this one pan. Otherwise, use a big skillet and a heavy casserole.

Sauté chicken and pork in oil until nicely browned; sprinkle with salt and paprika. Add a few onion slices to oil to prevent spattering. Add garlic cloves. When garlic is soft, press with tines of fork to crush. Remove chicken and pork. Add remaining onion, parsley and pimiento. Cook until soft. Add rice; stir to glaze with oil. Add strained chicken stock a little at a time, bringing to a boil after each addition.

If using a paella pan, add shrimp or lobster and peas to rice; stir to mix. Replace chicken and pork in rice. Place scrubbed mussels or clams in rice so that they stand up. Continue cooking until all liquid is absorbed, the rice is fluffy and mussels have opened. If rice becomes dry on top, lay a cloth or paper towel over it for 5 minutes. Serve from the paella pan.

If using a casserole, after sautéing ingredients in skillet transfer all ingredients to casserole; place a cloth over the top; put casserole in oven to complete cooking, about 20 minutes longer. Remove cover; brush top with a mixture of 1 tablespoon olive oil and 1 tablespoon sherry. Serve with lemon wedges, the juice sprinkled over the rice at table. Makes 8 servings.

**Paella Variations.** Canned snails, fitted into shells, may be added instead of mussels. Other meat products that may be used instead of pork include cut-up veal, diced ham or sausage (butifarra or Italian sausage are interesting additions), chicken livers, sliced squid, or chorizo. For the vegetable, chick peas (cooked or canned), artichoke hearts or cut-up green beans may be added instead of green peas.

# Rosetxat

This is another unique rice dish of southeastern Spain. I found the recipe in a book picked up in Valencia, containing 100 rice dishes of Spain.

| | |
|---|---|
| ¼ cup olive oil | 1 pound butifarra sausage |
| 1 garlic clove | or sweet Italian sausage |
| 2 medium tomatoes, | 1½ cups long grain rice |
| chopped | ½ to 1 teaspoon salt |
| 1 medium onion, chopped | ¼ teaspoon saffron, dissolved |
| 1 tablespoon minced parsley | in 3 cups beef broth |
| ¼ cup ham, minced | 1-pound can garbanzos |
| 1 teaspoon paprika | (chick peas), drained |

Heat olive oil in large heavy skillet or casserole; add whole garlic and tomato. When garlic is soft, press with tines of fork to crush. Add onions, parsley, ham and paprika. Cook until onion is soft; add sausage; cut into 1-inch lengths; brown lightly. Add rice, salt and boiling-hot saffron-flavored beef broth. When water has again come to the boil, add drained garbanzos. If skillet will not hold all ingredients, transfer to casserole. Finish cooking in moderate oven with a cloth laid over top of casserole until all liquid is absorbed and rice is fluffy. Makes 6 servings.

# Risotto alla Milanaise

Saffron is not generally used in making Italian rice dishes, but Risotto alla Milanaise is an exception.

| | |
|---|---|
| 1 small onion, minced | 2 cups uncooked rice |
| 6 tablespoons butter | 5 cups chicken or beef broth |
| ¼ cup chopped beef marrow, | ¼ teaspoon saffron |
| if available; or two chicken | 1 cup freshly grated |
| livers, chopped | Parmesan cheese |

Gently cook onion in half the butter (3 tablespoons) until soft and golden. Add beef marrow or chicken livers. Heat broth with saffron; keep at the boil. Add rice to the onions; stir to glaze. Add ½ cup boiling broth; bring again to the boil. Add more broth; cook 5 minutes; repeat, each time bringing broth to a boil. When all liquid is absorbed and rice is fluffy, transfer to serving dish. Cover with rest of butter, melted, and with the cheese. Toss to mix well. Serve immediately as an entrée. Makes 6 servings.

# PASTA CASSEROLES

It is claimed that Italy has at least 347 different shapes and sizes of pasta available commercially, to say nothing of those made by ingenious cooks in Italian homes: wolf's eyes, cock's combs, stars, wheels, hats, bows, wide noodles, thin noodles, short and long. For a long time, macaroni was used as the generic name for all pastas, though it has come to mean the tubular-shaped pasta larger than spaghetti.

D'Annunzio was once so enraptured by a dish of *tagliatelle* (wide flat noodles) prepared by a poet friend that he composed a sonnet in its honor. Boccaccio, in the *Decameron*, described a village situated on top of a mountain of Parmesan cheese, whose people lived entirely on macaroni and ravioli. Tomato sauces today are more popular than any other kind, but in the days before the tomato was known in the Mediterranean, garlic and herb sauces were the rule, and there are a number of these, containing not a whiff of tomato, that are noteworthy.

Whatever the shape or size of the pasta, it must be precooked in a large quantity of boiling salted water, at least 6 cups water (1½ quarts) for every pound of pasta. The length of cooking time depends on the size of the pasta and also on how rapidly the water keeps boiling, so it's best to make taste tests after 8 minutes for fine noodles or after 12 minutes for larger pasta. The pasta should be firm enough to be felt with the teeth when bitten (*al dente*), not soft. Drain thoroughly in a colander before adding sauce or using in a casserole.

# Spaghetti Olivetana

2 or 3 garlic cloves, crushed
2 large onions, minced
2 ounces slab bacon; or
   4 bacon strips, diced
2 tablespoons olive oil
4 anchovy fillets, chopped
2 tablespoons capers

½ cup chopped black olives
2 cups homemade tomato
   sauce or spaghetti sauce
½ teaspoon oregano
Salt to taste
Freshly ground pepper

Sauté garlic, onion and diced bacon in olive oil until onion is soft and bacon is lightly browned. Add anchovies, capers and olives; cook 5 minutes longer. Crush anchovies and garlic with back of spoon to blend with other ingredients. Add tomato sauce and seasonings to taste. Cook 5 minutes longer. Add to freshly cooked spaghetti. Makes a little more than 2 cups sauce.

# Fettucini al Ciro

This superb dish was prepared for us on the *Cristoforo Colombo* by the assistant head waiter whose name was Ciro. He did the whole thing with a chafing dish, which is fun for those who like to be a bit dramatic at table.

½ pound egg noodles
   (fettucini), cooked
4 to 6 tablespoons butter
1 cup shredded chicken
   breast
1 cup shredded ham,
   preferably prosciutto

1 cup heavy cream
Freshly ground black
   pepper
Salt to taste
½ cup grated Parmesan or
   Romano cheese

Keep noodles warm over a candle or hot tray while sauce is being prepared. Melt butter in blazer of chafing dish. Add chicken first; sauté 2 or 3 minutes; then add ham. Sprinkle with pepper and just a little salt; then add cream and cheese; allow the sauce to simmer until somewhat reduced and thickened. Add to the noodles; toss well. Makes 4 servings.

# Fettucini with Chicken Livers

| | |
|---|---|
| ½ pound egg noodles, cooked | ½ teaspoon salt<br>Freshly ground pepper |
| 1 pound chicken livers | ¼ cup red wine |
| 6 or 7 tablespoons butter | ¼ cup grated cheese |
| ¼ pound fresh mushrooms, sliced | ¼ cup light cream |
| | 2 eggs, beaten |

Drain cooked noodles thoroughly; keep warm. Sauté livers in 3 tablespoons of the butter until well browned. Push to one side of pan. Add mushrooms; brown lightly. Add salt, pepper, and wine; lower heat; simmer 3 minutes. Place noodles in bowl; add remaining 3 or 4 tablespoons butter, cheese and cream; toss to blend well. Add eggs; toss again. If noodles are still warm, this should be enough to cook the eggs. If not, place over hot water, covered, until eggs are cooked. Arrange fettucini around edge of platter or casserole. Place liver-mushroom mixture in center. Serve immediately or place in casserole, top with buttered crumbs and reheat 4 inches below broiler. Makes 4 servings.

# Lasagna

Lasagna, the extra-wide flat noodles, are best used in casseroles. All sorts of leftovers—meat, chicken, vegetables or scraps of cheese—may be added. Start with a Bolognese Sauce, add to it crumbled sausage left from breakfast, chopped ham or the very end of a roast, chicken giblets or a bit of ground meat. Among leftover vegetables that make good additions are chopped spinach, green beans, carrots or peas.

If you don't have sufficient leftovers, buy either ground meat or sausage or an inexpensive piece of pork or lamb, cut fine. Sauté meat in fat until browned, add onion and garlic, continue with the usual ingredients for Bolognese Sauce.

Cook lasagna in boiling water about 15 minutes or al dente. Drain thoroughly. Arrange in a greased casserole in layers with Bolognese Sauce and meat; add chunks of ricotta or cottage cheese and a generous sprinkling of Parmesan to each sauce layer; save out enough sauce to cover the top. Over the top sprinkle more Parmesan; then add slices of mozzarella. Bake in a moderate oven until the cheese is melted and the sauce is bubbling.

(The same recipe can be followed using any pasta. You need approximately 3 cups sauce for a pound of cooked pasta. Vary the sauce according to taste.)

# Pasta alla Siracusa

Syracuse was the Greek city-state in Sicily that was noted in antiquity for its luxurious dining habits. Today Sicily, after having been occupied through the centuries by first one conqueror and then another, is an extremely poor little island and its people must use great ingenuity in making delicious dishes with lowly ingredients. Almost any long pasta may be used for the following.

| | |
|---|---|
| 2 cups diced eggplant | 1 cup minced lamb or pork |
| 6 tablespoons olive oil | 6-ounce can of tomato paste |
| 2 onions, chopped | 2 cups water |
| 2 garlic cloves, minced | 2 teaspoons beef stock |
| 2 green peppers, seeded and diced | concentrate |
| | Salt, pepper |
| 1 tablespoon chopped basil; or 1 teaspoon dried basil | 1 pound spaghetti, linguine, or fettucini |
| ½ teaspoon oregano | 1 cup grated caciocavallo or provolone cheese |
| ½ cup chopped black or green olives | |

Salt the eggplant; let stand 15 minutes; then drain well. Heat oil in large skillet or pot; add eggplant; cook until well browned and soft, stirring occasionally. Add onion, garlic and green peppers; cook until lightly browned. Add basil, oregano and chopped olives. Add meat (any uncooked trimmings of roast or chops, or any cooked meat may be used); cook until lightly browned. Add tomato paste, water and stock concentrate; simmer 10 to 15 minutes. Adjust seasonings to taste. Cook pasta in boiling salted water; drain well. Toss with ½ cup of the cheese. Arrange on plates. Spoon the eggplant mixture over the pasta. Pass remaining cheese. Serve with escarole salad and a rough red wine. Makes 4 to 6 servings.

# Pastichio
*(Greek meat and macaroni custard)*

| | |
|---|---|
| 1 pound elbow macaroni, cooked | Thyme, parsley, or crumbled bay leaf |
| 6 eggs | 1 cup tomato sauce |
| 2 pounds ground beef or lamb | **Sauce** |
| 1 cup chopped onion | ¼ cup flour |
| ¼ cup olive oil | 4 tablespoons butter |
| ¼ teaspoon cinnamon | 1 quart milk |
| ⅛ teaspoon black pepper | Salt, pepper, nutmeg to taste |
| 2 teaspoons salt | 1 cup grated Parmesan cheese |

Cook macaroni in boiling salted water; drain thoroughly. When macaroni is lukewarm, beat three of the eggs; blend into macaroni. Sauté the meat and onions in olive oil until onion is soft; add cinnamon, pepper, salt and herbs as desired; stir in tomato sauce. Separate remaining 3 eggs. Add the 3 egg whites to the meat mixture when latter is somewhat cooled. For the sauce, melt butter in saucepan; stir in flour. Slowly add milk; stir with whisk until thickened and smooth. Season to taste. When cooled, stir in remaining 3 egg yolks.

Grease a 9x13x2-inch pan. Place half the macaroni mixture over the bottom. Add all of meat mixture. Spread about ⅓ of the sauce over the meat; add half the cheese. Cover with remaining macaroni and remaining cheese. This part can be done ahead. One hour before serving, spread remaining sauce over the top and bake in a preheated moderate oven (350°F.) for 1 hour. Serve immediately. Top will be golden yet soft. Makes 8 to 10 servings.

# Canneloni all'Etrusca

Another close relationship must be noted between what the French call Crêpes à la Florentine, what in Italy is called Canneloni all'Etrusca, and what, at the Corfu Restaurant in Athens, is called Kanelonia Toskana. Florence is the provincial capital of Tuscany. The latter owes its name to the Etruscans, who came to Italy from Asia Minor. The resemblance between these various dishes is not at all coincidental.

## Pancakes

| | |
|---|---|
| 1 cup sifted all-purpose flour | 1 cup milk |
| ½ teaspoon salt | 1 teaspoon oil or melted |
| 2 eggs, beaten | butter |

Sift together flour and salt into mixing bowl. Form a well in center; add mixture of beaten eggs, milk, and oil or butter. Beat with fork so that flour mixture is gradually added to egg mixture, until smooth and light, the consistency of cream, with no lumps. Refrigerate 1 to 2 hours.

## Filling and sauce

| | |
|---|---|
| 2 chicken breasts | 2 tablespoons flour |
| 5 tablespoons butter | 1 cup light cream |
| 2 or 3 chicken livers; or ¼ pound fresh mushrooms | 1 cup milk |
| | 1 egg yolk |
| 4 small slices prosciutto, minced | ½ cup grated Parmesan cheese |

Sauté chicken breasts in 2 tablespoons of the butter until nicely browned. Remove; cut off chicken meat; dice fine. Sauté livers or the mushrooms, sliced, in same butter until browned; remove; chop. Combine chicken livers (or mushrooms) and ham. Prepare the sauce: melt 2 tablespoons butter; stir in the flour; then slowly add cream and milk. Season with salt. Beat egg yolk; slowly add the hot sauce. To chicken mixture, add ⅓ cup sauce.

Make 12 large thin pancakes with the chilled batter, using a 7-inch crepe pan, if possible—next best is a small skillet. Moisten the pan with a small dab of butter; spoon 2 tablespoons batter onto pan and tilt so that batter spreads into a 7-inch circle. When batter is lightly browned, turn; as soon as firm on the other side, remove. Repeat until all batter is used.

Spoon about 1½ tablespoons of mixture into each pancake. Trim edges of pancakes so that they will roll up evenly; place in buttered shallow casserole with overlapped side down. Cover rolls with remaining sauce blended with ⅓ cup cheese. Sprinkle remaining cheese over top. Bake in a moderately hot oven (375°F.) until top is golden brown and sauce bubbly. Makes 12 canneloni or 4 servings.

# Kanelonia Toskana

For the filling, instead of a chicken mixture, use ½ pound or 2 cups ground veal and season with 2 tablespoons grated onion, ½ teaspoon salt and a dash of nutmeg. Blend with a beaten egg and a tablespoon of fine crumbs. Prepare 1 cup Bechamel Sauce (see Sauces and Seasonings chapter). Add ½ cup of the sauce and ¼ cup shredded Gruyere or Swiss cheese to the veal. Make thin pancakes as for Canneloni all'Etrusca. Place a spoonful of filling in each pancake; roll up; place close together in a long shallow baking dish. Combine remaining ½ cup Bechamel Sauce with another ⅓ cup cheese and pour over rolls. Sprinkle more Gruyere or grated Parmesan over the top. Bake in moderate oven 20 to 25 minutes or until top is golden and sauce bubbly.

# Crêpes à la Florentine

Make batter for thin pancakes as for Canneloni; refrigerate. For the filling, sauté 1 tablespoon minced shallots in 2 tablespoons butter. Add 1½ cups spinach that has been cooked just until limp, then chopped; or, use frozen chopped spinach, defrosted but not cooked. Be sure to press out all liquid from spinach. Season with salt and nutmeg. Prepare 1 cup Bechamel Sauce; blend ½ cup of the sauce with ¼ cup shredded Gruyere cheese;

add to spinach. Put 1½ tablespoons mixture in each pancake; roll up; place in buttered baking dish; cover with remaining ½ cup sauce blended with ¼ cup additional cheese. Bake as for Canneloni all'Etrusca.

# Cheese Blintzes

Make batter for thin pancakes; refrigerate. For the filling, use 1 cup creamed cottage cheese, ½ cup sour cream, ½ cup minced shallots or green onions, 1 egg, beaten, and salt and pepper to taste. Make pancakes as in preceding recipes, place 1½ to 2 tablespoons in each; roll up. Fry with overlapped sides down until golden. Or, place in baking dish side by side and brush melted butter over the top; then place in a hot oven until tops are browned lightly. Serve topped with sour cream and jelly.

(Blintzes may also be filled with a meat mixture, such as ground beef and onions, and served topped with yogurt blended with grated onion and mint. This makes them very much like the betzel of Algeria. See chapter on Appetizers.)

# Manicotta alla Napoletana

Prepare thin pancakes as in preceding recipes, or use largest size tubular pasta. For the filling, beat 1½ pounds ricotta cheese with 1 egg, a tablespoon of chopped parsley, ¼ cup grated Romano cheese and a little dried basil or chopped fresh basil. Place cheese-filled rolls in a shallow baking dish; cover with well-seasoned tomato sauce. Sprinkle ½ cup grated cheese over the sauce. Bake in a moderately hot oven until sauce is bubbling. Both manicotti and cheese blintzes may be prepared in advance, frozen, and reheated when needed—the former heated in tomato sauce in the oven, the latter by browning in butter in a skillet.

# Cous-Cous à la Viande

Cous-cous, the native dish of North Africa, is a formidable creation. It begins with semolina, similar to what is called cream of wheat in United States markets. In North Africa, every household has the utensils necessary to steam the semolina so that the grains do not touch the water. Yet I found packages of precooked, ready-to-use semolina for cous-cous in markets in Marseilles, and very likely a similar product can be found in those groceries in American cities that import food delicacies. (Otherwise, use cream of wheat.)

When I was staying at the Hotel Dar Zarouk in the resort of Sidi Bou Said near Tunis, the hotel's manager, M. Paul Albrecht, permitted me to watch the chef prepare the cous-cous, which I had ordered in advance. He explained that any kind of meat, fish or chicken may be used for the dish, or it can even be made with only vegetables.

First the semolina is moistened with a little water to swell the grains. Then broth is placed in a lower vessel and brought to boil. The moistened semolina is placed in a second upper vessel through which the steam of the broth rises. After 40 minutes of steaming, the semolina must be stirred with a fork to get rid of any lumps, moistened with more water and a little oil and seasoned with salt and pepper. Sometimes raisins are added as well. Back it goes to steam another 15 minutes.

Meantime, the meat (or other protein ingredient) is in preparation. The day I watched, a solid piece of boneless lamb was used. The meat was placed in the bottom of a heavy pot and covered with a paste of minced onion, tomato paste, crushed hot red pepper, crushed garlic, olive oil and paprika. Two cups of water, plus salt, were added, and the meat was simmered gently, tightly covered, for several hours. As the meat became tender, various vegetables were added according to the length of time required to cook them. Chick peas (presoaked) were added first, then onions, carrots and tomatoes, in this order. The vegetables that required only brief cooking were added last.

As important as the semolina and the meat-vegetable accompaniment is the sauce called *harissa*, which is sold already prepared in Tunis and Algiers. This is a mixture of red-hot pepper (like cayenne), coriander, cumin, garlic and olive oil.

| | |
|---|---|
| 1 pound semolina, ready to use | 1 small chicken, cut up |
| 3 pounds boned lamb or mutton; or 1½ pounds any desired meat | 3 quarts water |
| | 3 tablespoons olive oil |
| | Salt, pepper to taste |
| | ½ pound chick peas, soaked |

3 medium onions, peeled
4 tomatoes, peeled, seeded
  and chopped
4 small zucchini, sliced; or
  1 medium eggplant, cubed;
  or cubed yellow squash
2 stalks celery, diced
  Wedges of green cabbage

1 teaspoon paprika
  Black pepper
2 teaspoons mixed cinna-
  mon, cumin, mustard and
  ginger
1 tablespoon chopped fresh
  coriander or parsley
¼ teaspoon saffron
¼ cup raisins (optional)
  Harissa Sauce

Use a Dutch oven or other large heavy pot to cook the meat and vegetables. Place meat in pot with water, salt, and oil; simmer covered for 1 hour. Add chicken after first hour, if to be used; also add the chick peas; cook another hour. Add onions, tomatoes and carrots; cook ½ hour longer. During final half hour, add remaining vegetables and all remaining seasonings—three hours of cooking altogether.

Separately steam the ready-to-use semolina in a colander above a large kettle containing boiling water, covering with foil; or follow package directions. When semolina is cooked, stir in a little melted butter, a sprinkling of salt (if needed) and a pinch of cayenne. If raisins are to be added, first plump by soaking in hot water; then stir into semolina.

**Harissa Sauce.** Unless this can be purchased ready-to-use, make your own by crushing in a mortar 2 or 3 garlic cloves, ¼ teaspoon cayenne pepper, cumin, crushed coriander seeds, salt and pepper to taste. Dissolve in ½ cup olive oil.

Assemble the cous-cous on a large platter. Mound the steamed semolina in the center. Arrange meat and vegetables over and around it. Pass the Harissa Sauce in a sauceboat. Makes 6 to 8 servings.

# Bulgur bi Dfeen

What semolina is to North Africa, bulgur is to Asia Minor. In fact, cous-cous is sometimes made with bulgur in the Near East.

½  pound boned stewing
lamb, cut in small pieces
(use bits trimmed from
lamb for shish kebab)
3  tablespoons butter
3  onions, cut in sticks

1  teaspoon salt
1  large can chick peas
2½  cups water
1  cup bulgur
Cinnamon

Sauté meat in butter until browned. Add onions; cook until yellow. Add salt, chick peas with their liquid, and water. Cook 40 minutes. Rinse bulgur with water; squeeze out water with your hands. Add to meat; cook mixture 20 minutes longer or until liquid has evaporated. When serving, sprinkle cinnamon over top. Serve hot with yogurt or Tahina Sauce (see recipe in Appetizers chapter). Makes 4 servings.

# BEANS

# Cassoulet à la Toulousaine

This extravagant bean casserole of Languedoc has been the subject of many a poem and many a gastronomic quarrel. So many French gourmets have made it their specialty that recipes for it could fill a book. It is rich, garlicky and heavy. Nothing else is needed with it for the meal but a green salad and a light fruit dessert to follow. But its preparation will seem less formidable if you realize that it is basically a peasant dish and that you may improvise as you like.

Shop for the ingredients two days in advance. For the meat, you will need the following:

1  duckling
6  ounces garlic-flavored
sausage
½  pound smoked pork
sausage links

1  pound pork, cut in small
cubes
1  pound boneless lamb, cut
in small cubes
¼  pound salt pork, diced

In addition, buy 1 pound dried white haricot or pea beans. The remaining ingredients you will probably have on hand: a can of tomato paste, chicken bouillon cubes, the usual French soup herbs, onions and garlic—plenty of garlic.

The day before, roast the duckling (cut in half for easier handling) until nicely browned. Pour pan drippings into a narrow bowl so that the fat, rising to the top, will be easy to remove; chill. Cut up duck into small portions. Soak the beans.

Early the third day, the day the dish is to be served, start cooking the beans. Put them in a pot with several chopped garlic cloves, 2 onions stuck with whole cloves, a carrot or two, a bouquet garni of thyme, bay leaf and parsley, and the diced salt pork. Cover with 2 quarts water; add 6 chicken bouillon cubes. Simmer 1 hour after water comes to a boil. Drain, saving the broth.

Separate the chilled duck fat from the brown essence on the bottom. Put 2 tablespoons duck fat in the bottom of a large deep casserole, preferably of earthenware. Over this place the cubed pork and lamb and the diced sausage. (Since there is so much garlic in the dish, you may prefer to use only simple pork sausage links, precooked to draw out excess fat.) Over the meat lay a cup of chopped onion, 4 or 5 minced garlic cloves and a crumbled bay leaf. Next add the drained, partially cooked beans; insert into the beans the pieces of duck. Combine reserved bean broth with a can of tomato paste, the brown essence or glaze from the duck fat and salt and pepper to taste. The liquid should cover the beans; if it does not, add water. Some cooks also add a tablespoon of brandy. Melt 6 tablespoons of duck fat; pour over the top. (In France the fat from preserved goose would be used.) Cover the casserole; bake in a slow oven (300°F.) for 3 hours. Uncover; spread over the top 1 cup fine crumbs mixed with 2 tablespoons parsley. Continue baking until crumbs are browned. This can be kept warm in the oven for another hour with temperature reduced to 250° F. Serve from the casserole, giving each guest a little of each kind of meat. Makes 8 to 10 very hearty servings.

# Cholent

In Orthodox Jewish homes, no cooking is permitted on the Sabbath, so long-cooking casseroles are often begun the preceding Friday night, to bake all night long, or for 24 hours, in a very slow oven. In this respect, cholent can be compared to New England baked beans, which once served the same function for pious Yankee families who did no cooking on Sundays, their holy day.

| | |
|---|---|
| 2 cups dried faba or lima beans | 2 teaspoons salt |
| 3 pounds brisket of beef or mutton | ¼ teaspoon black pepper |
| | ¼ teaspoon powdered ginger |
| 3 tablespoons chicken fat | 1 cup pearl barley or millet |
| 3 onions, chopped | 2 teaspoons paprika |
| 2 garlic cloves, minced | Boiling water to cover |

Soak dried beans overnight or for 12 hours; drain. In an earthenware pot or deep heavy casserole, sear the meat in the chicken fat; then add onions and garlic and cook in the fat until lightly browned. Sprinkle with salt, pepper and ginger. Add drained beans and the barley or millet and sprinkle with paprika. Add boiling water to 1 inch above top of beans. Cover tightly; seal with flour paste around the cover if to be baked for 24 hours and keep oven as low as possible (250° F.); or bake for 12 hours at 300° F. Makes 8 to 10 servings.

# MEAT-VEGETABLE CASSEROLES

## Moussaka

This famous lamb and eggplant casserole is a specialty in both Greece and Turkey. It consists of three parts: the eggplant, fried first; the meat mixture; and the sauce, which serves as a soft golden custardy topping.

| | |
|---|---|
| 2 medium eggplants, about 1 pound each | 2 or 3 garlic cloves, minced |
| | Salt, pepper |
| ½ to ¾ cup olive oil | ½ teaspoon thyme |
| 1½ pounds lean ground lamb or beef | ½ teaspoon oregano |
| | 2 tablespoons chopped parsley |
| 4 medium onions, sliced | |

½ cup wine (red or white)
½ cup tomato sauce
    Fine dry crumbs, 6 table-
    spoons altogether

2 eggs, separated
3 whole eggs
3 cups Bechamel Sauce
    Dash of nutmeg
½ cup grated Parmesan
    cheese

Cut eggplant into ¼-inch slices; do not peel. Sprinkle with salt; let stand 15 minutes; then rinse or drain and pat dry. Pour enough oil into skillet to barely cover the bottom; then fry eggplant slices a few at a time until lightly browned on both sides. You will need to add more oil to skillet periodically. When all eggplant is fried, start the meat sauce.

Add more oil to pan; then add the meat, onions and garlic. Cook until onion is soft. Sprinkle meat with 1 teaspoon salt. Add herbs, wine, tomato sauce, pepper and 2 tablespoons fine crumbs. Let mixture cool in pan; then stir in 2 unbeaten egg whites, beating quickly to blend all through the meat mixture.

Grease a 13x9x2-inch baking pan. Sprinkle crumbs over the bottom in a fine layer. Place a layer of eggplant over the crumbs; sprinkle eggplant with a little salt; then add a layer of meat mixture and then more eggplant. Sprinkle ¼ cup cheese over the eggplant. Beat 2 egg yolks with the remaining 2 eggs. Prepare Bechamel Sauce (recipe in Sauces and Seasonings chapter). When sauce is smooth, beat some of the hot sauce into the beaten eggs; then combine with remaining sauce; season with nutmeg. Pour this sauce over the top of the eggplant-meat layers; the sauce must cover completely. Sprinkle remaining cheese over the top. Bake in a moderate oven until the top is golden, 45 minutes to 1 hour. Makes 8 to 10 servings.

# Eggplant Dolma

Meat may or may not be used in this stuffing. The dish is beautiful either way.

1 large eggplant, 1½ to
    2 pounds
    Olive oil
½ pound ground beef or lamb

½ cup chopped onions
½ cup chopped green pepper
    or pimiento

2 large tomatoes, peeled and chopped

1 cup chopped parsley or fresh coriander

½ teaspoon crushed cardamom, or mixture of cinnamon and nutmeg

Salt, pepper

3 tablespoons seedless raisins or currants

1 egg, beaten

1 cup cooked rice

½ cup fine crumbs

Cut a slice lengthwise down one side of eggplant; trim off blossom end, but without cutting into body of vegetable. Scoop out inside of eggplant, leaving a thick shell. Brush eggplant inside and out with olive oil; sprinkle with salt. Chop eggplant pulp, discarding seedier portions. Pour about ¼ cup olive oil in skillet; add meat, onion, green pepper and eggplant pulp. Sauté until meat has lost its pink color and eggplant pulp is well coated with oil. Add one of the two chopped tomatoes and the herbs, spices, seasonings, fruit and beaten egg. Simmer 5 minutes. Mix with rice; pile into eggplant shell. Sprinkle fine crumbs over the top and dribble oil over the crumbs. Place remaining tomato in bottom of shallow baking dish, along with another ¼ cup olive oil. Sprinkle salt and minced parsley over chopped tomatoes in pan. Place stuffed eggplant over tomato. Cover pan with foil. Bake in moderate oven (350° F.) for 40 minutes; remove foil; continue baking until top is nicely browned, at least 20 minutes longer. Serve with cold yogurt or hot Yogurt Sauce (see recipe in chapter on Sauces and Seasonings). Makes 4 to 6 servings.

For meatless stuffing, instead of meat, add 2 cups drained canned chick peas, or 1½ cups chick peas and ¼ cup chopped nuts to stuffing. Soft bread crumbs (1 cup) may be used instead of cooked rice, if preferred.

# Israeli Stuffed Peppers

6 large green peppers

1 medium onion, chopped

2 tablespoons pine nuts

2 garlic cloves, minced

4 tablespoons olive oil (altogether)

1 pound ground veal

⅓ cup uncooked rice

¼ cup seedless raisins

2 tablespoons honey

Salt, pepper, pinch of ginger

¼ teaspoon thyme, or
dried mint

1 ⅓ cups tomato juice
Fine crumbs for topping

Cut slice from top of each pepper. If necessary to make stand upright, cut a *very* thin slice from bottom of those peppers that tend to wobble. Remove all seeds and white membrane. Place peppers in boiling water for 2 to 3 minutes; then drain thoroughly. The meat should be put through the food grinder twice: it should be quite soft. Sauté onion, pine nuts and garlic in 2 tablespoons of the oil; add meat and cook, stirring, for 5 minutes. Add rice, raisins, honey and seasonings to taste. Moisten with ⅔ cup tomato juice. Fill peppers loosely with mixture (rice will swell). Sprinkle crumbs over top and dribble with oil. Brush oil over outside of peppers and arrange peppers in casserole, fitting the peppers so that all stand upright. Pour remaining tomato juice and 1 tablespoon oil in bottom of casserole around the peppers. Bake in moderately hot oven (375° F.) for 1 hour. Makes 6 servings. (This was served in a cafeteria in Jerusalem with Tahina Sauce on the side.)

# Calabacines Rellenos
(*Spanish stuffed zucchini*)

4 zucchini, each 6 to 8
inches long
1 pound ground beef
¼ cup fine dry crumbs
1 or 2 garlic cloves,
crushed
3 tablespoons chopped
parsley
1 teaspoon salt

½ cup olive oil
3 slices very stale bread
1 cup water
1 teaspoon paprika
5 or 6 toasted almonds,
crushed
1 hard-cooked egg
2 tablespoons tomato catsup
or purée

Scrape squash; cut a lengthwise slice from top of each; then scoop out centers. Blend zucchini pulp with meat, crumbs, garlic, 1 tablespoon of the parsley and salt. Stuff as much of the mixture as possible into the zucchini "boats." Make meatballs of remaining meat mixture. In a skillet, brown both the meatballs and the outside of zucchini in olive oil, quickly, without cooking through. Transfer to top-of-stove casserole or large saucepan. In same skillet, fry stale bread in olive oil until crisp on both sides; remove from oil; place in bowl containing 1 cup water. Pour off all but 2 tablespoons olive oil from skillet; add paprika, almonds, egg yolk forced through a sieve and the catsup; then add the bread with the water in which it soaked. Simmer this mixture 5 minutes to form a sauce (bread will dissolve and thicken sauce); pour sauce over the squash and meatballs. Cover pan. Simmer over low heat or bake in moderate oven for 20 to 25 minutes longer. Just before serving, sprinkle with remaining minced parsley and minced egg white. Serves 4.

# Dolmades, or Dolmadakia

Stuffed vine leaves are more often served as appetizers, or part of the mezes, than as entrées, but they are included here because of their relationship to other stuffed vegetables. Delicious as they are to eat, they are not attractive in appearance and can only be made so with artful garnishes, such as radishes, black olives, lemon slices and assorted pickles.

| | |
|---|---|
| 1 12-ounce jar vine (grape) leaves | 1 teaspoon salt |
| | ¼ teaspoon thyme |
| 1 medium onion, chopped | 2 tablespoons pine nuts |
| 1 pound lean lamb or beef, ground | ½ cup uncooked rice |
| | ½ cup boiling water |
| 2 garlic cloves, crushed | ½ cup olive oil |
| 3 tablespoons olive oil | ½ cup tomato juice |
| ½ cup chopped parsley | Lemon wedges |

Processed vine leaves can be purchased in Greek-American groceries; or if you have a grapevine in your yard, simply pick the right number of large, well-shaped leaves and dip them in boiling salted water to soften for 2 minutes; then drain well.

For the filling, cook onion, meat and garlic in oil until onion is soft and meat has lost its pink color. Add parsley, salt, thyme, pine nuts and the uncooked rice. Arrange the vine leaves on a board, using two overlapping leaves for each dolmade. Put a teaspoonful of filling in each leaf; fold over the ends; roll up like a cigar. Place rolls in layers, tight together, in an iron skillet or heavy kettle. Add water, oil and tomato juice. Place a plate over the rolls to keep them from floating; simmer uncovered about 1 hour. Cool slightly; then remove with slotted spoon. Serve cold (not chilled). Sprinkle with lemon when serving. Makes about 30.

Every day Iblis brought some new and rare dish to the impressionable young king. Most wondrous of all to Zohak was the egg. "What," he asked, "can be superior to this?"

— From the *Shah Nameh*,
legendary epic of Persia

Heraclides the Syracusan in his book on Cookery says that the best of all eggs are peacock's eggs and that the next best are those of the foxgoose, and the third best are those of common poultry.

— Athenaeus, *The Deipnosophists*

Soon we came to the [Cyclops] cave but we found him not within; he was shepherding his fat flocks in the pasture. So we went into the cave and gazed on all that was therein. The baskets were well-laden with cheeses . . . all the vessels swam with whey, the milk-pails and the bowls, the well-wrought vessels whereinto he milked.

— Homer, *The Odyssey*

# Eggs and Cheese

One of the supreme tests of a restaurant for me is whether its kitchens can produce a light, tender omelet. Making an omelet is such a simple thing to do, yet so few cooks know how. When I arrived in Tunis, exhausted after a jet trip from Beirut, and asked at my hotel in Sidi Bou Said for a simple omelet, I knew it was a good omen that the omelet brought to me a very short time later was tender and light as a cloud.

The two nationalities that seem to have mastered egg cookery most successfully are the French and the Spanish. French egg cookery is noteworthy for its delicacy. The Spanish are noted for ingenious and piquant combinations and for the ability to make a substantial entrée out of eggs combined with other lowly ingredients.

When it comes to cheese, the French again rise above all others. This I realized more than ever before when I reached Provence and in French restaurants was offered a choice of the fabulous French soft cheeses for dessert. Italy comes close behind; in fact, cheese is used more in cookery in Italy than in France, where cheese is more often eaten by and for itself. Greece, too, has a number of noteworthy cheeses, of which feta is almost the only one known elsewhere. Surprisingly enough, in other Mediterranean countries there are comparatively few cheeses and what few they have are little used in cookery.

Throughout the Near East, a soft cheese called *labanee*, made from yogurt and similar to ricotta cheese, is added to many things. It is used with eggplant and other vegetable dishes, used as a filling for tarts, put in salads, and it always is served for breakfast, instead of butter, with bread. Parmesan cheese is found everywhere, most of it exported from Italy, not locally produced. Spain has its *manchego*, a sheep cheese which can be buttery and semifirm when young, or very firm like Swiss when aged. Portugal has a number of sheep and goat cheeses, which can be very good but which vary so much in quality that one can never be sure what to expect. The most distinctive is *serra de estrela*, a runny-soft pungent dessert cheese, and its longer-cured counterpart, *serra currada*, which is firm and heavily crusted with paprika.

The custom of serving a selection of cheeses after the entrée, in addition to or in place of dessert, is observed in restaurants in all the countries on the northern Mediterranean shore. One of the most enthusiastic observations I found in my notebook after returning from my 'round-the-Mediterranean trip was this, after dining at a restaurant in Arles: "The cheese tray was the best part of the meal. The selection included Brie, Cantal, Roquefort, a wheel of Tome de Savoie and four different goat cheeses, of which I tried two. The Banon was divine! It was a small cheese wrapped in vine leaves, smooth, delicious, as creamy as custard."

Roquefort is a sheep cheese whose blue veining is caused by a mold or culture absorbed from the walls of the high mountain caverns where the cheese is stored for curing. The antiquity of the cheese can only be guessed at. The town of Roquefort lies not far from the Lescaux caverns in the province of Languedoc where the most beautiful of all prehistoric cave paintings have been found, and as mouflons, the ancestors of domesticated rams, are among the animals depicted in the paintings, it's likely that cheese from the milk of mountain ewes was being made and stored in the Roquefort caverns many centuries before Rome even existed.

Gorgonzola, the Italian blue-veined cheese, also gets its mold from the caves where it is cured, but the mold is a different culture from the one in the Roquefort caverns; it is a brownish-red in color when the cheese is young, turning green-brown, then green as the cheese ages. Roquefort is always made from the milk of sheep; Gorgonzola may be a blend of sheep's and cow's milk, or be made of cow's milk alone.

Curing cheese in caves has been the practice since earliest times because of the natural insulation afforded by cave walls, where the cheese may lie protected from extremes of heat and cold, winter and summer. The mystery of culturing has always been baffling. Yogurt is thickened by a culture absorbed into milk from the air; yeast, too, is a culture, and in primitive times it was made by allowing a thin gruel of crushed grain and water to ferment. Beer is made with still another culture obtained from fermentation, which is why beer dregs were used to make the original compressed yeast cakes.

When the curds of milk are drained without further curing, what results is a fresh cheese that is very perishable. These were the first cheeses. Curds that are pressed into shape and cured absorb a culture that acts as a preservative. Every kind of milk has been used to make cheese: that of water buffalo (the original mozzarella is an example), sheep, goats, cows and even camels. It's the combination of the kind of milk and the kind of culture absorbed from the atmosphere that determines the special flavor of the cheese. Its consistency, whether soft, firm, or hard, depends on how much liquid has been extracted from the curds, and on how long the cheese has aged.

The two cheeses most used in cookery in Mediterranean kitchens are Parmesan and Gruyere, or local cheeses similar to these two. In the United States, domestic Swiss may be used in recipes calling for Gruyere, though the imported natural Gruyere (different from the foil-wrapped packets of pasteurized process cheese marketed under the same name) is even better.

The Italians use many of their cheeses in cookery: provolone, mozzarella, ricotta, caciocavalla, and, of course, Parmesan and Romano. Ricotta is not always a soft cheese; in fact, it is sometimes hard enough to grate. When cured and aged it is called ricotta salada (meaning "salted"). There are dozens of soft dessert cheeses in Italy, many of which are unknown outside the country. Bel Paese and Taleggio are world-renowned. Incanestrato is a delightful sheep cheese (though sometimes made with a mixture of sheep, goat and cow's milk) bearing the imprint of the wicker baskets in which the cheese is pressed to be cured. Sometimes it is flavored with black pepper; or the curd may be blended with olive oil to give it still different flavor. Fontina, a semi-firm Italian cheese, is much used, notably for making fonduta, which is something like a Swiss fondue.

Caciocavalla, which translated means "horse cheese," and is said to have been made originally with mare's milk, is found not only in Italy but in Greece, Turkey and most of the Balkan countries. It's a firm cheese with a flavor a little like that of provolone.

# Oeufs sur le Plat

This simple French dish is wonderful for breakfast, lunch or supper. It requires ramekins (individual shallow casseroles), which come in two sizes, the small ones 5 inches, the large ones 6½ inches in diameter. The small ones hold one egg, the large ones two. Preheat the oven to hot (400° F.). Place a teaspoonful of butter in each ramekin; heat in oven until butter melts; then remove (be sure to use pot holders) and tilt each ramekin so the butter covers the bottom. Into each break one egg (for the small ramekins) or two eggs (for the large size). Sprinkle eggs with salt from shaker. Put dishes back in the oven and bake until the eggs are set but still soft. It's extraordinary how different these taste from poached or fried eggs, even though the ingredients are exactly the same.

# Oeufs sur le Plat au Fromage

Place dabs of butter in ramekins; then place a thin slice of ham in each; top with a thin slice of Swiss cheese; dot cheese with more butter. Place in oven until butter is melted; remove ramekins; break eggs into each; sprinkle eggs lightly with salt. You may, if you like, add 2 to 3 tablespoons cream to each, but this is not necessary. Bake until eggs are set but still soft; serve with toast or crusty rolls.

# Italian Eggs in Caper Sauce

These can be baked in ramekins, or poached in the sauce in a skillet. Add to a cup of tomato sauce, 6 or 8 chopped black olives, a tablespoon of capers, a little instant minced onion (or grated onion) and 2 tablespoons olive oil. Heat just to blend well; divide among 2 large or 4 small ramekins (or place in a 9-inch skillet). Break one egg into each small ramekin, two into each large ramekin; or break 4 eggs into the sauce in a skillet. Bake uncovered in a preheated hot oven until eggs are set; or poach, covered, on top of stove until eggs are set. Makes 2 or 4 servings.

# Huevos a la Flamenco

This Spanish version of baked eggs is definitely an entrée; each serving is a "one-dish meal." Sauté 1 cup minced onion and 1 or 2 minced garlic cloves in 2 tablespoons olive oil until soft; add ½ cup chopped ham; cook until lightly browned. Add a little minced parsley, some chopped pimiento and a can (1 pound) of tomatoes. Cook until well blended and thickened; chop tomatoes as they cook. Add seasonings to taste. Divide mixture among 4 large ramekins. Break 1 egg into each. Arrange frozen tiny peas around the eggs (1 cup altogether), or, place 2 asparagus spears (fresh cooked, or frozen) on either side of the eggs. Bake in preheated hot oven until eggs are set but still soft. Makes 4 servings.

# OMELETS

# French Omelet

The making of a French omelet, as observed in the introduction to this chapter, is the simplest thing in the world—yet more horrors have been served by the name omelet than can be counted. One important thing is to use a well-seasoned skillet or an omelet pan that will not stick. Those who serve omelets frequently should keep a pan aside especially for the purpose and never wash it after use. Instead, the pan should be wiped thoroughly with a paper towel until it is clean.

No matter how many people are to be served, it's best to keep each omelet small, repeating if necessary to make as many as needed. Small omelets are much easier to handle, and will be more tender. Beat 3 or 4 eggs in a narrow bowl with a fork (not an egg beater), using a cupping motion so that whites and yolks are blended without bubbles. Beat in ¼ teaspoon salt and 2 tablespoons water. In the pan, melt (but do not brown) 1 to 1½ tablespoons butter. The pan must be *hot* when the eggs are added; then the heat must be instantly turned to low. As the egg firms, lift it up with a spatula to allow the moist egg to run under. The omelet can be rolled over slowly as the egg firms or allowed to remain like a pancake until all the egg is firm but still moist. Do not try to brown the omelet; it will be more tender if still yellow on the bottom. This process takes perhaps 2, perhaps 3 minutes for each omelet. Serve immediately.

# Omelette au Fromage

Sprinkle ⅓ to ½ cup shredded Swiss cheese over the beaten egg after it has been poured into the pan. Continue as in previous recipe.

# Omelette aux Fines Herbes

Add a tablespoon of chopped parsley or other *fresh* herbs (dill, chives, basil, or chervil) to the beaten egg mixture.

# Omelette aux Champignons

Sauté 1 cup sliced fresh mushrooms in 2 tablespoons butter until mushrooms are lightly browned. Add about a tablespoon of very finely sliced onion as well, if liked. To this add the beaten egg mixture, as in the basic recipe. Serve sprinkled with minced parsley or minced chives.

# Tortilla Española

In Spain, the word for omelet is tortilla, and the most typical Spanish omelet is one made with potatoes, sometimes called tortilla con patatas, sometimes Tortilla Española. Potatoes alone may be added, or potatoes and onion; or, potatoes, onion and diced bacon or ham. Other vegetable combinations may also be added to a tortilla, but the basic technique of preparation is the same.

Peel and chop 1 large potato, or 2 medium potatoes. Add potatoes to olive oil (¼ inch deep) in skillet or omelet pan. Peel and chop 1 large onion; add to pan. Cook, turning occasionally, until vegetables are very soft and golden, or very lightly browned. Sprinkle with salt from a shaker. Beat 5 large or 6 smaller eggs with egg beater or whisk; add ½ teaspoon salt and 3 tablespoons water. Add half the egg to the pan; lift up with spatula as it firms to allow moist egg to run under. When firm, add remaining egg; repeat. Make sure omelet is not sticking by slipping a spatula under as it starts to brown. When nicely browned (you can tell by lifting it up at one side), loosen all across the bottom with the spatula, then invert by holding a plate over the top of the skillet, and turn over. The omelet should slip out easily. Remove any sticky bits that have stuck to the pan, add more olive oil, then slide the omelet back with the moist side under. Cook until lightly browned; cut into wedges. Serve hot or cold. Makes 2 to 4 entree servings, depending on appetites.

(Inverting the pan is easier than it sounds. Some cooks roll up the omelet as it firms on the bottom, so that the moist egg is pushed forward, but this requires more oil in the pan and I find it more tricky to do successfully. Olive oil is the best fat to use because it does not stick. It may shock the manufacturers of Teflon-coated utensils to hear me recommend this, but I find a Teflon-coated skillet with sloping sides is the perfect utensil for making a Tortilla Española, and slightly less oil then may be used than for making it in an ordinary skillet.)

# Italian Macaroni Omelet

One of the great uses of eggs is to bind together leftovers: this can be done with macaroni, spaghetti, Spanish rice or even cooked beans or lentils. The method is the same as that for Tortilla Española. First sauté the ingredients in oil; then add beaten seasoned eggs. The omelet will be easier to handle if ingredients have been chopped into small pieces.

When leftover pasta is used this way, it need not be sautéed, especially if there is some leftover sauce to mix with it. Moisten the bottom of the skillet with oil or fat, enough to prevent sticking; add the cooked macaroni or spaghetti and cook and stir until it is thoroughly hot. If you do not have sauce, only the pasta, sauté the pasta in about 2 tablespoons of fat or oil; add 2 or 3 tablespoons of chopped parsley. Beat 5 or 6 eggs until frothy; season with ½ teaspoon salt; thin with 2 tablespoons water. Add about ⅓ of egg mixture to pan at first, lifting up mixture as egg firms on bottom to allow moist egg to run under. Continue with remaining beaten egg until a thick cake is formed. Cover with grated Parmesan. Slip spatula under the omelet to loosen it, slide out, browned side down, on to a heatproof platter or shallow casserole. Place 4 inches under broiler until cheese is lightly browned. Serve immediately.

# SOUFFLÉS

# Cheese Soufflé

When and by whom the first soufflé was invented, I haven't been able to learn. Custards, called cheesecakes, were popular with the Greeks and Romans; Apicius has a recipe for a "cheesecake" that is in reality a baked custard. The trick of separating the yolks from the whites was known by Apicius, too. But the creation of a high frothy soufflé with its characteristic "top hat" would seem to belong to an era of reliable ovens and standardized casserole sizes.

| | |
|---|---|
| 3  tablespoons butter | Dash of nutmeg |
| 3  tablespoons flour | 4  large or 5 small eggs, |
| 1  cup milk | separated |
| 1  teaspoon salt | 1½  cups shredded Swiss or |
| ½  teaspoon freshly ground | natural Gruyere cheese |
| black pepper | Butter, about 2 teaspoons |
| | Flour, about 1 tablespoon |

Make a Bechamel Sauce (recipe in Sauces and Seasonings chapter) with the butter, flour, and milk; melt butter, stir in flour, let cook a few seconds, then slowly add milk, salt, pepper, and nutmeg. Beat egg yolks with a whisk until thick and smooth; add sauce to yolks a little at a time. Stir shredded cheese into mixture. This part may be done ahead. Preheat oven to 325° F. (moderate). Butter bottom and sides of a 1½-quart casserole or soufflé dish; dust flour over the buttered surface; then shake out excess flour. Beat egg whites with egg beater or mixer until stiff; fold into yolk mixture, blending well but with a gentle motion. Spoon into casserole. Make a groove around the edge, 1 inch from the outside, with a spoon. Bake about 45 minutes until puffed high above the top of the casserole and until it is golden. Serve immediately. Serves 4.

For a soufflé to serve 6, increase all ingredients by half (4½ tablespoons each butter and flour, 1½ cups milk, 6 large eggs, 2½ cups cheese). Either use a 2-quart straight-sided casserole or soufflé dish or make a 2-inch cardboard "collar" to stand up around the edges of a smaller casserole to protect the soufflé as it shoots up. This collar can be held together with paper clips. It, too, should be greased and floured, like the casserole.

# Dairy Eggplant Soufflé

I found the foods served in dairy restaurants in Israel to be wonderfully imaginative. According to kosher dietary laws, milk products may not be served in any meals containing meat; in fact, the same utensils may not be used to cook meat and milk, and so "dairy restaurants" are those that serve no meat at all, in any form, but use cheese, butter, and milk in many interesting ways.

| | |
|---|---|
| 1 small to medium eggplant | 6 tablespoons butter or |
| 4 eggs, beaten | margarine |
| 2 cups shredded Gruyere | Salt, pepper |
| or Swiss cheese | 2 tablespoons flour |
| | ½ cup milk |

Peel the eggplant and cut in very thin slices; sprinkle with salt; let stand 15 minutes; then squeeze out or rinse off bitter juices. Pat dry with towel. Sauté the slices in butter until lightly browned; arrange half the cooked slices over the bottom of a greased

9 x 13 x 2-inch baking pan; sprinkle with flour. Combine beaten eggs with cheese; stir in milk. Pour into baking dish. Place remaining eggplant slices over the egg mixture (they will float until the egg firms). Bake in a slow oven preheated to 325° F. until set. This is more like a custard than like a French soufflé. Cut in squares to serve. Makes 6 servings.

# Cheese-Potato Croquettes

|   |   |
|---|---|
| 3 cups mashed potatoes | 1 teaspoon grated onion |
| ¼ teaspoon black pepper | 1½ cups shredded firm cheese |
| ½ teaspoon salt | Fine dry crumbs |
| 2 tablespoons butter | Oil for frying |
| 1 egg, separated | |

Beat potatoes until light, adding pepper, salt and butter. Beat in the egg yolk and the grated onion. Add cheese, blend well. Mixture must be firm. Shape into fat "fingers" 2 inches in length. Roll croquettes in egg white that has been beaten only until soft (not stiff); then roll in crumbs. Chill. Heat oil, 2 inches deep, to 375° F. (until a square of bread browns in 60 seconds). Drop croquettes into hot oil; cook until browned on all sides (do not crowd pan). Serve hot with catsup or Tahina Sauce (see recipe in chapter on Appetizers). Makes 4 to 6 servings.

# CHEESE PIES

Cheesecakes receive more attention in the pages of Athenaeus' third-century book, *The Deipnosophists*, than any other one subject except wine. The book's author, Athenaeus, allows his banqueteers to discuss lovingly the many ways of preparing this delicacy, until it becomes clear that what they mean by cheesecake is something quite different from the soft creamy dessert pastry we call by that name today. The recipe for tyropitakia (little cheese pastries), given elsewhere as an appetizer, is one kind of cheesecake. The following Tyropita is another. In the Sweets chapter will be found a honey-and-cheese pie which is still a third.

# Tyropita
*(cheese luncheon pie)*

| | |
|---|---|
| Pastry for 2-crust pie | 1 cup milk |
| 4 tablespoons butter | 6 eggs, beaten |
| ¼ cup grated or minced onion | 1 tablespoon cornstarch |
| | Dash of cayenne pepper |
| ¼ pound grated kefalotyri or grated Romano cheese | ¼ teaspoon dried dill weed |
| | ¼ teaspoon nutmeg |
| 1 pound feta cheese, crumbled; or 1 pound pot cheese | ¼ teaspoon salt |

Prepare pastry dough, using a favorite recipe or pie crust mix. Divide dough in two unequal parts; roll out the larger portion as thin as possible, and stretch to fit bottom and sides of a 10-inch round Pyrex baking dish or a 10-inch layer cake pan. Brush this dough with 2 tablespoons melted butter. Melt a third tablespoon of butter in a skillet or saucepan; add the grated cheese and stir until well blended but not browned. Mash the feta cheese or force pot cheese through a sieve; beat cheese in blender with the milk. Add the grated cheese blended with butter, the beaten eggs, cornstarch and seasonings. Mix until well blended. Spoon into pie crust. Roll out remaining pie crust and fit over top, making slashes in the center. Moisten edges and crimp together to seal. Brush top with remaining tablespoon of melted butter. Bake in oven preheated to 375° F. (moderately hot) until pastry is crisply golden and a knife inserted through the slashes comes out clean. Cut into 8 to 12 wedges, depending on whether this is to be served as a luncheon entrée or a snack. Good both warm and cold.

# Onion Flan

The word "flan" has quite a different meaning in Spain than in France and Italy. In Spain it means the caramel custards served for dessert. In France, it's a kind of pie. In Italy it is a custard baked in a pie shell but not a dessert custard. The following could be compared to a Quiche Lorraine.

Pastry for a 1-crust pie
4 large onions, sliced
3 tablespoons olive oil or
   butter
3 slices bacon, diced

¾ cup milk or light cream
2 eggs
   Salt, pepper
1 tablespoon flour

Prepare pastry with a favorite recipe or with 1 stick pie crust mix. Roll out; fit into pie pan. Brush a little beaten egg over bottom. Bake in a hot oven for about 3 minutes; remove. Reduce oven heat to 350° F. Cook onions with bacon in olive oil until soft and golden. Sprinkle with flour, salt and pepper. Add milk or cream and continue to cook until slightly thickened. Allow to cool.

Separate eggs; beat yolks; blend with onion mixture. Beat egg whites until stiff; fold in. Spoon mixture into pastry and bake until top is golden and the filling firm and the pastry is golden and crisp, about 30 minutes. Makes a nice luncheon entrée with a green salad. 4 servings.

Four persons are wanted to make a good salad, a spendthrift for oil, a miser for vinegar, a counselor for salt, and a madman to stir them all up.

—Spanish proverb


The near end of the street was rather dark and had mostly vegetable shops. Abundance of vegetables—piles of white and green fennel, like celery, and great sheaves of young, purplish, sea-dust-colored artichokes, nodding their buds, piles of big radishes, scarlety and bluey purple, carrots, long strings of dried figs, mountains of big oranges, scarlet large peppers, a last slice of pumpkin, a great mass of colors and vegetable freshnesses. . . .

—D. H. Lawrence, *Sea and Sardinia*

# Vegetables and Salads

The three regions of the world where vegetable cookery is supreme are China, India and the Mediterranean, and in all three, vegetables are cooked in oil rather than in water. It's a healthful method because the oil seals in nutrients and flavor, the vegetables cook more quickly than in water, and, because the oil becomes part of the sauce, no vitamins are washed down the drain. In many cases, the amount of fat used is no more than would be added to boiled vegetables, so that cooking with oil isn't necessarily more fattening, either.

The one big difference is in the kind of oil used. In the Mediterranean, it's usually olive oil; in the Orient, peanut or soy oil. (Sesame oil is used differently, as a flavoring or sauce rather than for frying.) It's quite possible that the method of cooking vegetables in oil was imported from India along with such vegetables as eggplant, haricot beans and certain types of squash and such spices as ginger, pepper, nutmeg and cinnamon, all of which are used frequently in Mediterranean kitchens to season vegetables.

177

In every Mediterranean country, vegetable stews are popular, and often the only difference between a dish served in Damascus and its counterpart in Marseilles is in the name bestowed upon it. Ratatouille, the Provençal vegetable stew, is strikingly similar to what is called ciambotta in southern Italy, batinjaan bi zayt in Lebanon and Syria, and pisto manchego in Spain. In fact, using the basic method, any number of different vegetables may be turned into one of these delicious stews, which are as good cold as hot and may be served as relishes, side dishes or the entrée for the meal.

Deep-fried vegetables also are to be found in different Mediterranean countries, as they are in the Far East. In Italy, batter-fried vegetables are called frito misto. In Lebanon, the name for virtually the same thing is maqaali. Dolma, a word that was first used by the Persians, is the name given to any stuffed vegetable (and also to stuffed grape or vine leaves) throughout the Near East.

Religion has had much to do with the glorification of vegetables in the Mediterranean. Devout Christians abstain from meat throughout the forty days of Lent, and while the pope has in recent years relaxed the stipulation for Roman Catholics that Fridays should be meatless days, Christians of the Eastern Orthodox faith continue to fast on holy days throughout the year. Kosher dietary laws, which forbid the eating of meat and any milk products in the same meal, have inspired Jewish cooks to develop intriguing vegetable dishes for dairy meals. Moslems are forbidden to eat pork or pork products at any time, and the entire month of Ramadan is one of severe fasting.

Vegetarianism was introduced among the Greeks in the fifth century B.C. by the philosopher Pythagoras, who had been inspired, during a visit to India, in both his philosophy and his eating habits, by Buddhism. A banquet once prepared for Pythagoras by his followers featured nothing but figs, grapes, cheese and cucumbers prepared in a multitude of ways. Undoubtedly Pythagoras brought back from India recipes for preparing vegetables deliciously.

Outside of religious scruples, a good reason for making use of vegetables is a matter of economy, for the poorest peasants can raise a few vegetables of their own and keep a few hens for eggs.

Because of the warm climate of the Mediterranean, vegetables and fruits grow in abundance everywhere, and cooks make use of a number of vegetables rarely seen in American supermarkets, such as fresh okra, fennel, Swiss chard and celery knob. Even well-known everyday vegetables become exotic when prepared the Mediterranean way.

# EGGPLANT AND ZUCCHINI

## Ratatouille

| | |
|---|---|
| 1 eggplant, about 1 pound | 3 large ripe tomatoes, peeled |
| Salt | and chopped; or 1-pound |
| 2 or 3 small zucchini or | can of tomatoes |
| yellow squash | 1/4 teaspoon thyme or |
| 1 large onion, sliced or | oregano |
| chopped | 2 tablespoons minced |
| 2 or 3 garlic cloves, minced | parsley |
| 1/2 cup olive oil | 1 green pepper, seeded and |
| | chopped (optional) |

Slice or cube eggplant and sprinkle with salt; let stand 1/2 hour; then drain well. (Whether or not to peel the eggplant is a matter of individual preference. I never peel it, for to me the peel is the most flavorful part.) Partially scrape squash with edge of sharp knife; cube. Cook onions and garlic in olive oil at moderate heat until onion is soft and golden; add eggplant and squash; cook, uncovered, until eggplant is delicately browned, turning occasionally. Add remaining ingredients, including salt and pepper to taste. Simmer, uncovered, 1 hour or until all vegetables are soft and sauce has thickened. Usually served warm but equally good cold (at room temperature, not chilled). Makes 6 to 8 servings.

# ıan bi Zayt

ın Lebanon, the tiny eggplants, about the same size as small zucchini, are more frequently used than the larger ones in making this stew, though a large eggplant may be used. With a kitchen fork, make incisions lengthwise in the peel; sprinkle with salt; do not cut up small eggplants. Larger ones should be cut in lengthwise pieces. Fry in a cup of olive oil until very soft. Then add sliced onion to the oil and crush *six* (yes, six) garlic cloves along with 1 teaspoon salt and add this to the oil. Cover with 3 or 4 sliced tomatoes. Add ¼ teaspoon cinnamon and ½ cup water. Cook uncovered very slowly until a thick sauce has formed and vegetables are very tender. Always served cold.

## Pisto Manchego

This dish is more frequently made with squash than with eggplant, though both can be added if desired. As in making Ratatouille, cook the chopped vegetables slowly in plenty of olive oil with onion, garlic and tomato. The Spanish add only parsley for seasoning, but plenty of it, plus salt to taste—no black pepper. Sweet red peppers (pimientos) are also frequently added.

Pisto means "stew" in Spanish, and like most stews, this one can be varied infinitely. Often it appears made with meat, usually diced pork: the pork is browned first, then the vegetables added. I've had it also garnished with strips of scrambled egg and have found recipes in Spanish cookbooks that describe it as a kind of omelet, that is, beaten eggs are added to the cooked vegetables. (What I sometimes do is to add a cupful of leftover Pisto Manchego to beaten eggs to make into a Tortilla con Legumbres.)

## Aubergine en Scabech

Escabeche, a word frequently used in Spanish to mean "pickled," comes from the Arab cisbech (or siquisbe in Persian). This Algerian dish is served cold as a relish or salad with meat. Its uniqueness is due to the cumin flavoring.

2 pounds eggplant, preferably the small ones
Salt
⅓ cup olive oil
6 garlic cloves

1 tablespoon paprika
Pinch of cayenne
1 teaspoon crushed cumin
2 tablespoons wine vinegar

Score or cut strips lengthwise in the peel of the eggplants; sprinkle with salt; let stand ½ hour. (Leave small eggplants whole; cut large one in strips.) Place eggplant strips on rack over boiling water and steam 15 minutes. Drain; pat dry. Cook in hot oil with the garlic until garlic is soft; crush garlic with tines of fork and remove. Add seasonings to eggplant; continue to cook uncovered until tender, turning until browned on all sides and very soft. Add vinegar; cook 2 minutes longer. Chill. Serve cold. Makes 8 to 10 servings.

# Fried Eggplant or Zucchini

In many recipes, zucchini may be substituted for eggplant, or vice versa. Zucchini is the Italian name for the squash the English call marrow and the French call courgette. Its Arabic name is kousa. These two vegetables are quite different in flavor but, because the pulp is of the same consistency and the rind or peel of both may be eaten, they lend themselves to the same treatment.

Peel eggplant or not, as you prefer; scrape outer rind of zucchini lightly. Cut in ¼-inch slices; sprinkle with salt. Let eggplant stand 15 minutes; then drain. (Draining is not necessary with zucchini.) Fry the slices just as they are in hot olive oil, until lightly browned on each side. Or, dip in a batter (made with 1 cup biscuit or pancake mix, 1 egg and ¼ cup milk), then add to deep hot oil (2 inches deep) and fry until browned on each side. Serve hot with catsup or Tahina Sauce, or Hummus (recipes in Appetizers section).

# Eggplant Parmigiana

Layer fried eggplant in a casserole with ricotta or cottage cheese between layers; over the top spread a cup of well-seasoned tomato sauce and a thick layer of grated Parmesan cheese. Bake in a moderate oven until top is golden, about 30 minutes. (A similar Greek casserole made with fried eggplant layered with cottage cheese is topped with Bechamel Sauce and grated cheese, then baked.)

# Zucchini Parmigiana

Layer fried zucchini slices with ricotta cheese, top with tomato sauce and grated Parmesan, and bake in the same way.

# Calabaza a la Española

This dish can be made with either yellow summer squash or zucchini. Dice the squash (do not peel); cook with sliced onion and chopped green pepper or pimiento in olive oil until tender. For 1½ pounds squash, you will need about a cup of chopped onion, ¼ cup diced green pepper and ⅓ cup olive oil. Season with salt, pepper, minced fresh tarragon or parsley. If you wish, you may also add a peeled, chopped tomato—but no water. (With zucchini, pimiento is more attractive than the green pepper.)

# OKRA

Okra is extremely popular in the Eastern Mediterranean, but it is not as commonly used in the West. The Greeks call it bamies; the Arabic name is bamieh. Okra originated in Africa, where its name is gumbo. The Creole dish by this name was introduced to New Orleans by African slaves who brought some of their favorite vegetable with them in the slave ships.

In Egypt, okra has been used since ancient times, as it has in India, where the gummy substance the okra juice produces is considered a good thickening ingredient in soups and stews.

During the Moorish period in Spain, bamiyah, as it was called, was treasured, but it has since fallen out of favor among the Spanish.

Okra must be carefully trimmed. When the glutinous consistency is not wanted, trim away the stem without cutting into the pod at all. Also, okra should be washed and dried before adding to liquid, and always cooked briefly. Frozen okra is already trimmed and ready for the pot. A little lemon juice does much to bring out the unique okra flavor.

# Bamies Yahni
(*okra Greek style*)

Cook about a cup of sliced onion in olive oil until very soft and golden. Add 2 cups tomato juice or a cup of canned tomatoes and a cup of water. Season to taste with salt, pepper and thyme. Add a teaspoon of lemon juice and some grated lemon peel. Cook 20 minutes. Add a package of frozen okra pods or 1½ cups fresh trimmed okra pods; continue to cook until okra is tender, 10 to 15 minutes longer. Makes 4 servings.

# Bamieh bi Zayt

The Lebanese prepare an okra dish made with the same ingredients as the Greek one, plus coriander and garlic. Trim, wash and pat dry the okra pods; then fry in deep fat or oil until tender but still green, about 4 minutes; remove with slotted spoon; drain on absorbent paper. Add sliced onions to ¼ cup of the same oil in a top-of-stove casserole; crush to a paste 3 or 4 garlic cloves with ½ teaspoon salt and a tablespoon of chopped fresh coriander (or 1 teaspoon crushed coriander seeds). Add this mixture to the onions. Cook over low heat until onions are soft; then add 3 sliced tomatoes and the okra. Sprinkle with ¼ cup lemon juice blended with ½ teaspoon sugar; add ½ cup water. Cook, covered, 15 minutes; remove cover and continue cooking until most of liquid is gone. Adjust seasonings to taste. Serve chilled. Makes 6 servings.

# CABBAGE, CARROTS, CAULIFLOWER

## Lahana Yahni

Lahana yahni is the Greek way of braising cabbage. Cut half a head of Savoy (curly) cabbage in wedges. Cook 2 chopped onions in oil until soft; add 3 peeled chopped tomatoes (or a 1-pound can), 2 tablespoons minced parsley, 1 or 2 carrots scraped and diced, the cabbage and salt and pepper to taste. (No water—the cabbage and the tomatoes furnish enough liquid). Cook covered for 20 to 30 minutes. Makes 6 servings.

## Lahana Kuzulu

Lahana kuzulu means "braised cabbage" in Turkish. Shred green or white cabbage as for cole slaw. First cook 2 large onions, chopped, in 4 tablespoons butter until soft; then add 4 cups shredded cabbage, ½ teaspoon salt, a dash of pepper and a pinch of ginger. Chopped pimiento is also good with this. Cook over low heat, tightly covered, about 15 minutes, shaking the pan now and then to prevent sticking. When cabbage is tender, drain well, then add ½ cup yogurt or sour cream and blend lightly. Makes 4 or 5 servings.

## Glazed Carrots, French Style

Scrape carrots and cut lengthwise into quarters or sticks. Cook carrots in 1 cup chicken broth (made with a chicken bouillon cube or stock concentrate and water) until barely tender, 5 to 7 minutes. Remove carrots with slotted spoon. Boil to reduce broth to ½. Add to the broth 3 tablespoons butter and 2 tablespoons sugar; continue boiling until reduced and shiny. Serve carrots in the sauce. (If making the broth with stock concentrate, use only ½ teaspoon powder to a cup of water; when broth is reduced this will be quite salty enough.)

# Carrots Agridolce
*(Italian sweet-sour carrots)*

Scrape and quarter carrots; cook in 1 cup salted water until barely tender. Remove carrots, saving broth. Melt 3 tablespoons butter; stir in 1½ tablespoons flour; then slowly add ¾ cup carrot broth, 2 tablespoons sugar and 3 tablespoons vinegar. Continue to cook until sauce is reduced and thickened. Replace the carrots in the sauce.

# Carrot Tzimmes

This honey-sweetened Jewish fruit and vegetable mixture is delicious with roast meat; also nice for a buffet. Sometimes diced beef is added to it (cooked with the onions in shortening or oil), which makes it almost a one-dish meal.

| | |
|---|---|
| 1½ pounds pitted prunes | Salt to taste |
| 3 cups boiling water | ¼ teaspoon cinnamon |
| 2 to 3 tablespoons shortening or oil | ¼ teaspoon cloves |
| 2 onions, chopped | 2 or 3 medium sweet potatoes, peeled and |
| 3 or 4 carrots, scraped and cubed | cubed |
| | ½ cup honey |

Soak prunes in water ½ hour. Heat shortening in heavy pot; add onions; cook until soft and golden. Add carrots, prunes and water in which they soaked; also add the salt and spices. Simmer over lowest heat, covered, for 1 hour. Add sweet potatoes and honey; continue to cook until potatoes are very soft and mixture is well blended. Makes 6 servings.

# Cauliflower Avgholemono

Cook cauliflower (whole or in sprigs) in boiling salted water until tender. Serve topped with Avgholemono Sauce (see recipe in chapter on Sauces and Seasonings).

# Deep-Fried Cauliflower

This is served in a number of different Mediterranean countries. Break cauliflower into sprigs; dip the raw sprigs into batter (like that for Fried Eggplant, or use the batter for Fried Scampi). Drop into deep hot fat and cook until golden. Serve immediately.

# FENNEL

Fennel when cooked is an intriguing vegetable, though its licorice flavor does not go with everything. It's best to serve it with other mild-flavored foods. The green bulbs look like a curious form of celery and the texture is much like celery, too. Cut in half through the bulbs; trim off the feathery tops. (These may be used as an herb; freeze in a plastic bag to have on hand when wanted.) Cook the fennel until barely tender in boiling salted water, about 20 minutes. Drain; arrange in a buttered casserole and cover with Bechamel Sauce (recipe in chapter on Sauces and Seasonings); top with grated cheese; sprinkle breadcrumbs over the top. Bake until top is lightly browned. Very nice with roast lamb or beef pot roast.

# ASPARAGUS

Asparagus is more often seen white than green in Mediterranean markets. I admit to a prejudice in favor of the green, perhaps because of fond memories from childhood when we had an asparagus bed in our garden and the tender shoots of green asparagus on the table were a sure harbinger of spring. When young and fresh, the spears need the briefest cooking. I prefer to break off the tough ends of the stem and discard them, then cook the tender part, laid horizontally in a skillet, barely covered with salted water. Put a lid over the skillet, but see that it is only partially covered, so that steam may escape. Otherwise, the spears lose much of their bright green color.

When the spears are tender, remove them and place immediately on toast; spoon just a bit of the cooking water over them; then dot with butter. The toast soaks up the broth, which makes it as good as the asparagus itself.

The Romans were inordinately fond of asparagus, and writers of antiquity claimed that some grown at Ravenna, in the north of Italy, weighed three pounds each, though why anyone should want such monsters, I don't know. I personally prefer the slenderest of stalks, and I suspect the Romans did, too, for they had a saying that when a thing could be done quickly, "it takes no more time than to cook asparagus"—a maxim that could only be applied to comparatively slender spears.

# Asparagus Milanaise

Break off the tough ends; cook the spears just until fork-tender, 5 or 6 minutes. Remove with slotted spoon and place over toast, 3 or 4 spears per serving. Place a poached egg over each serving and sprinkle the egg with grated Parmesan cheese. A very nice luncheon dish.

# Asparagus Omelet

This is an Italian recipe that can be made with frozen asparagus spears. First melt 2 tablespoons of butter in a skillet or omelet pan; place the frozen thawed spears over the butter (no precooking needed), in spokes like a wheel. Beat 3 eggs until light; season with ¼ teaspoon salt; add 3 tablespoons cream and ¼ cup grated Parmesan cheese. Pour the egg mixture over the asparagus, ½ at a time, lifting up at the edges with a spatula as the egg firms, but without moving the spears. When omelet is firm on the bottom, place the pan under the broiler, 4 inches from the heat, until lightly browned. Serve in the pan, cutting in wedges.

# Asparagus Maltaise

Serve tenderly-cooked green or white asparagus spears topped with Sauce Maltaise (the recipe is in the chapter on Sauces and Seasonings).

# ARTICHOKES

Artichokes are plentiful throughout the Mediterranean, both the tiny ones and the big purplish-tinted heads. It's the babies I particularly like, for they can be cooked quickly and many have no thistles (chokes) inside at all. They only need trimming, cutting off the stems close to the bud. Then cut them in halves or quarters. If there is any choke, it can be detected quickly and easily removed. Drop at once as cut into water acidified with lemon juice to blanch; drain; then cook in salted water containing more lemon juice until tender, about 12 to 15 minutes. Drain; serve with Vinaigrette Sauce, with Hollandaise or with homemade Mayonnaise.

## Artichoke Bottoms

Artichoke bottoms are frequently served as the base for salad in France and also in Lebanon. For these, you need the larger artichokes. Pull away the tough outer leaves; trim the inner leaves by cutting across the top with scissors. Then push the leaves apart so that you can get at that thistlelike choke inside and remove it with a sharp knife. Drop into lemon-scented and salted water to boil until tender, which may require 40 to 50 minutes. When tender, remove from water and drain upside down.

All the leaves may be gently removed, leaving only the solid base, the most delicious part. Or the leaves may be left on and stuffed with a salad mixture. In any case, marinate in an oil-lemon sauce at least half an hour before adding salad mixture or topping.

Suggested salad mixtures: Salpichon de Mariscos, Celery Salad alla Colombo or Potato-Shrimp Salad (see Pastel de Gambas). Or, arrange overlapping shrimp over the top of each artichoke bottom and garnish with mayonnaise and pimiento strips. Very pretty and delicious as a first course.

## Yakhnit el Ardishawki
(*artichoke stew*)

12  baby artichokes; or 2 boxes frozen artichoke hearts
10  small white onions

3  small carrots, scraped and cubed
1  cup diced leftover meat (optional)

½ cup olive oil

2 cups water

1 teaspoon salt

1 teaspoon minced dill or mint

2 tablespoons lemon juice

1 teaspoon sugar

1 teaspoon flour or cornstarch

If fresh artichokes are used, cut away stems and tough outer leaves. Cut each artichoke in quarters; remove thistlelike choke in center. Frozen artichokes merely need defrosting.

Peel onions; sauté onions, carrots and meat (if used) in oil until lightly colored, turning occasionally. Add water, salt and dill or mint; simmer covered 15 to 20 minutes. Add artichokes, lemon juice and sugar blended with flour. Continue cooking, covered, 7 minutes for frozen artichokes, for fresh artichokes about 12 minutes or until a fork will easily penetrate the largest. Reduce sauce by boiling until thickened; serve the vegetables in the sauce. Makes about 8 servings.

When I examined Yakhnit el Ardishawki in a Lebanese cookbook, it seemed familiar. When I tested it, I discovered it is very much like the Greek dish called Anginares a la Polita which I used to enjoy at Zonar's cafe in Athens. The Greek dish never has meat in it, but often has small potatoes that have been cooked with the carrots and onions. It is much more delicious than it sounds, and I like it better cold than hot.

# SPINACH

Spinach is more often served as part of another dish than by itself in Mediterranean cookery, and when served by itself, it is usually creamed. Or, it may be dressed with Vinaigrette Sauce (see Sauces and Seasonings chapter). The Greeks serve it this way, cold, calling it a "cooked salad."

However it is served, the important thing about spinach always is brief cooking. Soak fresh spinach in a sinkful of water for about 15 minutes; then shake each cluster as it is removed from the water; break off the stems; drop the leaves in a kettle. No further water is needed. Sprinkle lightly with salt; cook, tightly covered, until leaves are just limp, about 3 minutes. Drain thoroughly and chop well.

For chopped frozen spinach, an Italian recipe may be adapted: partially thaw the package of spinach; then place it in a heavy saucepan with ½ cup red wine (no water) and sprinkle with salt, pepper and nutmeg. Cook over low heat, tightly covered, removing lid occasionally to stir the spinach to prevent burning. Needs only a few minutes of cooking after it is completely thawed. Dress with 3 tablespoons butter.

# SWISS CHARD

Swiss chard is much used in the Mediterranean, and I learned when I had a vegetable garden that this is an extremely easy vegetable to grow; in fact, it is often perennial. Only the green leaves should be used—though some very provident European cooks cook the white stems separately, since the stems require longer cooking). Chard requires more water and somewhat longer cooking than spinach, about 10 minutes for boiled chard. It may be dressed either with butter or with oil and vinegar; I lean to the latter. The leaves may also be used for stuffing.

# Spinach or Swiss Chard Catalán

Cook a pound of spinach as previously described; chop well. (Or, cook frozen chopped spinach according to package directions; drain well.) Sauté a little chopped onion, about 2 tablespoons, and 2 slices of bacon, diced, in oil or butter until lightly browned. Add the cooked spinach, ¼ cup pine nuts, ¼ cup seedless raisins or dried currants; salt to taste. Cook just until spinach is heated through. A most delicious and unusual dish, excellent with either pork or lamb. Makes 4 servings.

(When Swiss chard is used, first cook the green leaves with ½ cup water until tender, about 7 minutes; drain well and chop.)

# TOMATOES

## Domates Dolması
*(Turkish stuffed tomatoes)*

| | |
|---|---|
| 8  medium or 6 large tomatoes | ¼  cup currants or seedless raisins |
| Salt | ½  teaspoon dried mint |
| 6  tablespoons olive oil | 2  tablespoons chopped parsley |
| 1  cup chopped onion | 1  cup uncooked rice |
| 1  stalk celery, diced | 1  cup water |
| ¼  cup pine nuts | |

Scoop tomatoes for stuffing, but save the cut-off top slice and the scooped-out pulp. Sprinkle insides of tomatoes with salt and a little oil. Add 2 tablespoons oil to a skillet; cook onion, celery and scooped-out tomato (seeds removed) until onion is soft. Add pine nuts, currants, mint, parsley, rice, 1 teaspoon salt and water; cook 5 minutes. Place mixture loosely inside tomatoes (rice will swell further with cooking). Replace tops on tomatoes. Brush outside of tomatoes with remaining oil and sprinkle with remaining salt. Fit tight together inside a casserole so that the tomatoes will remain standing. Bake for 45 minutes in a moderate oven (350° F.). Serve cold with the sauce from the casserole. Makes 6 to 8 servings.

   (Green peppers or zucchini may be filled with the same stuffing. Top with buttered crumbs before baking. Serve hot.)

## Grilled Tomatoes

Cut medium-sized tomatoes in half; sprinkle over the top of each a mixture of minced chives and minced parsley; dot with butter and sprinkle with salt. Broil or bake in a very hot oven for 10 minutes until butter is melted and tomatoes are lightly browned. Or, use a mixture of crushed garlic, salt, chopped coriander or basil and a little thyme; sprinkle with fine crumbs and dot with butter. (You may do the same with canned plum tomatoes that have been well drained of their juice.)

# POTATOES

Considering that white potatoes were regarded with such disdain, even fear, when first introduced to the Mediterranean via Spain in the sixteenth century, it is extraordinary how important they have become since. Every country, of course, serves what Americans call "French fries," often in too much abundance. The French and the Italians do the most interesting things with white potatoes. Sweet potatoes are used in unusual ways in Spain.

## Truffade

¼ pound (4-5 slices) lean bacon, diced
2 tablespoons olive oil or 5 potatoes, sliced or diced

1 garlic clove
1 or 2 tomatoes, peeled and chopped
Salt, pepper
Parsley

Cook diced bacon in the oil until nicely browned (but take care bacon does not burn). Remove bacon with slotted spoon. Add sliced or diced raw potatoes to fat, also a garlic clove. Cover pan; turn heat low; cook about 25 minutes, shaking pan occasionally to prevent sticking; or, uncover occasionally and turn over with spatula. Uncover when potatoes are tender; remove and discard the garlic clove; add the tomato; stir to mix with potatoes. Sprinkle parsley and cooked bacon over top. Continue cooking uncovered over low heat without stirring until potatoes are glazed on bottom; then turn out like an omelet. Makes 4 to 6 servings.

## Gratin de Pommes
(*escalloped potatoes with cheese*)

6 medium potatoes
1 garlic clove (optional)
Salt
Freshly ground pepper

⅔ cup shredded Gruyere or Swiss cheese
1⅓ cups milk; or 1 cup milk and ½ cup cream
1 egg, beaten

Peel and slice potatoes very thin; dry on paper towel. Rub inside of 1½-quart casserole with cut side of garlic. Place potatoes in casserole in layers, sprinkling each layer with salt from shaker, pepper and a little of the cheese. When all potatoes have been added, there should still be an inch of space at the top of the casserole. Combine milk, egg and remaining cheese; pour over potatoes. Bake in slow to moderate oven 45 minutes to 1 hour until potatoes are tender (test with fork) and sauce has thickened. Makes 6 to 8 servings.

# Patatas a la Castellana
(*potatoes Castilian style*)

| | |
|---|---|
| 4 or 5 potatoes, peeled and sliced very thin | ¼ teaspoon saffron |
| 4 onions, thinly sliced | ½ teaspoon salt, or to taste |
| 1 pimiento, cut in strips | ¼ cup coarsely chopped blanched almonds |
| ¼ cup olive oil | |

Place potatoes, onions, and pimiento in oil in heavy skillet; sprinkle lightly with salt. Dissolve saffron in a tablespoon of hot water; add to pan. Cover; cook over low heat, removing cover to stir once or twice to prevent sticking, for 20 to 25 minutes. After 15 minutes, add the almonds. Makes 6 servings.

# Garbanzos a la Sevillana
(*chick peas with sweet potatoes*)

| | |
|---|---|
| 1 small onion, sliced | ¼ cup uncooked rice |
| 1 or 2 garlic cloves, minced | 2 sweet potatoes, peeled and diced |
| 2 tablespoons olive oil | 1 cup water |
| 1 cup canned tomatoes | ½ teaspoon salt, or to taste |
| 1-pound can chick peas, drained | Minced parsley |

Cook onion and garlic in oil until soft; add tomatoes, chick peas, rice and sweet potatoes, water and salt. Cover; cook 20 minutes or until potatoes are tender. Sprinkle with parsley to serve. Delicious for luncheon or supper with ham or cold cuts, or as part of a vegetable meal. Makes 4 to 6 servings.

# SALADS

## Salada de Legumbres
(*hot vegetable salad*)

This is a dish served in both Portugal and Spain and no doubt in other countries by other names. A mixture of cooked vegetables is dressed with olive oil and a little vinegar and served hot as a side dish. Leftover or canned vegetables may also be combined or heated in oil. All the vegetables should be diced or cut in small pieces.

The following vegetables are all suitable: carrots, potatoes, green beans (broken in 1-inch lengths), green peas, tiny white onions, mushrooms, cauliflower, artichoke hearts, okra, squash and turnips. Cubed beets or brussels sprouts may be added at the end, but should be cooked separately and not even be tossed with the others. A little diced pimiento is good with potatoes and green beans. Chopped hard-cooked egg may be sprinkled over the top with or without chopped parsley for garnish. For the sauce, add the usual proportions of three parts oil to one part vinegar, with salt and pepper to taste.

## Greek Salad with Feta

Salad means simply greens tossed with oil and vinegar, unless otherwise specified, in most Mediterranean countries. This may be varied by adding tomato, or cucumber, or both to the greens. Watercress is a popular salad green and in the early spring, the Italians are fond of dandelion greens; other locally abundant greens may also go into the salad bowl. The sauce invariably is the simple oil and vinegar dressing plus salt, mustard and sometimes herbs. Roquefort cheese is occasionally added to salad greens in France, and Gorgonzola in Italy, but this is a modern innovation. Once in Marseilles I had lettuce tossed with chopped walnuts, but I have a suspicion that this is a reflection of American influence. The best of all mixed salads is to be met with in Greece, what the Greeks themselves call simply "Greek Salad."

Wherever we traveled in Greek-speaking towns or islands, this bountiful and wonderful salad was served. The ingredients vary, but there will always be tomatoes, cucumber, green peppers, black olives and feta cheese in chunks, dressed with fresh fragrant olive oil and lemon juice (or vinegar). Some mixtures include white beans (cooked or canned), cooked artichoke hearts, chopped scallions or thinly sliced onion. In hot weather it's a fine lunch by itself, needing only good crusty bread and, if you can arrange for a siesta afterward, a small carafe of light local wine for the beverage.

# Salade Algerienne

| | |
|---|---|
| 4 green peppers, seeded and diced | 4 to 6 anchovy fillets, chopped |
| 4 to 6 tomatoes, chopped or quartered | 2 hard-cooked eggs, quartered |
| ½ cup sliced cucumber | Fresh basil, chopped |
| 2 small onions, thinly sliced | 3 tablespoons olive oil |
| 1 cup black olives | 1 tablespoon vinegar |
| | Salt, pepper |

This is much like Greek Salad but without the feta cheese. All ingredients may be combined in a bowl and tossed; or, crush in a mortar the anchovies, egg yolks and basil until pastelike, blend this with oil, vinegar and seasonings, and pour over the vegetables to toss. Makes 6 servings.

# Salada Frita
(*grilled green pepper salad*)

| | |
|---|---|
| 4 to 6 green peppers | 3 garlic cloves |
| 7 or 8 small ripe tomatoes | ⅓ cup olive oil |

Dash of cayenne pepper        1 to 2 tablespoons vinegar
Salt, pepper

Grill peppers over an open fire or the flame of a gas burner until outer skin is blackened; or sauté in oil until this thin skin burns. When cool, peel off the blackened skin; seed and chop the peppers. Do the same with tomatoes; hold with a fork over a flame until the skin is blackened; then peel the skin. (If done over a charcoal fire, the tomato acquires a smoky flavor.) Crush garlic in a bowl with a pestle; add some of the oil. Work in tomatoes one at a time, after squeezing out as many seeds as possible. Add more oil; then mash the peppers in the same way. When all has been well blended, season with cayenne, salt, pepper and as much vinegar as liked. Cumin is also sometimes added, which makes this dish similar to what the Tunisians call la mechouia. Serve as a salad or a relish with grilled meats.

# Fennel and Celery Salad

Sliced raw fennel and sliced or julienned celery hearts (2 cups each) are combined in this Italian salad, with a dressing of ½ cup heavy cream, salt, pepper and a few drops of lemon juice. (Or use sour cream and omit lemon juice.) Chopped walnuts may be sprinkled over the top for garnish.

# Ensalada Valenciana

This Spanish salad is one of my favorites. Thinly slice a small onion into the salad bowl and add to it ¼ cup each, olive oil and vinegar. Peel an orange and cut into segments; add to the onion-oil mixture; also add salt, pepper and, if liked, some strips of pimiento. Marinate an hour at least before serving; then add salad greens at the last moment and toss lightly. The orange and onion combination is what makes the dressing so delicious. Stuffed green olives may also go into the bowl; they make a pretty touch and the flavor combination is good, too.

# Fagiolini all'Agro
*(Italian bean salad)*

Break string beans into 1-inch pieces; cook in boiling salted water just until tender. At the same time, hard-cook 1 or 2 eggs. Rub the salad bowl with a slit clove of garlic. When beans are cooked, drain thoroughly and add while warm to the garlic-seasoned bowl. Shell the hard-cooked eggs; chop; add to the beans. Toss mixture with olive oil and vinegar in the usual proportions and season to taste. Serve at room temperature but not chilled.

# Salade de Pamplemousse
*(grapefruit salad)*

| | |
|---|---|
| 2 grapefruit | 2 tablespoons olive oil |
| 1 cup black olives | Pinch of sugar |
| 1 teaspoon paprika | Salt, pepper to taste |
| 2 teaspoons powdered cumin | |

Cut each grapefruit in half and carefully remove segments so that the grapefruit skin is kept whole. The empty halves will be used as "baskets." Cut grapefruit segments so that inner skin and seeds are removed and segments are either chopped or left whole. If there are many seeds, it is best to chop the fruit. Remove seeds from olives; combine grapefruit, olives, and remaining ingredients; toss to blend and return to grapefruit shells. Sprinkle minced parsley over top. This is an Algerian salad. Makes 4 servings.

# Insalata alla Calabrese
*(Italian tuna salad)*

| | |
|---|---|
| 1 can white meat tuna | 1 medium onion, sliced |
| ½ cup ricotta cheese | 4 celery stalks, diced |
| 2 large tomatoes, quartered | 12 large black olives |

12  pimiento-stuffed green
    olives
    Watercress, about 1 cup

4  basil leaves, chopped; or
   ¼ teaspoon dried basil
   Salt, pepper
½  cup Vinaigrette Sauce

Drain tuna, break in pieces. Break cheese with fork. Combine in salad bowl with remaining ingredients and toss lightly. Serve with toasted garlic bread. Makes 4 servings for a luncheon entrée.


# Poitou Salad

2  cups cooked rice
1  4-ounce can sliced mushrooms, drained
1  small onion, very thinly
   sliced

2  tablespoons minced green
   pepper
2  tomatoes, peeled and
   chopped
½  teaspoon dried tarragon
¼  cup Vinaigrette Sauce

Combine all ingredients, toss to blend. Serve chilled over lettuce, as a summer luncheon salad with cold cuts and crisp French bread and cheese. Makes 4 to 6 servings.


# Tabbouleh
(*Lebanese wheat salad*)

1  cup fine bulgur
   Water
1  cup minced onion
   Salt, pepper to taste
1  cup minced parsley
½  cup minced fresh mint; or
   1 tablespoon dried mint

1  cup lemon juice, or to taste
¾  cup olive oil
1  cup peeled chopped
   tomato
   Crisp lettuce leaves

Wash bulgur with cold water; then drain and squeeze out any remaining water with your hands. Place in a bowl with remaining ingredients except lettuce; toss to mix very well. Taste for seasoning and add more lemon juice if liked (it is supposed to be quite tart). Serve on individual plates surrounded with crisp small lettuce leaves, which are used to scoop up the salad (the more timid are permitted to use forks, if preferred). This is so popular in Lebanon that it is rated a national dish, as popular as kibbe. Makes 8 to 10 servings.

# Cucumber and Yogurt Salad

Slice cucumber; sprinkle with salt; let stand ½ hour; then drain. Toss with yogurt and a little chopped fresh mint (or dried mint if the fresh is not available) and add, if liked, a little thinly-sliced onion or crushed garlic, plus salt and pepper. One of the most popular of all side dishes in the Near East, served with meats, or as an hors d'oeuvre. (Dill may be used instead of mint.)

Niçoise Salad and Salade Russe are not to be forgotten. Recipes for these will be found in the chapter on Appetizers.

Tis a hard thing, beholding Cyprian loaves,
To ride by carelessly, for like a magnet,
They do attract the hungry passengers.

— Athenaeus


Such was the size, O master, of the *nastus,*
A large white loaf: it was so deep, its top
Rose like a tower quite above its basket.
Its smell, when that top was lifted up,
Rose up, a fragrance not unmixed with honey,
Most grateful to our nostrils, still being hot.

— Athenaeus, *The Deipnosophists*

# Cereals and Breads

The word "bread" usually means to us today a loaf of wheaten flour, soft and white within a brownish crust. But long before the first cereal grains were cultivated, primitive men made breads with acorns, chestnuts and even seeds. The cultivation of wild grasses into grains that could be harvested in large quantities and stored for daily use marked the first transition from nomadic into settled community life.

Archaeologists now believe that Jericho, in the hills of Judea near the Dead Sea, may have been the world's first city. Some 9000 years ago Jericho had a population of at least 2000 people, their homes spread out over ten acres. Gathering and processing salt from the nearby Dead Sea was Jericho's industry. Salt was valuable because it could be used to preserve meat and fish, and it also helped to make their crude hearth bread more palatable. But they couldn't have developed an industry without bread, "the staff of life," which could be baked when needed from grains conveniently stored within the city walls. The grain storage pits in the 9000-year-old rubble of Jericho reveal how important a part bread already played during the dawn of civilization, 6000 years before Joshua appeared on the scene with his trumpet to "fit the battle of Jericho" and cause those mighty walls to "come tumblin' down."

201

The first breads were similar to what is called chapati in India, or like the tortillas of Mexico: crushed cereal grains blended with water, rolled or stretched out as thinly as possible and baked on hot stones.

The first leavened bread was created by accident in Egypt— at least, that's the legend. A baker in the royal kitchens at Thebes left his bread dough in a bowl in a darkened corner and forgot it. When he found it next day, the dough had ballooned into a ball. There wasn't time to make a fresh batch, so the terrified baker shaped his loaves and put them in the oven hoping for the best—and out came delicious light leavened bread.

The spore or starter for making raised bread can be made simply by allowing an infusion of grain and water to stand in a moist place until it ferments. This is the principle behind the salt-rising bread and the sourdough bread of our pioneer ancestors in America. It was the method used before commercial yeast cakes were invented. In many Mediterranean villages today, housewives still keep a roll of dough aside from each batch of bread to use as a "starter" for the next baking.

Wandering through the markets in Beirut and Tunis, I noted that most of their breads are flat and round and that several kinds of pancakes were also for sale in the stalls, cold, ready to be used in making such things as the brik of Tunisia and the blintzes of Israel.

I must confess that I was not won over to a liking for the chewy Arab flat bread, finding it palatable only when toasted. Yet I'm sure that for those who have known such bread from childhood, khubuz is treasured. In the museums one may see the big colorful woven mats on which the dough is kneaded. Even the women who prepare the dough at home send it to public ovens for baking: balls of the dough are shaped into circles and pressed flat, carried by little boys on huge trays to the bakeshops. As they bake, the "loaves" rise in the center, but they fall again when taken from the oven. This leaves a soft pocket in the center, which, when the bun or loaf is slit open, can be used to hold meat, cheese, pickles and sauces, like a hamburger bun. These were the buns being used for the barbecue I happened upon in old Jaffa, in Tel Aviv.

According to Athenaeus, there were more than fifty kinds of bread known to the Greeks of his time, some leavened, some unleavened, some made of "the best wheaten flour," others of groats, rye, millet, oats or barley—and some of chestnuts or acorns. There were "pan loaves" and cheese bread, and a bread made with "a grain raised in Ethiopia which resembles sesamum." The Cappadocian loaf was made with "milk and oil and a fair quantity of salt." This was often eaten while still hot from the oven. Still another bread was "plastered with poppy seeds . . . when placed in the oven, with groats spread under it on the tile, it gets a most beautiful color, like cheese which has been smoked." "Unsifted wheat" full of bran was often used to make a black bread—and still is in the mountain villages. Anise seeds, sesame seeds and honey were also ingredients added to special breads in antiquity as is still the case today. A favorite child's snack food in the Near East is the semileavened Arab bread sprinkled with anise seeds, thyme and powdered sumac (a non-poisonous variety of sumac) before baking.

Wheat made into a porridge—which is what is done with bulgur and semolina—might be classified as a kind of "boiled bread." The polenta of Italy, cornmeal porridge, is in the same class. So is rice, another cereal grain. Each of these basic starch foods is as sustaining in family meals as the baked "staff of life" we call bread.

# PASTAS

## Basic Pasta Dough

Sift, then measure 2 cups all-purpose flour with ½ teaspoon salt. Place in a mixing bowl; make a well in the center of the flour. Beat together 2 eggs and 2 tablespoons water; pour into center of flour. With a fork, gradually mix flour with eggs, forming a stiff dough; then knead with hands until the dough is smooth and elastic, about 10 minutes. Cut in half; roll out half at a time on a floured pastry board until paper-thin.

## Noodles

Fold over the basic pasta dough, or roll up in a tight, even roll; then cut all the way through in whatever width is desired

(¼ to ½ inch), using a very sharp knife. Unroll; spread out cut noodles on a freshly floured board and cover with a towel; let stand one hour; remove towel; then drop noodles into a kettle of salted rapidly boiling water (use plenty of water!). Stir once to make sure all strands are separated. The larger or thicker the pieces of pasta, the longer the boiling time. Test a piece periodically to see when it is done to your taste. Drain thoroughly.

# Easy Pasta Sauces

**Fettucini Alfredo.** Prepare one recipe Basic Pasta Dough, or use 1 pound commercial fettucini; when cooked and drained, add to the hot noodles a cup of grated cheese, a cup of sweet butter and 2 tablespoons heavy cream. Toss quickly to melt the butter. (Freshly ground black pepper and a dash of nutmeg may also be added, if liked.)

(This same butter-cheese sauce may be added to any hot pasta, including spaghetti or elbow macaroni.)

**Garlic-Oil Dressing.** Rub a deep serving dish with a cut clove of garlic, crushing until only shreds remain (the garlic flavor is in the juices clinging to the dish). Add hot pasta to the dish; then pour over the pasta ¼ cup olive oil (for 1 pound of pasta) and ½ cup grated cheese, plus some chopped parsley. Toss to blend.

**Pesto Genovese** or **Aïllade** are both excellent sauces for dressing spaghetti, noodles, or any of the smaller or thinner pastas. (See chapter on Sauces and Seasonings.)

**For a quick tomato sauce**, heat together 1 cup of canned tomato sauce, 2 tablespoons olive oil, a teaspoon of instant minced onion and ¼ teaspoon oregano. Enough for ½ pound cooked pasta.

**Strascinate.** This makes a good dressing for any thin or small-shaped pasta such as linguine, thin spaghetti, fettucini, elbow macaroni, shells, bows, etc. As pasta is cooking, fry 8 slices bacon until crisp; remove and, when cool enough, crumble bacon. Cook a garlic clove or two in the bacon fat until soft;

then crush into fat with tines of a fork. While the co
is still hot, add the crumbled bacon, the *hot* bacon
if it has cooled), 1 raw egg, a cup of grated cheese ...  _
tablespoons butter. Toss rapidly with a long-handled fork. The
egg should cook by the heat of the pasta and the bacon fat;
if it does not, place in oven for 5 minutes. A little chopped
parsley, a pinch of thyme, basil or oregano may also be added,
if desired. As soon as the pasta has been tossed, it must be
served promptly. One pound of cooked pasta makes 4 to 6
servings.

**Mushroom Cheese Sauce.** Sauté ½ pound sliced mushrooms in
6 tablespoons butter until lightly browned. Add a fistful of
chopped parsley, ½ cup grated Parmesan or shredded Gruyere
or Swiss cheese, salt, pepper and ¼ cup heavy cream. Add
this to a pound of hot cooked pasta; serve at once, or transfer
to a greased casserole, top with crumbs and more cheese and
bake until crumbs are browned. Makes 4 to 6 servings.

# Ravioli

Make Basic Pasta Dough; divide dough in half; roll out each
portion in turn until very thin, stretching it to make it as thin
as you possibly can. Fold over first sheet of dough and put
aside while rolling the second sheet. Place teaspoons of filling
1½ inches apart on the second sheet of dough. Cover with the
first sheet of dough so that the two fit exactly together; trim
edges. Cut into squares with a pastry wheel, around the little
piles of filling. Sprinkle flour from a sifter lightly over the cut
ravioli; let stand thirty minutes. Turn each filled square; sprinkle
with flour on the other side. Refrigerate until time to cook, if
desired. The ravioli may now be cooked in broth or fried in deep
fat to be served as appetizers.

To cook in broth, use at least 2 quarts beef or chicken broth
(made with concentrate) with a little tomato paste added to the
broth. Or, boil in salted water and drain well. Cook 10 minutes
after broth or water has returned to the boil.

Reheat in Sauce Bolognese and serve topped with cheese;
or, place in a buttered baking dish, cover with Mornay Sauce
and top sauce with grated cheese (recipes for sauces are in

Sauces and Seasonings chapter). Bake in a moderate oven until lightly browned. Makes 24 to 30 ravioli, for 6 to 8 servings.

### Meat Filling for Ravioli

1¾ cups minced meat, chicken giblets, liver; or whatever meat is desired

1 egg, beaten
1 tablespoon grated cheese
Seasonings to taste

### Spinach Filling for Ravioli

1 cup chopped cooked, or frozen spinach, seasoned
2 tablespoons butter or ricotta cheese

4 tablespoons grated Parmesan cheese
1 egg, beaten
¼ teaspoon nutmeg

# Kreplach

Make Basic Pasta Dough and roll out very thin. Cut into 3-inch squares. Place a teaspoon of filling in center of each square; fold over into triangles and moisten the edges; press with tines of fork to seal. Cook in 2 to 3 quarts rapidly boiling salted water for 15 to 20 minutes; remove with slotted spoon. When cooked, may be reheated by browning in fat, to serve as an entrée or a snack; or add to clear soup.

### Meat Filling for Kreplach
1 tablespoon chicken fat
½ cup minced onion
½ pound ground beef
Salt, pepper

### Chicken (or Turkey) Filling for Kreplach
1 tablespoon chicken fat
1 small onion, minced
1½ cups minced cooked chicken or turkey
1 egg yolk
Salt, pepper, minced parsley

For either filling, sauté the onion in fat; add meat or chicken; cook until lightly browned; then add remaining ingredients. Makes 30 to 40 kreplach.

# PIZZAS AND RELATED SNACKS

The Italian word pizza is derived from the Greek pita, both of which are sometimes used to mean "pie." (Pizza is a specialty of the region that was Greek in ancient times.) Pizza dough can also be used to make a flat bread somewhat like the flat Arabian bread of the Near East, which I found to be called pitta in Cyprus.

## Pizza Dough

| | |
|---|---|
| 1 envelope active dry yeast | 2 tablespoons olive oil |
| 1 cup warm (not hot) water | 3½ cups sifted flour |
| 1 teaspoon salt | ½ teaspoon sugar |

Dissolve yeast and sugar in water; stir in salt and oil; gradually add flour and knead until smooth. Turn out on floured board and continue kneading until very smooth and elastic. Place in warm spot free from drafts (like the inside of an unlighted oven); let rise until doubled. Then divide dough in half to make two pizza shells; or use as directed in any of the recipes that follow. For pizza shell, press and stretch dough to fit pan or baking sheet; brush with oil first; then add any desired topping. Bake in very hot (450°F.) oven for 20-25 minutes or until golden. Makes 2 large pizzas.

## Pissaladiere

This is a Riviera pizza. For each large pizza, slice 4 or 5 onions; cook over low heat in ⅓ cup olive oil until very soft, about 40 minutes. Spread onions over shaped pizza dough; cover with a thin layer of tomato sauce or chopped peeled tomatoes seasoned with salt, pepper and oregano. Then arrange spokes of anchovy fillets over the onions and place pitted black olives between. Bake in a very hot oven until crust is golden.

# Pidoni

A Sicilian snack. Roll out Basic Pizza Dough with a rolling pin to very thin; cut into 4-inch squares. Place a spoonful of filling in each square (see following filling suggestions); fold over into triangles; press edges together to seal. Let stand in warm place until dough has doubled in bulk. Fry in deep hot fat until golden on each side; or, brush with oil on both sides and bake in preheated hot oven. (To freeze, bake first; freeze; then reheat, brushing with oil first, when wanted.)

**Escarole Filling.** Sauté equal quantities chopped escarole and onion in oil or butter until soft; season with salt, pepper and a dash of ginger. Over each spoonful of filling, place a dab of ricotta cheese.

**Meat Filling.** Sauté ground raw or chopped cooked meat and chopped onion in fat, add chopped fresh coriander or parsley, salt and pepper.

**Cheese Filling.** Combine equal quantities ricotta and Parmesan, or ricotta and mozzarella, and for each cup cheese mixture, add a beaten egg, freshly ground pepper and chopped parsley, cress or dill.

# Arabian Flat Bread

| | |
|---|---|
| 2 packages active dry yeast | 1 teaspoon salt |
| 2 cups warm (not hot) water | ½ cup Aunt Jemima pancake |
| ¼ teaspoon sugar | mix |
| 5½ cups unbleached flour | 3 to 4 tablespoons olive oil |

Dissolve yeast in ¼ cup of the warm water; add sugar. Place flour, salt and pancake mix in a large bowl; make a well in center and work in the yeast, the remaining warm water and 3 tablespoons of the olive oil, beating until flour is completely moistened. Knead until smooth and pliable; then shape into one large ball and let stand in warm place until doubled. Turn out onto board dusted with pancake mix (instead of flour) and knead again until smooth. Divide into 16 even portions. Shape each into a ball the size of an orange. Let "rest" 1 hour, at room temperature. Cut 16 squares of foil, each 7x7 inches. Preheat oven to 450°F. (moderately hot). Pat each ball into a circle no more than ½ inch high. Brush remaining oil over top. Bake 2 at a time until lightly browned and puffed, 5 to 6 minutes. Remove and allow to cool. (The loaves will fall, creating a soft pocket in center.) When loaves are completely cold, slit so that the pocket is opened and fill inside with sandwich ingredients; or slice in half and toast to serve with kebabs. Loaves not used immediately may be frozen to be reheated later. Makes 16.

# Shortcut Arab Loaves

Prepare pizza dough with a commercial mix according to directions. When dough has doubled in volume, knead until smooth; then shape into 8 to 10 separate orange-sized balls. Pat each into thin (½ inch) circles; place on squares of foil or on baking sheets. Press sesame seeds over top of each, if desired. Bake in hot oven until lightly browned and puffed, 5 to 6 minutes. When cool, slit as described above. Makes 8 to 10.

# Anchoiade

These may be made with pizza dough, rolled thin and cut into 4- or 5-inch squares, or with thickly-sliced bread brushed on both sides with olive oil or melted butter. Spread dough or bread with a mixture of crushed garlic, anchovy and olive oil (or see Pesto Genovese or Aïllade). Over this place sliced tomatoes; sprinkle tomatoes with salt, pepper, garlic salt and any desired herbs. Over the tomatoes place thin slices of quick-melting cheese such as mozzarella or Swiss. Bake in a hot oven 10 minutes.

# Pan Bania

This is a hearty sandwich made with French or Italian bread sliced lengthwise. First brush the bread liberally with olive oil;

then place inside the bread layers of sliced tomato, sliced onion, chopped sweet green or red peppers, a chopped anchovy fillet or two and pitted sliced green or black olives. Sprinkle with vinegar; douse with more oil. Press the bread tight together, weighted down with a heavy cooking utensil, for about half an hour; then cut into serving portions.

Variations of this are sold in every Riviera snack bar, and you may choose your own fillings from dishes set out on the counter. Fillings may include tuna fish, chicken livers, bacon, various kinds of sausages, cold cuts and sautéed vegetable mixtures like Ratatouille. (The sandwich is also good with no other filling than ripe tomatoes, brushed liberally with olive oil, sprinkled with salt and pepper.)

# Croute Suisse

This is an open-faced sandwich, a popular item at Marseilles snack bars. Square-trimmed slices of bread (thickly sliced) are first sautéed in olive oil; then sliced Swiss cheese is placed over the top. The slices are then placed under the broiler until the cheese melts. It's the olive oil flavor combined with the Swiss (or Gruyere) cheese that makes this sandwich different.

# Fried Bread Fingers

For those who, like me, find the aroma of olive oil a lovely thing, bread fried in it until crisp makes a beautiful garnish or soppit for eggs, salads and other luncheon-type dishes. Of course, for those who don't like olive oil, the bread may be fried in bland oil, or in butter or margarine, with perhaps a garlic clove allowed to brown in the fat at the same time. (This makes it Fried Garlic Bread.) And for those who don't like garlic — well. . . .

Olive oil is like garlic in one respect. Those who like it, adore it. Those who don't like it, abhor it. There doesn't seem to be any middle ground. So be it. It would be a dull world if everyone had exactly the same tastes.

# RICE, BULGUR, AND CORN MEAL

A Turkish recipe for preparing pilaf suggests first rinsing rice through several changes of water to wash off excess starch. Then melt butter in a large saucepan and, when it is melted, add 2 cups chicken broth (for each cup uncooked rice) and bring to a boil. Then the rice should be added and cooked until all broth has been absorbed and holes can be seen through the rice. "Test with a wooden spoon; if it stands upright the rice is cooked." But a final step is even more important, says this recipe: place a napkin over the saucepan, put the lid of the pot over the napkin, and keep in a warm place for 30 to 35 minutes to fluff up the rice.

In each country there are favorite methods of cooking rice, and each has its merits. The Italians add only a half-cup of boiling broth or water to the rice at a time, bringing the liquid to the boil after each addition. In Spain, the rice is glazed first in olive oil to keep the grains separate; then the liquid is added. There are still some cooks who add rice to a large quantity of boiling water, and when it is cooked, drain the rice in a colander. This method is rapidly dying out, however.

Very important is choosing good rice. Most packages of rice in American markets contain cooking instructions on the package, though whatever they advise, I usually glaze the rice first in butter or oil before adding liquid, finding this always helps to keep the grains separate. Two cups of liquid for each cup of rice should be enough. If broth is used rather than water, less salt is needed. Rice that is still moist when served is almost as annoying (to me) as gummy-soft rice. A napkin or cloth towel over the top in the last minutes of cooking, or while it rests, helps to absorb excess moisture; a few minutes, say 10 or 15, in the oven before serving also helps to fluff and dry the rice.

# Pilaf me Bizelia
*(Greek rice with peas)*

| | |
|---|---|
| 2 tablespoons butter | 2 cups water |

2 teaspoons chicken stock concentrate (or bouillon cubes)
½ teaspoon salt
1 cup long grain rice

1 10-ounce package frozen peas
1 cup tomato sauce (optional)
¼ cup grated Parmesan

Melt butter in 2-quart heavy saucepan; add water, chicken stock concentrate (or bouillon cubes) and salt; bring to a boil. When boiling rapidly, add rice and peas; stir once. Cook covered at low heat for 20 minutes or until all liquid is absorbed and the rice fluffy. Prepare tomato sauce separately (use any pet recipe or prepared sauce), and pass sauce and the cheese at table to be spooned over the rice. May be the entrée in a meatless meal, or a side dish with meat. Makes 4 servings.

# Atzem Pilaf

Sauté a chopped peeled tomato in 2 tablespoons butter; add ¼ teaspoon cinnamon, 1 teaspoon salt and a dash of black pepper. Add 1 cup rice and 2 cups water; bring to a boil; cover tightly; lower heat and cook until all liquid is absorbed. Very nice with either pork or veal.

# Portuguese Tomato Rice and Carrot Rice

For each cup Tomato Rice, use 1 cup canned tomato, 1 teaspoon salt and 1¼ cups water; chop the tomatoes before adding to the pot. Carrot Rice is made with ½ cup scraped, grated carrot, 2 cups water or broth, salt and 1 cup rice. Both are good with fish.

# Saffron Rice

Dissolve ¼ teaspoon saffron and ½ teaspoon paprika in 2 cups boiling chicken broth; in saucepan, heat 1 tablespoon oil; add

1 cup rice; stir until rice is glazed with oil; then slowly ad
boiling hot broth. Bring again to a boil; lower heat; cook t⸋...꜀y
covered until all liquid is absorbed.

# Rice and Chick Peas

This combination is served in many Mediterranean countries.
First sauté some chopped onion, about ½ cup, a minced or
crushed garlic clove and some chopped pimiento in 2 tablespoons
olive oil. Add 1 teaspoon salt, a cup of rice and a 1-pound can of
well-drained chick peas to the onion mixture. Cook about 2
minutes; then add 2 cups water, 1 cup at a time, bringing to a
boil after each addition. Cover; cook until all liquid is absorbed.
A little minced parsley added with the chick peas is also nice,
both for color and for flavor. Good with ham or chicken; also
good for a barbecue grill. Makes 4 or 5 servings.

# Riz Creole

A side dish frequently served with meats and poultry in southern
France. Sauté a little minced pimiento, minced green pepper,
mushrooms and onion in butter; add rice and liquid, season and
cook in the usual way.

# Bulgur bi Banadoura
*(Lebanese-style cracked wheat with tomatoes)*

| | |
|---|---|
| 1 cup bulgur | 1 teaspoon salt |
| ½ cup clarified butter | ¼ teaspoon pepper |
| 1 cup minced onions | ¼ teaspoon cinnamon; or |
| ¼ cup pine nuts | 1 teaspoon crushed |
| 1-pound can tomatoes | coriander seeds |
| 2 cups water | |

Wash bulgur well and drain thoroughly, pressing out water. Sauté
onions and pine nuts in 2 tablespoons of the butter until lightly

browned. Chop canned tomatoes; add with their juice to the onion; cook 2 or 3 minutes. Add water, salt, pepper and cinnamon or coriander; bring to a rolling boil; add bulgur and cook covered over medium heat until all liquid is absorbed. Uncover; cook until fluffy. Melt remaining butter; spoon melted butter over the top and stir lightly. Makes 4 to 6 servings.

# Gnocchi

| | |
|---|---|
| 2  cups water | ¼  teaspoon nutmeg |
| 2  teaspoons salt | 2  eggs, beaten |
| 1  cup corn meal | ¼  cup butter, melted |
| ⅔  cup grated Parmesan cheese | |

Heat salted water to boiling; stir in corn meal and continue to cook, stirring, until thick and smooth. Remove from heat. Beat in half the cheese, the nutmeg and the eggs, beating vigorously so that eggs are thoroughly blended. Chill 1 hour. Generously flour a pastry board; turn out cornmeal mush onto the board and press out to ½ inch thick. Cut with a 2-inch biscuit cutter into rounds; sprinkle each round with flour. Lay in overlapping rows in a lightly greased shallow baking pan. Sprinkle with remaining cheese mixed with melted butter. Bake in oven preheated to 375°F. (moderately hot) until top is golden, about 30 minutes. Makes 4 to 6 servings.

# BAKED BREADS

Few Mediterranean women bake bread at home any longer, though some prepare the dough at home and take it to public ovens for baking. The big stone ovens do a better job than home ovens can, because there is moisture and circulation of air that makes the crust more crisp and chewy. Still, the fragrance of home-baked bread is the surest of all ways to a man's heart; it is the delight of children, too.

The secret of the wonderful French loaves, so crisp and full of wheat flavor, is twofold: first, the flour that is used is not as heavily refined as American all-purpose flour and therefore is more flavorful; second, the moistness of the ovens in which the bread is baked. Those who want to try making French bread at home would be well advised to buy flour at a health-food store, or, next best, to use a combination of cracked wheat and all-purpose flour.

# French Bread

| | |
|---|---|
| 1 cup warm water | 2½ cups unsifted unrefined |
| 1 package active dry yeast | flour |
| 1½ teaspoons salt | Corn meal |
| 1 teaspoon sugar | |

Measure warm water into warmed mixing bowl. Sprinkle in yeast; stir to dissolve. Add salt and sugar. Add flour ½ to 1 cup at a time. Beat vigorously with a wooden spoon, adding additional flour if necessary to make a smooth pliable dough. Cover bowl; let stand in warm place until doubled. Sprinkle pastry board with corn meal; turn out dough onto it and let it rest 10 minutes. Then divide the dough in half. Roll out each to an oblong ¼ inch thick; fold the ends of the oblong to the center, overlapping slightly; then seal by pinching center seam and ends together. Twist slightly. Pull out dough to make loaves long and slender, for the more crust exposed to the moist oven heat the better. Dust a baking sheet with corn meal; place shaped loaves on sheet. Cut diagonal gashes over the top of each loaf. Brush with water. Cover; let rise again until doubled. Preheat oven to 400°F. Place a pan of water in bottom of oven, under the baking sheet containing the shaped loaves. Bake about 40 minutes until loaves are golden and crusty. Cool on racks. Do not slice until completely cold. Makes 2 long narrow loaves.

To make commercial French or Italian bread more crisp, sprinkle with water, place in a hot oven for about 8 minutes, serve warm.

# Challah
(*Jewish egg bread*)

| | |
|---|---|
| 1¼ cups lukewarm water | 1 package active dry yeast |

| | |
|---|---|
| 2 teaspoons sugar | 2 tablespoons oil |
| 4½ cups sifted all-purpose flour | Pinch of saffron |
| 2 teaspoons salt | 1 egg yolk |
| 2 eggs | 4 tablespoons poppy seeds |

Place ¼ cup of the lukewarm water in a small bowl; add yeast and sugar. Let stand 5 minutes. Sift flour and salt into a second bowl. Make a well in center of flour and drop the eggs into it. Add oil, remaining water in which a pinch of saffron has been dissolved and the yeast mixture. Stir flour into egg-water-yeast mixture from the sides, working until a soft dough is formed. Knead on a floured surface until smooth and elastic. Place in a greased bowl and brush top with oil. Cover with towel and set in warm place to double (1 hour). Punch down; cover again; let rise once more until doubled. Divide dough in 3 parts. Lightly flour palms of hands, take up one third of the dough at a time and roll between palms into evenly shaped long rolls. Braid the three together and place in a long deep baking pan, twisting the ends to meet. Cover with a towel, let rise again. Brush with egg yolk blended with a little water and sprinkle with poppy seeds. Place in oven preheated to moderately hot (375°F.) and bake 50 minutes or until golden and firm. Cool on a rack.

# Lambropsomo
(*Greek Easter bread*)

| | |
|---|---|
| ½ cup milk | 8 to 9 cups sifted all-purpose flour |
| 2 teaspoons salt | Grated rind 1 orange |
| ¼ cup sugar | Olive oil |
| 2 packages active dry yeast | ½ cup sesame seeds |
| 2 cups lukewarm water | 5 eggs, dyed blood red |

Heat milk to scalding with salt and sugar; stir to dissolve sugar. Dissolve yeast in ½ cup lukewarm (not hot) water; add the milk mixture (cooled to lukewarm) and 1 cup of flour. Cover; let rise ½ hour. Place 7 cups of flour in mixing bowl; add yeast mixture along with remaining 1½ cups lukewarm water and the orange rind. Knead until smooth; replace in greased bowl. Cover; let rise until doubled. Take out half the dough; shape it with hands into a long roll. Brush board with olive oil; then sprinkle with ½ of the sesame seeds; roll the dough over the seeds so that they will stick to the dough. Place loaf on a greased baking sheet. Divide remaining dough in half; treat each portion like the first but form longer, thinner rolls. Roll each in sesame seeds. Arrange these two rolls around the first, forming a kind of wreath. Press ends together. Cook eggs to soft (3 minutes). Cool, then dye red with Easter egg dye. Press one of eggs in center of the big loaf; the remaining four in the smaller outer ring. Let dough rise again until doubled. Bake in oven preheated to moderately hot (375°F.) for 45 to 50 minutes until bread is golden. This is the traditional loaf always served in Greece at Eastertime. Makes 1 large loaf.

After we had washed our hands in the Damascus basin, we crouched cross-legged beside the immense brass tray and there was a moment of thrilled expectation while another slave lifted the lids of a dozen dishes. . . bowls of sweetmeats, stiff puddings of all colors adorned with almonds, junket made of the milk of newly lambing sheep, all sorts of date concoctions, cous-cous made with raisins and sugar, a white, sticky cream flavored with mint. Always there were bowls of sweet hot milk and piles of thin, crisp, heavy bread fried with butter and eaten hot with sugar.

— Rosita Forbes, *The Secret of the Sahara*

Next they filled him with pastries, including cream tarts, fruit squares, sweet biscuits, sugar plums, fritters, tarts of sixteen varieties, waffles, pancakes, quince rolls, curds and cream, whipped cream, preserved myrobalans or prunes, and jellies.

— Rabelais, *Gargantua and Pantagruel*

# Sweets

Honey and *defrutum* (fruit juice boiled down to a syrup) were the only sweeteners known to Mediterranean cooks until the tenth century, and for another four hundred years or so after that no other sweetening was in use in the capitals of western Europe, either. Sugar cane "from a far country" was known in biblical times, but Pliny dismissed it as an "herb" useful chiefly as a medicine. It wasn't until the process of extracting and refining the sugar from the cane was invented that the stuff we now call sugar came into common use and then it was mostly cream-colored or light brown, not white, and a solid cone, not granulated.

The Arabs planted sugar cane in Sicily and southern Spain in the eleventh, or it may have been the twelfth century—no one seems to know the exact date. Crusaders returning to London and Paris from the Holy Land proclaimed the wonders of sugar, and when sugar was finally accepted by the fourteenth century, it was looked upon as a treasure greater than black pepper. Fantastic sculptures were made of sugar, some so immense that they had to be carried into banquet halls on the shoulders of six or eight knights. Considering that all refined sugar at that time was imported from the Far East, its cost must have been even more staggering than the weight of those molded

219

landscapes complete with castles, soldiers, kings and bishops all in glittering edible white.

To this day, in all the Arab lands, cloyingly sweet syrup pastries are adored. Our word candy comes from the Arab *qand,* meaning sugar.

For myself, I find it hard to wax enthusiastic about Arabian pastries or, for that matter, any very sweet concoctions, for I must confess to lacking a taste for sweets. For this reason, the dessert section of a cookbook is the hardest for me to compile. I am content with fruits, or fruit and cheese, at the conclusion of a meal, and much prefer the European custom of having pastries by themselves at teatime rather than for dessert. Yet I am very much aware that there are many people who are quite the opposite, who rate sweets as the most interesting and important part of any meal. So for the benefit of those with sweet tooths, I have collected some representative Mediterranean sweets.

The fruits of the Mediterranean region are especially luscious because of the year-round growing season. In every month of the year there is an abundance of fruit in the markets. When peaches have run their course, melons of all kinds are to be seen piled in pyramids in markets and fields, ripening on peasant roofs, being carried in truckloads down highways. When the supply of melons wanes, oranges and small, juicy tangerines are at their sweetest and most abundant. Spring brings with it strawberries and raspberries, then cherries, plums and apricots follow in succession. I am not one to bewail the unavailability of January strawberries or March peaches; on the contrary, there is excitement in seeing the first strawberries in April and knowing it's peach time again when peddlers' carts suddenly appear loaded with this lusciously juicy golden fruit. And how different is the flavor of freshly picked fruit from that of the cold-storage bounty shipped from distant markets!

Canned fruits in America, on the other hand, are probably the best in all the world. This is especially true of peaches, pears and apricots, which makes it easy for American cooks to produce compotes with a turn of the can opener. For this reason, I almost hesitate to suggest the making of a compote with fresh fruit simmered in syrup. Yet there is a tantalizing wine flavor about peaches or pears cooked with lemon slices in a thin syrup. The result is less sweet than the canned fruit—which makes it more appealing to me, and it's surprising how many people are sure there must be wine in the sauce, when there's none.

Compotes made with dried fruits can also be delicious, especially with a bit of spice added to the syrup. As for fruit salads, make them of whatever fresh fruit happens to be in season, a different combination every time. Fruit desserts never need be mundane.

# Fresh Peach-Pear Compote

Dip the fruit into boiling water to soften the skins; peel carefully with a sharp knife so that only the outermost peel comes off. Cook whole, or cut in halves and remove stones first before cooking—whichever seems easier. In a large (3-quart or larger) saucepan, prepare a syrup of 1 cup sugar to 3 cups water; add 1 lemon, thinly sliced. Bring to a boil; add the fruit and simmer about 10 minutes. Depending on size, approximately 3 peaches and 3 pears at a time can be cooked in this amount of syrup. If you want a larger compote, remove the cooked fruit with a slotted spoon and add more fruit to the same syrup. When all fruit is cooked, pour remaining syrup over the fruit and allow to cool; then chill. The fruit should be soft, not mushy.

# Spiced Apricots

Stick each peeled apricot with 2 whole cloves before adding to syrup. Or, use canned apricots; heat in a mixture of 1 cup of the canned syrup and ½ cup white wine plus ¼ teaspoon dried cloves, a pinch of cardamom and a few drops lemon juice; simmer about 5 minutes, then cool and chill.

# Fruit Salad

Use any combination of fresh fruit; carefully peel and cut into small fairly even portions. Add sugar to taste. A tablespoon of brandy or almost any liqueur may also be added. For garnish, use shredded coconut, chopped nuts (walnuts, almonds or pistachio nuts), minced candied fruit (orange peel or preserved ginger) or chopped dates or figs.

Instead of using brandy, add table wine (red, white or rosé) to the fruit, or a mixture of canned fruit syrup and wine.

# Strawberries in Orange Juice

This is a Spanish combination, so lovely I can't praise it enough. Strawberries I adore by themselves, but I like them even better this way. Simply wash and hull the berries; sugar lightly; cover with freshly squeezed orange juice (not frozen juice). Serve in sherbet glasses. If you have some mint in your garden, a sprig of mint in each serving dish lends a pretty fragrance.

# Strawberries in Wine

The French way to serve strawberries. Cover trimmed sweetened berries with red table wine (or champagne, if you happen to have a bottle of champagne opened at the time). Very nice, but frankly I like the Spanish way better.

# Melon Delight

Almost any melon may be used: cantaloupe, Persian melon, honeydew or watermelon. Since melons differ greatly in size, use a larger melon when there are more people to be served.

Cut off a slice from the top of the smaller rounder types of melon; for watermelon, cut the slice lengthwise along one side. Scoop out the fruit, leaving a thick shell. Cut a thin slice of rind on the bottom to make sure the melon will stand upright and not wobble. Remove seeds; cut the rest of the fruit into balls with a melon cutter. Combine melon balls with other fruits such as sliced peaches, strawberries, white grapes (seeded or seedless), diced bananas or pitted black cherries. Cover fruits with a mixture of 1 teaspoon lemon juice, sugar to taste (some fruit needs more than others), a pinch of crushed cardamom or nutmeg and a cup of white or rosé wine. Return to melon shell; cover with the reserved slice of rind and chill in refrigerator until serving time.

# Baked Peaches Fenice

4 large ripe fresh peaches; or 8 canned peach halves
1 tablespoon brandy, rum or sherry (optional)

½ cup blanched almonds, minced or crushed
¼ to ½ cup sugar
2 eggs, separated

If fresh peaches are used, scald with boiling water to loosen skins; peel carefully; cut each peach in half and remove pits. Scoop out to make a deeper hollow. Sprinkle with brandy, rum or sherry and a little sugar. Combine almonds, the yolks of the eggs (put aside the whites) and sugar: ½ cup sugar for fresh peaches, ¼ cup for canned peaches or to your taste. Place mixture in center of peaches laid hollow-side-up in a shallow baking dish with cover. This can be done ahead; keep covered. About 40 minutes before dinner is to be served, preheat oven to moderately hot (375°F.); bake peaches, covered, for 20 minutes. Beat egg whites to a stiff meringue; fold in 1 tablespoon sugar. Remove baking dish from oven; uncover; pile meringue over peach halves; return to oven uncovered and bake until meringues are lightly browned. Serve warm but not hot. Makes 4 to 8 servings, depending on appetites. (To serve 2 persons, divide all ingredients by half, making 4 baked peach halves. To serve more than 6 or 8, multiply proportionately and use two baking dishes or pans.)

# Bananas Baked in Apricot Liqueur

If you don't happen to have any apricot liqueur in the house, use brandy, sweet port or sweet sherry for this delicious dessert—

but apricot liqueur makes the bananas really special. Peel 3 large or 6 small bananas; then slice them lengthwise. Lay the bananas in buttered shallow casserole; sprinkle with a mixture of ½ cup sugar, ½ teaspoon cinnamon, ¼ teaspoon powdered cloves and a dash of nutmeg. Dot with 2 to 3 tablespoons butter. Pour ⅓ cup apricot liqueur over the top. Bake in a moderate oven until bananas are glazed with the syrup. Serve warm topped with cream. Makes 6 servings.

# Prunes in Port

Soak a pound of pitted prunes in equal parts tawny port and water to cover for 24 hours. Add ¼ to ½ cup sugar (to taste), ¼ teaspoon nutmeg and 2 lemon slices. Bring to a boil; simmer about 4 minutes or until prunes are tender. Cool; then chill. Serve topped with heavy cream.

# Flan, or Crème Caramel

Small metal molds are sold especially for making these custards in every hardware shop and at all the fairs in Spain and Portugal. When made in these molds, the custard cooks more quickly and is more delicate in flavor than when baked in the larger Pyrex custard cups. It's a tip to food-minded tourists: look for these molds on your next trip to the Iberian peninsula. (And if you make inquiries, you may also find them in American gourmet shops.)

**For 8 small molds, or 6 Pyrex cups**

| | |
|---|---|
| ½  cup sugar, melted | 1  teaspoon vanilla |
| 2  cups milk | 2  extra large or 3 medium |
| ¼  cup sugar |    eggs, beaten |

Place ½ cup sugar in a small skillet, heat until sugar melts (turns golden-liquid) then promptly pour into bottom of the molds or cups, dividing equally. Heat milk with ¼ cup sugar and the vanilla until steaming—do not boil. Beat eggs until light; then stir to get rid of foam. Combine eggs and milk; divide among the molds. Place in a shallow baking pan; add water to depth of ½ inch; bake in oven preheated to 400°F. (hot) until tops are golden and knife inserted in center comes out clean, about 20 minutes. (For Pyrex cups, it may take 40 minutes.) Chill immediately. When cold, run a knife around the sides; invert each in turn on to a dessert plate; then tap the top and shake the two together (firmly holding the mold on the plate) until the custard slips out, with the caramel on top. Makes 8 small or 6 medium servings.

**Crème Caramel** is exactly the same thing as Flan but it is usually baked in one mold or a shallow baking pan or dish (Flan is sometimes so baked, too). First melt ¾ cup sugar, pour into a 9x9-inch baking dish or metal pan or a 3-cup mold. (For a larger pudding, use a 1-quart ring mold and increase ingredients accordingly, using 3 cups milk, 4 large or 5 small eggs, ⅓ to ½ cup sugar and a teaspoon of vanilla.)

Pour milk-egg mixture over caramel; place baking dish or mold in a roasting pan and add *boiling* water to come part way up sides of baking dish or mold. Bake in 350°F. (moderate) oven until knife inserted in center comes out clean, about 40 minutes. Chill. When completely cold, run a knife around the sides, invert over a serving platter, tap and shake to loosen. (A hot towel patted on the outside of a metal mold will help the custard to come out neatly.) Makes 6 to 8 servings.

# Leite Creme, or Crème Anglaise

| | |
|---|---|
| 2 cups milk | 4 egg yolks |
| ¼ cup sugar | 1 tablespoon flour |
| ½ teaspoon vanilla | Cinnamon |

Heat milk, sugar and vanilla in pan until sugar is dissolved (do not boil). Beat egg yolks until thickened; beat in flour. When milk has cooled to lukewarm, beat milk into eggs; then transfer to a saucepan and cook over lowest heat or over hot water, stirring with a whisk, until thickened and smooth; mixture should coat the back of a metal spoon evenly. Pour into serving dish. (Dish must be at room temperature, not chilled, and it would be wise to let the custard cool somewhat before adding to the dish; otherwise the dish might crack.) Serve this way for what the French call Crème Anglaise. To turn the dish into what the Portuguese call Leite Creme, sprinkle cinnamon in a pattern over the top when custard has set but is not yet firm. Place waxed paper over the top of the dish to prevent the formation of a heavy film. Chill. Makes 6 servings.

**Pêches aux Crème Anglaise.** Cut up fresh peaches; sprinkle with sugar and a few drops of lemon juice or brandy (to prevent discoloring). After Crème Anglaise is set, top with the sliced peaches and garnish with whipped cream.

**Framboise aux Crème Anglaise.** This is the same but with fresh raspberries instead of peaches.

# Torta di Ricotta
(*Italian cheese pie*)

| | |
|---|---|
| Torte pastry, or pie crust for 1-crust pie | 4 eggs |
| 1 pound ricotta cheese | Grated peel of 1 lemon |
| ½ cup sugar | Pinch of salt |
| ¾ cup toasted crushed almonds | ½ cup crushed macaroon crumbs |

Line pie pan with pastry, fluting edges. Place in freezer 5 minutes; then transfer to preheated hot oven (425°F.) and bake 5 minutes (this makes a flakier crust).

Force cheese through a fine sieve. Beat in sugar and almonds (crushed in a blender); then add the eggs, one at a time, beating until smooth after each addition. Add lemon peel and salt; beat again until smooth. Spoon mixture into partially baked pastry. Spread macaroon crumbs over the top. Return to hot oven; reduce temperature to 350°F.; continue baking until knife inserted in center comes out clean, about 40 minutes longer. Cool. Cut into 8 wedges (the filling is very rich).

## Torte Pastry

1½ cups sifted all-purpose
   flour
   Pinch of salt
  2 tablespoons sugar
   (optional)

½ cup butter
1 medium egg, beaten
  Grated lemon rind

Combine flour, salt and sugar (if used) in mixing bowl. Chop in butter until very fine. Add egg and lemon rind; work with fingers until smooth. Place ball of dough into 9-inch pie pan, and with heel of palm, stretch out to fit pan over bottom and up sides, as thin and smooth as possible. Flute around the edges. Freeze 5 minutes; then transfer to hot oven to bake briefly before adding a soft filling.

# Melopita
(*Greek honey-cheese pie*)

   Torte Pastry
1½ pounds sieved cottage
   cheese or ricotta

½ cup honey
¼ teaspoon cinnamon
5 eggs, beaten

Make Torte Pastry; fit into a 9-inch pie pan. Freeze; then bake 5 minutes; remove from oven. Combine sieved cheese, honey and cinnamon, blend well; beat in eggs one at a time until mixture is very smooth. Add mixture to pastry; return to oven; reduce heat to 350°F. and bake until knife inserted in center comes out clean, about 40 minutes longer. Cut into 8 wedges. (Not as sweet as if made with sugar; delicious for a between-meal, or teatime, snack or pastry.)

# Rice Custard Pudding

Every Mediterranean country has its own way of making rice pudding. The Arab versions are often flavored with rose water or orange blossom water (available in some drug stores), or they may be spiced with cardamom. One Turkish rice pudding has as a topping apples sautéed in butter and spiced with nutmeg. The Greeks often chill the cooked pudding in a ring mold and fill the center with sugared fresh fruit. The Portuguese pudding always has cinnamon sprinkled over the top. In Italy, chopped candied fruit may be added. A French pudding called l'Imperatrice also contains chopped candied fruit, and egg yolks and whipped cream as well. This recipe is inspired by several of these regional variations.

| | |
|---|---|
| ½  cup uncooked rice | 3  tablespoons chopped |
| 4  cups milk | candied orange peel; or |
| Pinch of salt | 2 tablespoons currants |
| ½  cup sugar | or chopped dates |
| 1  teaspoon vanilla extract | ¼  teaspoon crushed carda- |
| | mom, nutmeg or cinnamon |
| | 3  eggs, beaten |

Rinse rice with water to remove excess starch; drain well. Add to milk with salt and sugar; bring to a boil without stirring. Cook over very low heat until thickened, about ½ hour. Add sugar, vanilla, fruit and spice; continue to cook until rice is very soft. Remove from heat; beat in the eggs (one at a time) vigorously, to blend thoroughly. Allow to cool 10 minutes; then pour into crystal bowl or decorative serving dish. Top may be garnished with whipped cream, or with candied fruit or sugared fresh fruit (peaches or apricots)—but in this case, omit the fruit from the pudding itself. Or, sprinkle cinnamon in a pattern over the top, and omit cinnamon from the pudding. Makes 6 servings.

For a fluffier pudding, separate eggs; add yolks to warm pudding. Beat whites until stiff and fold in after all other ingredients have been added.

# Algarve Fig Pastry

If this delicious pastry has a name, I haven't been able to learn it. Prepare Torte Pastry (see Torta di Ricotta); divide dough in two parts. Roll out each as thin as possible (use waxed paper over the dough if it sticks) to fit a 9-inch pie pan. (It is not necessary to prebake this crust.) Combine ¾ cup each, chopped figs, chopped walnuts and a sweet, not bitter, orange marmalade; or, use 1 cup fig preserves and ½ cup chopped walnuts. Spread mixture over lower pastry; top with upper pastry; press edges together. Bake in hot oven (400°F.) until pastry is golden.

# Crêpes Flambées

## Crêpes

| | |
|---|---|
| ¾ cup flour | 1½ cups milk |
| ¼ teaspoon salt | 2 tablespoons melted butter |
| 1 tablespoon sugar | 1 tablespoon brandy or |
| 3 eggs | orange liqueur (optional) |

## Other ingredients needed

| | |
|---|---|
| 5 tablespoons melted butter | ¼ cup orange juice |
| 2 tablespoons brandy | Grated orange peel |
| 2 tablespoons Grand Marnier, Cointreau, or other orange liqueur | 3 tablespoons sugar |

Prepare the crêpes in advance: sift together flour, sugar and salt; beat eggs with fork just until whites and yolks are blended; then add flour mixture to eggs and beat until smooth. Add milk; beat again; then add 2 tablespoons melted butter and brandy. (Or, the mixing can be done in a blender: add eggs and milk to blender first, then flour and remaining ingredients. Beat at top speed 1 minute.) Let batter stand 1 hour at room temperature or 3 hours in refrigerator. It will thicken as it stands.

You need a 5- or 7-inch crêpe pan or a small skillet for making these. First melt a teaspoon of butter in pan, tilting so that all of surface is covered. Add 2 tablespoons batter; tilt to spread batter over the surface. When lightly browned, turn carefully and cook on the other side 1 minute (they need not brown on the second side). Moisten surface of pan with more butter each time. When all crêpes are cooked and cool enough to handle, roll up. Melt 5 tablespoons butter; pour into the blazer of a chafing dish; place the rolled crêpes in the blazer. Cover with waxed paper until shortly before dessert is to be served; then complete cooking at table.

Combine brandy, orange liqueur, orange peel and juice in a

small pitcher. Keep handy beside the chafing dish. Heat chafing dish over flame of alcohol burner; sauté rolled crêpes until lightly browned on all sides, turning with fork as they cook. Sprinkle sugar over top. When crêpes are lightly browned and sizzling, add the brandy mixture; heat until bubbles form in the liquid; then tilt the pan so that the flame of the alcohol burner ignites the brandy fumes. Spoon up sauce to keep flame alive; when it has burned out, serve the crêpes, with a little of the sauce spooned over each. Makes 4 servings.

# Mele in Gabbia
(*Italian apple dumplings*)

This dessert, served on the *Cristoforo Colombo*, reminded me of the apple dumplings I used to make back in Indiana when I was first learning to cook. I had always thought this an Anglo-Saxon dessert, but, after all, it was in the Mediterranean that pastry was first invented, and to use fruit and nuts inside pastry is as old as Egypt.

|  |  |
|---|---|
| Pie crust dough or mix for 2-crust pie | ¼  cup raisins or currants |
| 4  apples, peeled and chopped | ½  cup sugar |
| ¼  cup chopped walnuts or almonds | ¼  teaspoon nutmeg |
|  | 1  egg yolk thinned with water |

Roll out the dough ½ at a time; cut into 4-inch squares. Combine apples, nuts, fruit, sugar and nutmeg; place 2 tablespoons filling in each pastry square. Pinch edges of pastry together around the filling so that filling is almost but not quite completely enclosed. Brush outside of pastry with egg yolk thinned with a tablespoon of water. Bake on baking sheet in oven preheated to 400°F. until pastry is crisp and golden. Makes 6 servings.

# CAKES

What we call "sponge cake" is the most-used cake base in southern Europe, and I was amused to see it called pan de spagna in an

Italian cookbook. Another name is biscuit de savoie, after Savoy, which was an independent kingdom in the Middle Ages and later was incorporated into Italy. Pan was the Latin word for bread; biscuit originally meant a twice-baked bread, very dry, probably more like what we now call crackers than bread, or like unsweetened rusk. Such a bread was used by travelers in Charlemagne's time. Once again this suggests that at one time there was little difference between breads and cakes, until granulated or "powdered" (crushed) sugar came into general use and eggs were used for leavening.

Whether the first egg-raised sponge cake was created in a Spanish kitchen, or in the Savoy region, or whether such cakes evolved independently in each country, it would be hard now to prove. Americans accustomed to feathery high layer cakes made from packaged mixes tend not to care for sponge cake any longer, and it's hard to convince women accustomed to making cakes from package directions that sponge cake is as easy as any mix. But I, who am not a great cake expert, find sponge cake as easy to prepare as it is adaptable, and urge the timid to try this easy formula.

# Basic Sponge Cake

5 or 6 eggs, separated
1 cup sifted sugar

1 cup sifted flour, preferably cake flour
Grated rind of 1 lemon

Beat egg yolks with sugar until very thick and light (easiest in a blender). Beat in sifted flour about ¼ cup at a time; then beat in the lemon rind. Pour into an ungreased or very lightly greased pan or pans (according to specific recipe). Bake in oven preheated to 350° F. (moderate) until cake springs back when touched and has started to draw away from sides of pan. Remove from oven; cool in pan; then remove (unless otherwise directed for specific recipe).

# Bizcocho Borracho
(*Spanish tipsy cake*)

Bake sponge cake batter in lightly greased 10-inch tube pan for 35 minutes. Cool upside down in pan (invert over a milk bottle) for 10 minutes; loosen around edges with spatula. Turn out on cake rack. While still warm, dredge cake with syrup made of ½ cup sugar and ½ cup cream sherry cooked together about 4 minutes; add syrup a little at a time. Allow cake to cool; then place lacy doily over top and sprinkle with confectioners' sugar. When doily is removed, a lacy sugar pattern remains on cake. Do not cut until cake is completely cool.

# Zuppa Inglese
(*Italian rum-soaked cake*)

Prepare sponge cake batter, but divide among three 8-inch layer pans. Bake until cake springs back when touched, about 30 minutes. Cool in pan 5 minutes; turn out on racks. Sprinkle each cake layer generously with dark sweet rum, using ½ to ⅔ cup rum. Prepare 2 cups of a custard filling such as Leite Creme or Crème Anglaise (recipes in this section), or use packaged custard mix or vanilla pudding-and-pie-filling mix. Divide custard in thirds. To one third, add 1 ounce grated unsweetened chocolate (or, for a short-cut, a 1-ounce packet of chocolate-flavored baking product). Move the first cake layer to a platter or cake plate. Spread with one-third of the custard. Top with another cake layer; spread this with the chocolate-flavored third of custard. Add the final cake layer; spread with remaining custard. Chill overnight in refrigerator. Next day, spread chocolate frosting (this could be made with a small package of mix) around the sides. The cake will be so moist that its texture is more like that of pudding. Makes 10 to 12 rich servings.

# Brazo de Gitano
(*"gypsy's arm"*)

### Cake
| | |
|---|---|
| 4  whole eggs, separated | Grated rind 1 lemon |
| 2  egg whites | ½  cup sifted flour |
| ¾  cup sugar | Confectioners sugar |

Line a 13 x 9-inch pan with waxed paper; lightly grease the paper. Preheat oven to moderately hot (375° F.). Beat the 6 egg whites until stiff. (You need 6 eggs altogether, but put aside 2 yolks for the filling.) Separately beat the 4 egg yolks; beat in sugar until smooth and fluffy; then add lemon rind and flour. Fold egg whites into batter, using an up-and-over motion, until batter is well blended but fluffy. Spread evenly over waxed paper in pan. Bake 15 minutes or until cake springs back when touched. Loosen around edges with spatula; invert cake while hot onto waxed paper which has been sprinkled with confectioners sugar. Cover with moistened towel to keep pliable and warm.

### Filling and Topping

| | |
|---|---|
| ½ cup sugar | 2 tablespoons brandy |
| ¼ teaspoon cinnamon | 2 egg yolks |
| 2 teaspoons cornstarch | 1 tablespoon apricot jam |
| ½ cup orange juice | 1 cup heavy cream, whipped |
| ½ cup sherry | |

Blend sugar, cinnamon and cornstarch; slowly add orange juice, sherry and brandy; then add the 2 reserved egg yolks. Cook over hot water, stirring with a whisk, until smooth. Remove from heat; stir in jam. Whip cream; add half the whipped cream to the mixture. Spread two-thirds of the sauce over the cake; roll up like a jelly roll. Add remaining whipped cream to remaining sauce and spread over the top.

(Instead of this filling, a custard filling may be used, with chopped dates added, flavored with sweet sherry or brandy.)

# Biscuit aux Amandes

Prepare Basic Sponge Cake, using 6 eggs, but add ½ cup crushed toasted almonds with the egg yolks and use grated orange peel instead of lemon peel. Divide into 3 8-inch lightly greased layer pans; bake until cake springs back when touched, about 30 minutes. When cold, spread the first layer with ½ cup apricot jam thinned with a little brandy (or with Cointreau, Chartreuse, apricot brandy or another liqueur.) Spread second layer with whipped cream, the third layer with more apricot jam. Around the edges, frost with chocolate frosting or whipped cream.

# Torta de Laranja

This beautiful Portuguese dessert is unique. Its orange flavor is what makes it unforgettable.

| | |
|---|---|
| 6  eggs, well beaten | 1  cup sugar |
| Juice of 1 orange (⅓ cup) | Grated peel of 1 orange |

Prepare a 13 x 9 x 2-inch pan: line bottom *and sides* with one large piece of waxed paper (fit around edges as tightly as possible without cutting); grease bottom of paper. Combine all ingredients; beat with a light cupping motion until well blended and fluffy. Pour into pan. Bake in a preheated moderate oven (350° F.) until firm, about 25 minutes. Turn out on a pastry board dusted with either granulated or confectioners sugar. Quickly roll up with fingers, like a jelly roll. Dust top with sugar. Makes 4 to 6 servings.

# Roulade de Chocolate

| | |
|---|---|
| 5  large eggs, separated | 3  tablespoons strong coffee |
| ½  cup sugar | Cocoa, about 2 |
| 6  ounces semisweet | tablespoons |
| chocolate | 1  cup heavy cream, whipped |
| | and sweetened |

Butter an 18 x 12-inch baking sheet; line with waxed paper; butter again. Beat the yolks of eggs with the sugar until thick and light. Melt chocolate with coffee in a saucepan; stir into egg yolk mixture. Beat egg whites until stiff; fold into the yolk-chocolate mixture. Spread evenly over the buttered paper. Bake in oven preheated to 350° F. for 15 minutes or until knife inserted in center comes out clean (do not overbake). Remove from oven; lay a moistened towel over the "cake" for half an hour. Cut waxed paper large enough to more than cover the "cake." Lay flat on counter, sprinkle with cocoa. Turn out the "cake" onto the waxed paper, spread with sweetened whipped cream and roll up quickly like a jelly roll. This is very delicate and must be handled with extreme care. Spread more whipped cream over top for garnish, if liked. Cut in thick slices. Makes 8 servings.

# Baclava

Throughout the Eastern Mediterranean, this is the most popular of all desserts. It probably is a very old recipe, for the phyllo pastry is made with a flour-water dough stretched out paper thin, brushed with melted butter. (These pastry sheets can be purchased ready to use in Greek-American groceries.) The syrup used for a glaze probably in ancient times was pure strained honey.

12 sheets phyllo pastry
1½ cups chopped walnuts, or blanched chopped almonds

½ cup sweet butter, melted

**Syrup**
½ cup honey
1 cup sugar

1 cup water
1 stick cinnamon
Thin slivers of lemon peel

For the pastry, line an 8 x 8-inch greased baking pan with phyllo pastry, brushing each of the first 9 sheets with melted butter, and sprinkling each with 2 to 3 tablespoons of nuts. For the last three sheets, brush only with butter (no nuts). Bake in preheated moderate oven (350° F.) until pastry is golden. Remove from oven; cool.

Combine ingredients for syrup; bring to a boil; cook 2 minutes until syrup spins a thread. Remove cinnamon and lemon peel. Pour syrup over baclava in pan. When cooled, cut pastry with a sharp knife into diamond shapes. Serve when cold. Makes 8 to 10 servings.

# Greek Walnut Cake

¾ cup sweet butter, softened
½ cup sugar
4 eggs
3 cups sifted flour
1 teaspoon baking powder
1 teaspoon cinnamon
Pinch of salt

¾ pound shelled walnuts, crushed

**Syrup**
¾ cup sugar
1 cup water
½ cup brandy

Cream butter and sugar together until fluffy (this can be done in a blender). Separate eggs; add yolks one at a time to butter-sugar mixture. Sift together flour, baking powder, cinnamon and salt; add mixture gradually to butter-cream mixture; then add all but 2 tablespoons of walnuts. Beat egg whites until stiff; fold into batter. Spread evenly in greased 8-inch square baking pan; sprinkle top with remaining walnuts. Bake in oven preheated to 350° F. (moderate) until cake pulls away from sides of pan, 35 to 40 minutes. Prepare the syrup as the cake is baking: boil sugar and water together until it falls from the spoon in a sheet, about 15 minutes. Add brandy; keep hot. The moment cake is removed from oven, pour hot syrup over it in the pan. Leave at room temperature. Next day, cut into small squares while cake is still in pan and remove each piece with a spatula. Makes 16 very rich, very sweet servings.

# Panettone
(*Italian yeast-raised fruit cake*)

| | |
|---|---|
| ¼ cup warm (not hot) water | Pinch of salt |
| 1 package active dry yeast | 4 eggs, beaten |
| 4 cups sifted all-purpose flour | 1 egg yolk |
| | ¼ cup lukewarm milk |
| ½ cup sugar | ½ cup chopped mixed candied fruit |
| 8 tablespoons butter or margarine, softened | ½ cup currants or raisins |

Place warm water in mixing bowl; sprinkle yeast over it; allow to soften. Add ½ cup of the flour and a teaspoon of sugar; stir. Cream together butter and sugar until fluffy. Add eggs one at a time; put in the egg yolk. Add this mixture to the yeast mixture. Add remaining flour and the milk (heated to scalding, then cooled to lukewarm) to make a soft dough. Turn out on floured pastry board; knead in the fruit until well distributed. Place in a warm spot free from drafts (such as an unlighted oven). When doubled in bulk, knead again. Butter a 9 x 5 x 3-inch loaf pan; place waxed paper to fit in bottom and grease that. Spoon dough into the pan. Or, grease two smaller loaf pans and divide dough between them. Make collars of strong paper (cardboard or heavy brown paper) to rise above the pan or pans; fasten with paper clips or pins to stay in place. Let dough rise again; then bake in oven preheated to 350° F. (moderate). Place a pan of water on a shelf below the pan containing the cake batter—this makes the top crust glossy and crisp. Bake until cake tester inserted in center comes out clean, about 40 minutes for smaller cakes, up to 1 hour for large cake. Cool in pan 10 minutes; then turn out on rack. When completely cold, cut in slices to serve. This is usually served with afternoon tea or coffee, or it may be served for breakfast.

# Bombe Lucullus

Bombe is the French name for molded ice cream. The following is based on a superb ice cream dessert served at the Hiely-Lucullus Restaurant in Avignon. It is fairly easy to make if one has a deep freeze, but the freezing compartment of a refrigerator is not cold enough and generally not large enough, either.

| | |
|---|---|
| 1 quart finest quality chocolate ice cream | 1 pint pistachio ice cream Hot chocolate syrup |
| 1½ cups crushed macaroons | |

You need a 1-quart metal mold, or a 9-inch spring form pan. Soften the ice cream at room temperature until it can be easily handled. Spoon ¼ at a time into the mold; over each layer spread ½ cup crushed macaroons, with ice cream for the top layer. Press down until very firm. Freeze for 24 hours or longer. Remove from freezer to refrigerator about ½ hour before serving so that it will not be too difficult to cut in serving portions. Loosen from mold by patting outside with a warm towel. The pistachio ice cream should be moved from freezer to refrigerator 1 hour before serving so that it will be soft enough to use as a sauce-like topping. When serving, top each portion of the bombe with the pistachio ice cream; over this dribble hot chocolate syrup (a commercial syrup may be used, heated shortly before serving). Makes 6 servings.

(To make 10 or 12 servings for a larger party, use a 2-quart mold; double ingredients.)

Wine, O Menelaus, was made by the gods for mortal men as the best means of putting care to flight.

—Homer, *The Iliad*

The ancients did not ask what a man was before drinking, but afterwards.

—Athenaeus

They have in Turkey a drink called Coffee, made of a Berry of the same name, as Black as Soot, and of a Strong Scent, but not Aromatical; which they take, beaten into Powder, in Water, as Hot as they can Drink it; and they take it, and sip at it in their coffee houses which are like our taverns. The drink comforteth the brain and heart and helpeth digestion.

—Francis Bacon

# Beverages

## WINES

Wine has been gladdening Mediterranean hearts since the days of the cavemen—seeds of *vitis vinifera*, the same grapes still considered the best for wine-making today, have been found in prehistoric cave dwellings in northern Italy. Noah, as everyone knows, planted a vineyard as soon as the flood had subsided and, with wine from the first pressing of grapes, got himself shamefully drunk.

Next to water and milk, wine seems to have originally been the basic family beverage, the mainstay—not a luxury drink as it is now considered. In fact, fermented beverages were drunk before milk cows had been domesticated. When it wasn't wine from grapes, it was barley wine—what the Egyptians called bouza—or a drink fermented from honey or dates.

But there's a world of difference between a sour drink drawn from fermented fruit and the smooth elixir of an aged wine of outstanding vintage for which connoisseurs are willing to pay fantastic prices. It was the Greeks of the Homeric world who first mastered the technique of making wines that would grow more luscious with age. In *The Odyssey*, Homer tells how Nestor "prepared a bowl of mellow wine" from a jar that had stood in his cellar for ten years "before the maid undid the cap."

239

The British wine historian, Warner Allen, says that the reason the Greeks could age wines successfully was that they knew how to make a nonporous pottery that protected the maturing wine from the destructive effects of oxygen, and, long before cork was used to stop up the necks, they sealed their amphorae with wax. But the Greeks had also learned such things as which were the best grape varieties for wine, which soils were best (because the poorest soil, dry, rocky or chalky, produces better wines than rich earth) and how to cultivate and prune for the most bountiful yield.

The earliest treatise written on wine-making was contained in Hesiod's *Works and Days*, compiled about 700 B.C.; Hesiod was a Boeotian farmer-poet who spelled out rules for planting and pruning vines. It was already known how to treat the "must" after it had ceased bubbling and seething in the vats, and what signs to look for to determine which wines ought to age well and which had better be drunk while young.

Vintage wines were highly prized in that long-ago time, so much so that the date ("in the time of so-and-so," since years were not yet reckoned by numbers) and place of origin were often stamped on the amphorae, the pottery jars in which wine was stored and shipped. When it was a famous wine, the amphorae might also be marked with a special symbol: Chios wines, for example, were known by the picture of a sphinx holding a goblet. In the museum of the ancient agora in Athens, adjoining the Acropolis, a fascinating collection of wine artifacts from that time is on display, along with a map showing the routes covered by the Greek wine trade, which included every Mediterranean port, from Troy and Tyre in the eastern Mediterranean, to Gades in the west. No other wines were rated as highly as the wines of Greece, especially those of Lesbos, Chios, Thrace, the Malvasia wine from the Peloponnesus and Saprias wines of which Dionysius wrote, "When the stopper has been pulled, there rises the scent of violets, the scent of roses, the scent of hyacinths. A divine fragrance fills the whole house to its lofty roof, ambrosia and nectar in one." Pramnian, a very sweet wine made of grapes allowed to remain on the vine until their juice oozed from them, was also treasured. Many of the sweeter wines are still produced by this method, what vintners today call "the noble rot."

The earliest vines were allowed to climb to the tops of trees, which made harvesting so hazardous that a contract with vineyard workers in Campania, in southern Italy, specified that the master would take care of the workers' funeral expenses in case of accident. There are places in the Mediterranean where wine grapes still grow high; the Vinho Verde vines of northern Portugal are deliberately so trained, in order to produce a tart, light wine (and also because it's more economical in an area where holdings are small and land dear, as other crops can be planted around the base of the vines).

But for heavier, more full-bodied and sweeter wines, the Greeks had learned that grapes needed to be closer to the ground, to capture the reflected heat of the hard-baked soil. It was for this reason that they pruned the vines heavily, a practice still carried out in most of the world's vineyards.

It's extraordinary how many of the techniques the Greeks developed then are still in use. Vineyards on slopes near the sea, where the vines might be harmed by rough salt-laden breezes, were protected by low cane fences—exactly like the fences still put up to protect the Colares grapes of Portugal, in vineyards that produce one of Portugal's finest table wines. Spain's sherries have a small dose of gypsum added to the must to give the wines characteristic crispness—as the Greeks used to add potter's earth or even crushed marble to some of their wines. A picture on a Greek vase of 450 B.C. shows a boy with a wine dipper in his hand that is fashioned exactly like the long-handled dippers called *venencia* still used in the bodegas in Jerez to dip out small samples of sherry from the casks for tasting.

One of the peculiarities of fino sherry is that a yeast blanket called a "flor" forms on the wine as it lies in the cask. Archestratus, the cookbook author and friend of Pericles, once described a wine of Lesbos as having "liquid locks thickly overgrown with flower." It's now believed that Greeks planted the first vineyards in Jerez; some historians have found Homer's description of a vineyard in the "land of the Phaeceans" extraordinarily similar to Jerez and to some of the methods used in producing this unique Spanish wine.

The first Greeks settled in southern Italy in 750 B.C., which date might be called the beginning of Italy's wine industry. Wherever Greeks settled, there vineyards were planted. It was about 150 B.C., however, before Italian wines began to come into their own and, when Julius Caesar ordered four different wines served at a banquet in 46 B.C., one was Italian (Falernian wine), another was Sicilian and the remaining two were Greek.

Greek wines were so in demand in Gaul as early as the sixth century B.C. that Diodorus reported the Gauls "were prepared to barter for an amphora of Greek wine the slave who served it."

Yet the Greeks rarely drank their wine unwatered. According to Athenaeus, the proportions of water added to wine ranged from 3 to 1, up to 20 to 1, and it was considered in bad taste to drink wine straight. Nor did their wines have the clarity connoisseurs now consider such an important characteristic. It was common to strain the wine at table as it was served, to clear it of the lees. Greek goblets were of gold, silver or pottery, not glass, so the gleaming jewel-like reflection of wine in delicate crystal was unknown. This would change, of course, when the Romans introduced crystal goblets and the making of fine glassware developed into an important Roman industry.

Wine was being introduced in other lands throughout this time; in fact, wall paintings in Egyptian tombs show workers pruning grape vines with curved knives like those still in use and women picking the grapes and dropping them into wicker baskets to be carried on men's backs—baskets identical in size and shape to the wine baskets still used to carry the grapes from high terraced slopes in Mediterranean vineyards. There are also Egyptian frescoes showing workers trodding the grapes in the fermenting vats, clapping their hands in rhythm.

Phoenician wines are frequently mentioned by Athenaeus. The wines of Byblos were famous for their potency, giving rise to the word "bibulous" for a drunkard. As early as 2000 B.C., in Babylon, the Code of Hammurabi stipulated conditions under which wine could be bought and sold, ordering that any seller who gave short measure was to be thrown into the sea. Wine is mentioned 165 times in the Bible, and vineyards were rated as important in the biblical world as olive groves and wheat fields ("every man shall have his vine and his fig tree"). But it was the Greeks who raised viniculture to an art and who made viniculture the most profitable of all agricultural pursuits. The Romans, inheriting the Greek know-how, later turned Italy into the world's chief wine-producing nation, a role which Italy maintained until the French, nearly a thousand years afterward, caught up with and surpassed them.

Today Italy produces more wines than any other nation in the world, but most of it is consumed by the Italians themselves who are content with local wines drawn from a butt or vat, or matured in their own cellars. Vines grow everywhere in Italy, hanging from trees, festooning fences, forming canopies over trellised patios; but only a small proportion of what is produced is bottled as vintage wine of superior quality from controlled wine regions.

However, the rare Brunello Bioni-Santi wines from the Mantalcino region of northern Italy are among the most prized wines in the world, and the 1888 vintage has come close to equaling the record of the famous Falernian wines of antiquity. A few precious bottles of this vintage, now nearing 85 years of age were proclaimed still to have "miraculous" flavor and bouquet when last opened and tasted (a ceremony that has been performed once every 25 years, after which the bottles are recorked and returned to their sanctuary). Wines in the same vineyard are still being produced, and the great-grandson of the founder has predicted that the 1970 vintage will be "the best of this century." Not surprisingly, these are among the most expensive wines anywhere: a single bottle was sold not long ago for $415.

Falernian wines were reputed to be drinkable for a hundred years. Trimalchio, the rich but vulgar Roman merchant whose banquets were described in nauseating detail by Petronius, once served each of his guests a jug labeled "100-year-old Falernian." A wine called Falerno is still being produced in the same area, and it's a pleasant wine, but far from great, and not even noted any longer for its longevity.

How was it possible that in antiquity wines could remain not only drinkable but superb for 100 years? Warner Allen says it was due to that extraordinary pottery the Greeks knew how to make, which was air and waterproof. He says that after the fall of the Roman Empire, when the wine trade also fell into trouble, wine was aged in wooden casks through which oxygen could penetrate to sour the wine. The secret of making the Greek nonporous pottery was lost, and from that time until glass bottles with cork stoppers were invented it was no longer possible to successfully age even wines of superior growth. The wines of Jerez, protected from the souring microbes of the air by their yeast blanket, could remain drinkable longer, but at the same time the yeast blanket robbed them of alcoholic content so that before they were blended, as in today's solera system, they became increasingly weaker and more insipid with the years.

Yet wine remained a symbol of delight; connoisseurs continued to argue the merits of one vintage over another; and, in the monasteries of the Middle Ages, wine traditions were rediscovered, expanded and carried to new heights.

The first wines of note in France were those planted near the banks of the Rhône in Provence, a region now most noted for its Châteauneuf-du-Pape, a wine named after the popes who lived in Avignon during the years when the papacy made its headquarters in Provence rather than in Rome. When in 1377 the papacy was about to be moved back again from France to Italy, Petrarch told the pope, "Most Holy Father, the princes of the church esteem the wines of Provence, and know them as more rare than the holy water at Rome."

Rabelais, the French Benedictine monk, so adored the simple wines produced by his monastery that his toast was, "Empty your full glass. Fill your empty glass. I cannot bear to look at you with your glass either empty or full."

Blending of wines has always been practiced, since the earliest days of wine-making, but in about the thirteenth century, when brandy was introduced by the Moors in Spain, a whole new chapter in wine-making began.

The followers of Mohammed are forbidden to drink any alcoholic beverages; but, like all other alcoholic prohibitions that have ever been laid down, this one is as frequently ignored as obeyed. In all the Arab countries that border the Mediterranean, excepting Egypt and Libya, wine-making is pursued, and wines are drunk by the Arabs, not only by the Christian Arabs, but also by many of the followers of Islam. Both in Lebanon and Tunis there are excellent native wines, as I was to discover on my recent trip. When the Moors invaded Spain, some vineyards may have been destroyed by zealous followers of Mohammed, but most of them were maintained, and many a poem was written in Arabic to the beauty of this heart-gladdening liquid.

Presumably neither the Greeks nor the Romans had ever distilled wine into brandy, yet the process had been known in China for thousands of years, and it is hard to believe no one in the Mediterranean had learned about it in the course of the centuries, with all the travelers who had visited India and China. The Arabs with their Far Eastern spice trade certainly would have been exposed to such knowledge, and undoubtedly the Moor who first distilled or "burned" the wine in Spain to collect a concentrated essence knew what he was about. Ironically, the distillation was not wanted as a beverage but as a stabilizer for perfumes and cosmetics. The Arabs were inordinately fond of perfumes; they liked both their dining rooms and their private chambers to reek of the essence of flowers. And the ladies of the harem had a favorite cosmetic for painting their eyelids, which they called kohl, a preparation which in some way was rendered more attractive with the addition of the distillate, which from that time on was known as alkohl.

Sometimes, drinking the cheaper brandies of the Mediterranean, I find them to be too perfumy in both taste and bouquet and could wish the processors of "burnt wine" had not been quite so successful. Yet when skillfully blended and properly aged, a fine brandy can be a lovely thing.

It was British wine merchants in Spain who first blended the alkohl concentrate with the light wines of Jerez so that the wines would hold up better when shipped across rough seas to England. And because the British taste was for sweeter beverages, the wines were blended at the same time with a sweet concentrate called arropo (our word syrup comes from *xaropo*), which, like the Roman defrutum, was made by boiling down grape juice to one-tenth its original volume. A naturally sweet wine, Pedro Ximenez, was also blended with the tart, saline sherry. The wine thus blended became so popular with the English, who called it sack (from the Spanish verb *sacar* meaning "to export") that grape brandy would later be used to fortify other wines—Port, Malaga and Madeira, and the aperitif wines flavored with herbs and bitters, all of which now are technically classified as vermouths.

(The solera system of aging, blending and again aging Spanish sherries is unique in wine production. Every Spanish sherry, whether dry, medium dry or sweet, or one of the many shades of differing sweetness between, undergoes the same system of blending. For each named sherry there is a special *referencia*, or formula, jealously guarded by the bodega that produces it. There is no "vintage sherry," because every sherry contains a little of a "mother wine" that may be fifty or more years old. There is no young sherry, either, because all sherries are aged at least two years in the cask before the first stage of blending begins.

Many centuries before a wine called port was produced, there were vineyards rising above the banks of the Douro River in Portugal. This is a magnificently wild region of rocky mountain slopes rising above the winding ribbon of a river that arises deep in Spain to wend its way to the Atlantic. The Romans called the city on the northern bank of the river's estuary simply "the port"

(*O Porto*). The settlement on the other side was called Gallo (from which the country's name, Portugal, was later derived). Wines from this region had always been locally consumed and might never have gained fame had it not been for a war between England and France in the eighteenth century, which forced the British to do without the clarets from Bordeaux, of which they were so fond. The Douro wines were too tart for British tastes, so a clever British wine man tried adding grape brandy to the must while it was still fermenting in the vats, to halt the conversion of natural grape sugar into alcohol. It worked; this produced both a sweeter and a more potent wine, one perfect for the British tastes of that day.

But still another innovation in port wine production was to have wide-reaching repercussions throughout the wine world. Wines of outstanding vintages, after two years maturing in wood, were transferred to glass bottles that were corked. Later, bottles that could be laid stacked on their sides to save storage space were invented. When the bottles were opened a number of years later, it was discovered that an extraordinary change had come over the wine, rendering it superbly smooth and velvety, with a heady, wonderful bouquet. The secret of long aging of wines, which had been known in antiquity but lost during wine's "dark ages," was thus rediscovered. A mature wine with firm character, if enclosed in a nonporous container, sealed and stored in a dark cellar with controlled temperature, would develop into "nectar," the kind of wine the poets of ancient times described so eloquently.

The greatness of French wines, like the greatness of French cooking, is not a matter of originating their own but of adapting and improving the techniques of others. The secret of aging vintage port was applied to the table wines of Bordeaux and Burgundy, the two wine regions that by that time were producing the finest table wines in the world. But table wines are never fortified; they are temperamental and unpredictable. Some continue to improve up to five years, then start to deteriorate even when sealed and corked; some do not reach the peak of perfection until they are ten years old; a few continue to mellow and improve up to 25, 30 or even 50 years in the bottle. Then there are those wines that showed early promise of greatness, only to turn sour unexpectedly after a few years. The French made a science out of viniculture, studying and recording all those factors affecting wines, as much of a science as is possible with a product of such temperament. Science (or discipline) applied to and combined with art is the French touch.

Yet one of the important lessons about wine to be learned from the Mediterranean countries is that simple wines from a pitcher are sometimes quite as good as highly touted and expensively priced vintage wines about which so many books have been written. The expensive bottle of 1964 Châteauneuf-du-Pape served to me at a Michelin-starred three-forks restaurant in Arles (the wine served with cork floating in it) was no better than another Châteauneuf-du-Pape served from an open carafe at another restaurant in Avignon two days later, yet the latter cost a quarter as much.

Another important lesson, for those who care to appreciate the best wines, is that a great deal of drinking of simple wines is the best apprenticeship there is. By a "great deal," I mean having ordinary, inexpensive wines with lunch or dinner, often enough so that wine is taken for granted. After you become accustomed to the taste of ordinary wine, the more luscious taste and the more fragrant bouquet of finer wines is truly appreciated. And what is often nonsense about vintage years and famous labels may be seen for what it is, a great deal of fuss about nothing.

Nor is all the elaborate equipment now used to produce wines necessarily an improvement. Men who have been in the wine business a long time say that there is no equipment for pressing the must from the grapes as good as the gentle pressure of human feet in that "dance" of the vats. Only in small private vineyards is the must so extracted any longer; machinery is cheaper and more dependable. But when men do the pressing of the grapes, with nimble light dancer's steps, their arms linked as they move in slow rhythm backwards and forwards, the juice is squeezed out without breaking the pips, the color is extracted from the skins with less tannin, so a smoother more mellow wine is possible. (And anyway, the alcohol kills all germs, and when the wine is racked all impurities are cleared.)

Methodically and conscientiously I've tried to learn which were the best of the Mediterranean wines in each country I've visited. My own taste preferences are prejudicial, which is always the case. What I rate best is not necessarily what others will like. The rosés, for example, I find for the most part too sweet, or too thin. I've observed that when I raved to my friends about a certain wine I found magnificent, they, to my astonishment, were cool about it. Or vice versa. This can even be true about those wines the experts report are "superior." If you like a wine, it's yours. No other criterion should be necessary.

From the list I give here, it will be seen that few are famous, or at least not from famous vineyards. I'm impressed with how many delightful wines come from small holdings little known outside their immediate regions.

# Southern France
*(the Mediterranean region)*

**Châteauneuf-du-Pape** is the most famous, subject to the most rigorous control of any wine in the south. It's a heavy, robust red wine, a blend of 12 different Rhône valley growths. I liked what I had on my recent visit, but some bottles of Châteauneuf-du-Pape that I've bought in America were disappointing.

**Tavel Rosé** is considered one of the best of the French rosé wines. It is fruity and exceptionally high in alcoholic content for a table wine, pleasantly dry (for a rosé).

There are dozens of local wines of Languedoc and the Riviera coast that are pleasant, though none renowned enough to be singled out by name. Because this is a region where all the natives drink wine every day, and they are gastronomically critical, the vin du maison served in an open bottle at a good restaurant is usually a safe bet.

In every good French restaurant, all the renowned wines of France are available, and anyone eager to learn more about what to order will find a French wine information center in nearly every town on the tourist routes, with more specific information about those fabulous wines of Bordeaux and Burgundy. I will not attempt to discuss the latter here because they are not Mediterranean wines.

# Italy

**Souave, Bolla Classico**, is a soft, smooth white wine that I found beautiful. It was described in one of my wine books as "tasting like a clear summer day would taste if one could drink it," a very poetic and not ridiculous summary.

**Bolla Amarone 1964** was a deep, dark, robust red wine that I enjoyed on the *Cristoforo Colombo* as one of the best in their cellar.

**Barolo** is a lighter red wine from the Piedmont region, brisk and bracing.

**Brolio Classico** seems to be the most reliable of the chiantis. This is the most famous Italian wine outside Italy, but not by any means the best.

There are any number of other really lovely local wines in Italy, and "open wines" in a good Italian restaurant are usually worth a try. Ravello wines, both red and white, have a good reputation; a soft white dry wine in the Campania region that is very popular is Lacrima Christi, not to be confused with a wine with the same name in Malaga, which is a sweet fortified dessert wine.

# Spain

**Rioja** wines, the reds at least, are the best of the Spanish table wines. The cheaper ones are perfect for making Sangría; the more expensive ones can sometimes be as good as a fine red Burgundy. (When bottled for export to the United States, these now are sometimes called "Spanish Burgundy.")

**Monopole Cune** is the best of the Spanish white table wines (in my opinion). There are other agreeable table wines from the Valdepenas and Tarragona wine regions.

**Espumanta** is a pleasant Spanish champagne.

# Portugal

The Portuguese pink wines that have become world-famous through clever merchandising are the ones I like least. Mateus and Lancer's were both deliberately created to please the American market, and they have succeeded beyond expectations. If they bring pleasure to those who drink them, who am I to carp?

But there are some very fine Portuguese table wines that should be more appreciated. The **Colares** wines, from an ancient and quite small wine region near Sintra, have been the favorites of Portuguese kings since the twelfth century. The red wines from the Dao region can be excellent and age well, up to 20 years. The **Vinho Verde** wines are very light and tart with a natural "petulance," almost a sparkle; at a tasting of seven different white verdes, I was astonished to realize how they range from quite tart and thin to smooth and slightly sweet (which is a matter of comparison—none are really sweet). In addition, there are vins ordinaires from many vineyards not even officially recognized as "demarcated wine regions" that are very pleasant to drink. **Monopolio**, a dry white wine a bit like a Moselle; **Chamusca**, an inexpensive and robust red wine; **Serradayres**, good both in white and red; and a red wine called **Romeira**, which ages exceptionally well, are among Portuguese wines that have given me pleasure.

# Greece, Crete and Cyprus

**Retsina** (the white) means Greece to me. This is a generic name for table wine to which a little resin has been added to give the wine a bitter tang. It takes getting used to, and those who don't like it think it is dreadful. I lived in Greece long enough to get used to retsina, and one of the great joys in returning to Greece for a visit is the prospect of having as much retsina as I want while there.

The dry white wines of Greece are better than the reds; this is true in Crete, also. Most are very light in alcohol and very inexpensive. It's not necessary to know names or brands.

Cyprus has both red and white wines that are pleasant; the young wines are generally quite dry, though a number of sweet dessert wines are also produced.

# Lebanon

During my brief stay in Lebanon I was able to try only a few local wines, but all those I tasted were good, though quite heady, apparently high in alcohol. From the labeling on the bottles, it's clear that French vintners have left their influence here (not surprising, since Lebanon was under French rule for a long time). Two I particularly remember were **Domaine des Tourelles**, a full-bodied red, like a Burgundy, and **Ksara, Clos St. Alphonse.** The latter cost only 55¢ for a half bottle in a leading restaurant, and I can recommend it highly.

# Fortified Mediterranean Wines

**Sherries**, all produced in the area around Jerez de la Frontera in Spain (the only area in Europe legally permitted to use the name sherry), range from very dry to very sweet. When **viño de Jerez** is ordered in a Spanish cafe by the glass, without specifying the brand, the driest type is likely to be served. This is my favorite of all aperitif wines. Visitors are welcomed at the bodegas in Jerez, where they may sample the complete range of sherries and leave the place won over forever by the charm of the sherry men, who are the most delightful hosts in the world.

**Vermouths** are produced locally now in every wine country, regardless of the brand name on the bottle. Both the dry white and the red sweet vermouths are made with a base of dry white wine, a vin ordinaire blended with sometimes as many as 40 different herbs and spices, fortified with brandy. The red is also blended with sweeter wines and one of the spices prominent in its flavor is cinnamon. The Romans were making vermouth in Apicius' time when it was called absinthium, their name for the same herb that the Germans call wermut and the English know as wormwood. Other herbal wines popular as aperitifs in Mediterranean cafes include **Campari, Byrrh,** and **Dubonnet.**

**Ouzo** and **arak** are not wines but distilled spirits made from grain, flavored with anise. They look like water, but when water is added, the liquid turns milky white.

**Malaga**, from a word meaning "God's Harbor" in Arabic, is a sweet fortified wine created by English wine merchants in the nineteenth century in imitation of sherry. It may be drunk as an aperitif, but it's chief value is in the kitchen for making sauces.

**Ports** range from white ports called "dry" (though the driest are rather sweet) to tawny and ruby ports that are best as after-dinner wines. A true tawny acquires its color only with age and should be at least 10 years old. But rising production costs have led to the creation of "blended tawnies," younger wines selected for their color. All ports, though, are aged in wood at least two years before blending, and then in the bottle at least another year. Vintage ports are increasingly rare and increasingly more expensive. These are never blended; instead, the wine from a year of exceptional vintage is laid down in wood for maturing, then aged in the bottle from at least ten up to twenty-five years, during which time it acquires a characteristic sediment and must be decanted before serving. "Crusted port" is almost as expensive: this is a blend of outstanding wines, also aged for many years in the bottle when it, too, acquires a sediment.

**Brandies and liqueurs** are produced in every Mediterranean wine-producing region and they range from some so harsh and fiery they burn the throat, to others that are well aged, beautifully smooth and mellow. Only brandies from the Cognac district of France are legally called cognac, but the name is used everywhere, in other countries as well. A "brandy of the house" (or bar brandy) in France is called a fine; in Italy, the common name for brandy is grappa; in Portugal, aguardiente. Spanish brandies, most of them from the Jerez district, tend to be heavy and a little sweet; Greek brandies are even heavier and sweeter. Some of the Portuguese brandies are like perfume—but at least one (**Antigua**) can be compared favorably with **Armagnac**, the French brandy. As with wine, the choice of brandy is pretty much a matter of personal taste. Because cheap brandies are available in all these countries, brandy is used in cooking much as Americans use vanilla extract (and the alcoholic content is almost exactly the same, tablespoon for tablespoon). Fruit brandies and liqueurs are locally produced everywhere, too: cherry, apricot, peach, plum and orange being favorites.

# MIXED DRINKS

One reason for the prevalence of wine for everyday drinking in a hot climate in ancient times was because it was often safer to drink than water from a well, cistern or reservoir. Even when such water was not actually polluted, its taste could be unpleasant. For soldiers' rations, vinegar was often mixed with water; a popular family drink was made by combining honey, vinegar, rainwater and a bit of sea salt. This was called *oxymeli*, and Pliny, giving a recipe for it, explained that it should be boiled until it had bubbled in the pot ten times, then drawn off and stored "until old."

Fruit juices were often boiled down to one-third, making a syrup which could be diluted with water when wanted. Drinks called *sharbats* are still made this way in the Near East (our word sherbet comes from the Persian). Milk was rarely drunk by adults, perhaps because it soured so quickly, but yogurt, preserved from spoiling by its culture, was (and is) sometimes thinned with water and whipped to make a drink similar to buttermilk.

Hippocras, a drink named after Hippocrates, the Greek "father of medicine," and believed to be very good for the health, was popular from ancient times throughout the Middle Ages. Its base was often wine that wasn't much better than vinegar; so many spices were added that the original flavor was completely disguised. A medieval recipe reads: "Make Ypocrass for lords with gynger, synamon and graines, sugour and turnesol; and for comyn pepull, gynger, canell, long peper, and claryffyed hony."

Mulled wine has always been popular as a winter drink; it is mentioned by Martial, the gruffy Latin epigrammist. Certain of the more ostentatious Roman emperors had snow brought by relays of slaves from the mountain tops to chill their punches, a custom that Seneca regarded as "a sign of the impious and decadent luxury into which the world has sunk."

Pomegranate juice, date wine ("a pleasant drink causing headaches," as Xenophon described it), rosewater syrup and mulberry syrup were also used to prepare beverages in that long-ago time when carbonated drinks had not yet been dreamed of.

# Sangría

A Spanish friend of mine says the peasant way to make this popular summer wine punch is with vinegar "which is good for the blood," and that this explains its name. I prefer the modern urban way: combine 2 parts red wine, 1 part lemonade and 1 part club soda or sparkling water, plus any fresh fruits in season. (Peaches are especially good, crushed and sugared in the pitcher or bowl before the wine and lemonade are added.) A quick way to make Sangría is to use frozen lemonade mix. To make the punch slightly more potent, add brandy (¼ cup to a quart of wine).

# Andaluz

Another pleasant Spanish summer drink. Combine sherry and orange juice in any proportions liked, from ¼ cup sherry to a cup of orange juice; or half and half; or one third each sherry, orange juice and soda. Or make a big punch with a champagne base: to a fifth of champagne, add a cup of medium sherry (amontillado) and 2 cups orange juice. A very cheap champagne may be used.

# Mulled Wine

Heat together in a large saucepan or kettle a bottle of red wine, ¼ cup honey or sugar, 8 whole cloves, a cinnamon stick or ½ teaspoon cinnamon and a long spiral of orange peel. Do not let wine come to a boil; as soon as it steams, serve in mugs.

(To cure a cold, heat a cup of red wine with a tablespoon of honey, a slice of lemon, a dash each of cinnamon, cloves and nutmeg and a pinch of cayenne pepper. Get into bed, drink it steaming hot, and by next morning your cold may be gone. I've been told by Mediterranean friends that it's a sure cure. I can't vouch for this, but it does induce sleep, and that's something.)

# Miglee

This is a nonalcoholic spice drink served in Syria and Lebanon. Combine in a saucepan 4 cups water, 2 cinnamon sticks, 2 whole cloves, ¼ teaspoon ginger, a dash of nutmeg or a few cardamom seeds, 2 tablespoons sugar and a few lemon slices. Bring to a boil; simmer until water is the color of tea. It's a nice drink for children.

(Cucumber is sometimes added to fruit juice punches in the Near East, or a long spiral of cucumber rind. It adds a piquant fragrance.)

# COFFEE

According to legend, it was an Arabian shepherd who discovered the potency of the coffee bean, sometime around the ninth century. Noticing that his sheep gamboled wildly after munching on a certain plant, he chewed on the green beans himself and found it helped him to stay awake on drowsy afternoons.

"Teas" made from seeds and herbs were common (and still are) among the Arabs, so it was not surprising that someone thought of brewing the green coffee beans, though there's no record of when they were first roasted. Since the discovery of coffee occurred not long after Mohammed had forbidden his followers to drink any alcoholic beverages, it quickly found adherents among good Moslems in the Near East and Africa, but its acceptance was slower elsewhere. Some called it "the enemy of sleep and copulation," and certain Roman Catholic bishops condemned it as an instrument of Satan. But Pope Clement in Rome tasted the new drink sweetened with honey and liked it so much he declared, "This Satan's drink is so delicious it would be a pity to let the infidels have exclusive use of it. We shall baptize it and make it Christian."

The Arab name for coffee is *Qahwee*, and as they serve it, it is always thick, black, and very sweet. "Turkish coffee" is the name by which the brew is known everywhere. It's made with very dark-roasted beans crushed to a powder in a cylindrical brass instrument designed especially for the purpose, then combined with sugar before boiling. When coffee is ordered, it is customary to specify how sweet you want it; the most common proportions are a teaspoon of sugar for each tablespoon of powdered coffee and a measuring cup (8 ounces) of water. It's best to make it in the small long-handled brass coffee pots sold in all shops that carry Near Eastern products. Bring the water three times to the boil, pour into very tiny cups. There's not much liquid to be drunk; about half of the small cupful will consist of thick grounds. For this reason, dozens of cups of coffee are consumed in the course of the day in Greece, Turkey and throughout the Near

East and Egypt, where this is the favorite drink. Coffee is never consumed with meals, though, but only between and after meals.

# Cappucino

Named after the Cappuchian monks, this is a delightful Italian coffee drink. Combine equal quantities of hot milk and strong hot coffee; sweeten to taste, dust the top with cinnamon. Or, use a cinnamon stick to stir the sugar.

# Caffe Romano

Serve hot black coffee (dark roasted) in a glass with a twist of lemon peel. Pass sugar.

# Caffee Borgia

Combine equal parts hot chocolate and hot black coffee; add a sliver of orange peel and sugar to taste. Serve topped with whipped cream.

# Café Royal

Demitasse is the usual after-dinner drink in France, served in tiny cups, with lump sugar passed. To make a demitasse "royale," place a lump of sugar in the coffee spoon, fill it with brandy, then set the brandy alight and drop the sugar in the cup. (An easier way is simply to add a dash of brandy to hot coffee.)

# Café au Lait

Equal parts hot milk and hot coffee, poured simultaneously into the cup or mug. (This is served everywhere in the Mediterranean, known by the French name.)

# Galaõ

A Portuguese variation of café au lait: two-thirds milk, one-third very strong coffee, served in a tall glass, sweetened to taste.

# WATERS AND TEAS

Water is so vital to life that the earliest villages and towns were always clustered around springs. Jericho's spring is still today so powerful a source of water that the town appears as a brilliant green oasis in the midst of desert. The "sacred spring" of Byblos has never gone dry. Often primitive people believed the springs were inhabited by gods or goddesses, for no other explanation seemed adequate to explain the force of the "living water."

In Greece, the first time I was there, I was struck by how often the people would discuss the "taste" of the water from one spring as compared to another. I used to find this amusing, but no longer. City water has been made so bitter with purifying chemicals that the taste of pure spring water seems like nectar by comparison. Besides, water does have flavor, for in the purest specimens, there is always some mineral content.

Mineral waters were taken so seriously by the Romans that wherever they found lively mineral springs, health resorts were established around them and to this day, Europeans flock to "the springs" both for vacations and to "take the cure," which may be for anything from liver complaint (the favorite diagnosis of Mediterranean doctors when they don't really know what the trouble is) to gout, barrenness, impotence, high blood pressure, corpulence, lack of flesh, asthma or nervous instability. Bottled mineral waters are always sold in groceries and supermarkets in the display case beside the wines, and are served at restaurants with the same aplomb as the pouring of the wine bottle. Often the restaurant wine list contains a special section listing mineral waters, following the brandies, liqueurs and champagnes.

Artificially carbonated drinks were first introduced as a substitute for the natural mineral waters. Sparkling water, tonic and ginger ale were all originally promoted as beneficial for health (as was Coca-Cola). Today carbonated drinks vie with vermouths and lemonade at cafes throughout Europe, even though the cost is often exactly the same as for wine.

Teas, also, were originally introduced as healthful drinks. Tisanes, as herbal teas are often called, were served centuries before "China tea" was introduced to Europe by the Portuguese, who, by the sixteenth century, had replaced the Arabs as masters of the Far Eastern trade. (There was a time when Portuguese was the most-spoken language in the Far East, as English is today.)

Mint tea is the most-drunk beverage throughout North Africa. It's made much like other tea: fresh mint and sugar are infused with boiling water and allowed to steep four or five minutes before serving. Sometimes a little green tea ("China tea") is also added.

In Tunisia, in the principal cafe of the town of Sidi Bou Said, the mint tea was served with pine nuts floating in it. I can't say that the pine nuts were a great improvement, but it was an interesting variation. The cafe served only mint tea and coffee—and Coca-Cola, which seems to be available everywhere—and it was patronized only by men who sat cross-legged on the raised platforms (a few chairs were available for tourists). The male waiters all had flowers stuck behind their ears but we incurred their displeasure by asking for wine, so that only a scowl was visited upon us. Or was the scowl because women had penetrated their sanctuary?

In the Near East, tea is often made in a samovar. I saw a beautiful samovar in the museum at Acre (near Haifa in Israel) which the guide told me was the type used by the Greeks. In Portugal, there is a greater variety of teas for sale than in probably any other Western country outside England, and since as many herbs are sold for making tea as the black and green China varieties of tea leaves, I suspect even the English may be outnumbered. "Herbs" sold in Portugal for tea-making include dried orange blossoms, rosemary, mint, ginger and hundreds of strange-looking bundles whose names I have never heard elsewhere.

I'm told that teas are sometimes made with fresh wild violets, with nasturtium leaves and with rose petals. In winter hot tea is often sparked with rum or brandy to ward off chills.

# Zestos Hemos

| | |
|---|---|
| 4 cups freshly-brewed hot tea | 2 cups orange juice |
| | ⅓ cup lemon juice |
| 1 cup sugar | 1 cup brandy or cognac |

Dissolve sugar in hot tea; add strained orange juice, lemon and cognac; heat to steaming, serve hot in glasses with a lemon slice in each. Makes 12 servings.

# Index

# Recipe Notes

# Recipe Notes

# Recipe Notes

# Recipe Notes

# Recipe Notes

# Recipe Notes

# Recipe Notes

# Recipe Notes

1 2 3 4 5 6 7 ← P Y → 9 8 7 6 5 4 3